Freud, Jews and Other Germans

BOOKS BY PETER GAY

Art and Act: On Causes in History—Manet, Gropius, Mondrian
(1976)
Style in History (1974)
Modern Europe (1973), with R. K. Webb
The Bridge of Criticism: Dialogues on the Enlightenment (1970)
The Enlightenment: An Interpretation, volume 2, The Science
of Freedom (1969)
Weimar Culture: The Outsider as Insider (1968)
A Loss of Mastery: Puritan Historians in Colonial America (1966)
The Enlightenment: An Interpretation, volume 1, The Rise of
Modern Paganism (1966)
The Party of Humanity: Essays in the French Enlightenment (1964)
Voltaire's Politics: The Poet as Realist (1959)
The Dilemma of Democratic Socialism: Eduard Bernstein's
Challenge to Marx (1952)

Translations with Introductions

Voltaire: Candide (1963)
Voltaire: Philosophical Dictionary, 2 volumes (1962)
Ernst Cassirer: The Question of Jean Jacques Rousseau (1954)

Anthologies and Collective Works

The Enlightenment: A Comprehensive Anthology (1973)
Eighteenth Century Studies Presented to Arthur M. Wilson (1972)
The Columbia History of the World (1972), with John A. Garraty
Historians at Work, 4 volumes (1972, 1975), with
Gerald J. Cavanaugh and Victor G. Wexler
Deism: An Anthology (1968)
John Locke on Education (1964)

FREUD, JEWS AND OTHER GERMANS

Masters and Victims in Modernist Culture

PETER GAY

OXFORD UNIVERSITY PRESS
Oxford   New York   Toronto   Melbourne

OXFORD UNIVERSITY PRESS
Oxford London Glasgow
New York Toronto Melbourne Wellington
Ibadan Nairobi Dar es Salaam Cape Town
Kuala Lumpur Singapore Jakarta Hong Kong Tokyo
Delhi Bombay Calcutta Madras Karachi

First published by Oxford University Press, New York, 1978
First issued as an Oxford University Press paperback, 1979
Library of Congress Cataloging in Publication Data
Gay, Peter, 1923–
    Freud, Jews, and other Germans.
    Includes index.
    1. Germany—Intellectual life—Addresses, essays, lectures. 2. Jews in Ger-
many—Intellectual life—Addresses, essays, lectures. 3. Germany—Civilization—
Jewish influences—Addresses, essays, lectures. 4. Freud, Sigmund, 1856–1939
—Addresses, essays, lectures. 5. Brahms, Johannes, 1833–1897—Addresses, es-
says, lectures. 6. Hanslick, Eduard, 1825–1904—Addresses, essays, lectures. I.
Title.
DD67.G36   943'.004'924   77-76834
ISBN 0-19-502258-0
ISBN 0-19-502493-1 pbk.
UK ISBN 0-19-285085-9 pbk.

The following essays are reprinted by the kind permission of their original
publishers:

"Sigmund Freud: A German and His Discontents," originally published as
the Introduction to Berggasse 19 by Edmund Engelman; Basic Books, 1976.

"Encounter with Modernism: German Jews in Wilhelminian Culture," originally part of a symposium volume edited by Werner E. Mosse in collaboration
with Arnold Paucker: Juden im Wilhelminischen Deutschland 1890–1914,
Schriftenreihe wissenschaftlicher Abhandlungen des Leo Baeck Instituts 33,
J. C. B. Mohr (Paul Siebeck), Tübingen 1976.

"The Berlin-Jewish Spirit: A Dogma in Search of Some Doubts," originally
published by the Leo Baeck Institute, New York, as Leo Baeck Memorial Lecture No. 15.

"Hermann Levi: A Study in Service and Self-Hatred," originally published under the title of "Hermann Levi and the Cult of Wagner" by the Times Literary
Supplement, London.

"Aimez-vous Brahms? On Polarities in Modernism," originally published under
the title of "Aimez-vous Brahms? Reflections on Modernism" in Salmagundi
#36, Winter 1977.

"For Beckmesser: Eduard Hanslick, Victim and Prophet," originally published
in From Parnassus: Essays in Honor of Jacques Barzun, edited by Doris B.
Weiner and William R. Keylor; Harper & Row, Publishers, Inc., 1976.

Printed in the United States of America

To
Karl Dietrich and Dorothee Bracher
and
Wolfram and Elisabeth Fischer,
in friendship;
for changing me by being themselves.

PREFACE

While I wrote the essays gathered in this volume for separate occasions and across several years, they are unified, I think, by more than
being the expression of a single style of thinking, one man's way of
seeing. A collection of essays is something of a convenience and
something of an embarrassment; it is the first because it brings together publications once scattered and sometimes inaccessible; it is
the second because it invites their author to make claims for coher-
ence that the individual pieces, by themselves, can rarely sustain.[1]
But it remains true that these essays exhibit the convergence of two
interests that have dominated my thinking and my research for quite
some time, reaching back, in fact, to the very beginning of my writing for publication: German culture and the Modernist movement.
And the figure that stands at the heart of this collection, the German
Jew—or, more accurately, the Jewish German—unites in himself these
two interests in a kind of tragic completeness: he is at once German
and Modern, a symbol, to himself, to his admirers and detractors
alike, for the profound, often traumatic changes that made Western
culture what it is today; he is a metaphor for Modernity.

1. As my late friend, Richard Hofstadter, put it in introducing his articles and
lectures on the style of American politics: "The best case that can be made for
the unity of any such collection is a personal and informal one, and perhaps for
that reason is rarely resorted to: it is that the several parts, as the product of a
single mind, have a certain stamp upon them; they must be, at least in their
style of thought and their concerns, unified by some underlying intellectual
intent." *The Paranoid Style in American Politics and Other Essays* (1965),
vii.

I do not offer this mental image, this convenient clustering of ideas, values, and practices, as a literal report; this book is, implicitly but centrally, about metaphors—about the doors they open but also about the damage they do—and I want to say here, most emphatically, that while this particular image, the Jew as Modern, has some truth in it, that truth is distorted by exaggerations and diluted by sheer invention. I cannot insist often enough that the hackneyed saying, Where there is smoke, there is fire, is a most undependable guide to the historian, or, for that matter, to anyone else. In his recent study of the nineteenth-century industrial bourgeoisie in the Rhineland, Friedrich Zunkel has unwittingly documented the damage which, I have suggested, the uncritical application of metaphors can do. Speaking of the upward social mobility of bankers, he notes that among them were "also many Jews who, up to then of low social standing—*deklassiert*, tied to no social group through history and tradition, in special degree purposeful, ambitious, egotistical and strong-willed, supplied a large portion of the Berlin and Silesian 'parvenus' in this epoch."[2] In writing this, Zunkel had, not evidence before him but a picture in his head; a picture made sufficiently vivid, and plausible, for his readers by his adjectives—purposeful, ambitious, and the others: in other words, pushy, unscrupulous, rootless. This is the old, the all-too-familiar mixture: a bit of reality with a mass of prejudice, a morass of clichés kept from drying out entirely by a thin trickle of facts, pathetically annotated with a single reference: that outdated and discredited sociological tract by Werner Sombart, *Die Juden und das Wirtschaftsleben*, published a long, long lifetime ago, in 1911. The handful of Jews left in present-day Germany, recalling the unbroken ties that linked many of them to the German past, would doubtless reflect, if they read Zunkel's lines, that they have suffered far more from too much tradition, too much history, than from too little. And, as I shall have occasion to show in some detail, there was much about Jewish Germans that was not modern, and there is much about the glib assertion of their modernity that builds on ignorance and lapses, however unintentionally, into slander. It is to lay bare such slanders, and to dispel this ignorance, at least in part, that I finally thought it useful, indeed necessary, to gather these essays into a single volume. If some of them are about gentiles, that is all to

2. Zunkel, *Der Rheinisch-Westfälische Unternehmer, 1834–1879* (1962), 122. The passage that includes this "portrait" is conveniently reprinted in Hans-Ulrich Wehler, ed., *Moderne deutsche Sozialgeschichte* (2nd ed., 1968), 327.

the good: Jews lived in a world larger than themselves, and just as it is impossible to understand that larger world without its Jews, it is impossible to understand its Jews without their larger world. Masters and victims (and Jews were sometimes the first, normally the second) were locked into a single culture, German Modernist culture.

Visible and interwoven though my pervasive themes may be, I have underscored their interrelationships by revising and enlarging each of these essays, some of them substantially, and by adding an Introduction in which I elaborate the arguments I am adumbrating in this Preface. Yet I do not want to claim more for this collection than I have a right to claim: these essays are just that—essays. They are explorations in a region of our recent past of which we know much, and which is documented to an almost bewildering degree, but which we have mastered neither intellectually nor emotionally. It is, of course, neither possible nor desirable to segregate intellect from passion; but it should be possible to clarify the emotional stakes attached to my themes by laying bare their intellectual foundations—by contributing, that is, to the history of German Modernist culture with as much detachment as our—and my—inescapable engagement will permit.

Cautiously as I have here discriminated between detachment and engagement, the very distinction still leaves me uneasy. It evokes that value-laden polarity of private subjectivity (undesirable) and professional objectivity (desirable), a polarity against which I have polemicized elsewhere. In my *Style in History* (1974), I sought to demonstrate, exhibiting as my proof texts the writings of such historian-stylists as Gibbon, Ranke, Macaulay and Burckhardt, that private perspectives can be, in the right hands, a pathway to historical knowledge; that passion, even prejudice, may provide access to insights closed to cooler, more distant researchers. This demonstration is, for obvious reasons, particularly pertinent to the history of modern Germany; that history, as I will note again in the Introduction, is highly charged, even for those who have never seen the country. And the German historian, however bravely he attempts to see the whole picture and to see it plain, to see the pastness of the past in all its pastness, is bound to be emotionally involved in, and often crippled by, his materials. He, more than most historians, is exposed to the risk that psychoanalysts, wary of permitting their work to be distorted by feelings of affection or aversion toward their analysands, call counter-transference. The writing of German history is laden with, mainly unexamined, counter-transferences.

It is a risk but, as I have said, it is also an opportunity, though the risks are far more in evidence than the opportunities. Germans, for the past thirty years and more, have spoken a good deal about their need to master their past, but I can offer two recent instances suggesting how very hard it is—for anyone, not Germans alone—to achieve such mastery. Early in August 1976, I published, in two successive issues, a short article, "Thinking About the Germans," on the Op-Ed page of the *New York Times*. I began by reciting my credentials: refugee from Hitler, obsessed for years with hatred and thoughts of revenge on Germany and Germans, wresting from my experience and my friendships with Germans a more discriminating attitude, not of forgiving and forgetting, but of recognizing that there were, and are, several Germanies. I remembered those too young to have had any share in the making of the holocaust, and older Germans who had passively resisted or actively sabotaged the Nazi regime. I noted in my article that it had taken me many years to reach a set of conclusions that might strike others as rather obvious, but now that I had come to understand the folly of believing that the only good German was a dead German, I thought it my duty to point out to whatever readers I might find the only lesser folly of seeing every German as a movie villain, of refusing to buy German products or value German culture. The time had come, I suggested, to see Germany—I was always speaking of West Germany alone, of course—as a partner in the Western enterprise, as a democracy struggling with its traumas and seeking to define for itself the possibilities of freedom, the limits (in the face of terrorism) of liberality, and the blessings of decency.

The response was, at least to me, astonishing. I was invited to discuss "the ugly German" on German radio and television, and (in a memorable evening) with the members of a Reform Jewish congregation in Westchester; I had many emotion-laden discussions with friends and acquaintances. And I had mail—more than seventy-five letters and postcards ranging from demented denunciations and sly sick poems to pained dissents from my position and to a gratifying number of messages of agreement and support. And among the last, I was happy to see, the refugees from Hitler (including at least one survivor of Auschwitz) were most numerous. These were men and women who (with me) had not forgotten, still mourned (as I do) members of their families who had vanished in the Final Solution, but who (like me) believed that many Germans were neither secret nor potential Nazis and that the old, controversial love affair between Jews and Germans had not been a wholly one-sided, pathetic affair. The passions, both rational and irrational, that my article aroused, commonsensical and almost commonplace though it seemed to me, demonstrated to me, anew, the inexhaustible and terrifying vitality of the modern German trauma.

The piece that awakened all this excitement could be classified, crudely, as "pro-German." Yet I tried to emphasize in it, and my friendly correspondents agreed, that to mobilize historical understanding and to make discriminations did not mean to deny or to prettify what had happened. If some Germans did not need forgiveness, other Germans had committed crimes that could never be forgiven. For that reason I found it all the more necessary (and the Introduction will bear witness to this) to reserve some harsh words for historians—most, but by no means all of them Germans—who have made it their business to invent a more palatable past for themselves. The culture of the German Empire, around which these essays circle, was complex, varied, unfinished, rich in potentialities for many different futures; it was a culture, as I shall repeatedly argue in the pages that follow, which becomes opaque if seen from the perspective of later horrors. But it does not follow from this historical, historicist, maxim that Nazism was an accident, or really not so bad, or much like everything else in the modern world.

This brings me to my second, and even more sobering, experience: reading Ernst Nolte's book on Germany and the Cold War. While I say something about other German apologists in my Introduction, I concentrate on Nolte here because he is a prominent, even famous, though doubtless controversial, modern German historian, whose pronouncements are bound to lend respectability to the prejudices retailed by other, less respectable personages. I am not charging that Nolte wrote his book with full awareness of its implications, or that he was consciously compiling a pseudo-record for others, with hands less clean than his own, to exploit. But conscious or not, his *Deutschland und der kalte Krieg* (1974) amounts to a massive and sophisticated apology for modern Germany. I call his method "comparative trivialization," for at its heart lies the device of acknowledging Nazi atrocities but, as it were, "humanizing" them by pointing, indignantly, at crimes committed by others—crimes presumably as vicious as those perpetrated in the Third Reich. I think this a sophisticated technique, since it appeals to liberal guilt arising from real inhumanities committed by Frenchmen, or Americans, in other parts of the world. But its historical function is to cover over the special horror of German barbarity between 1933 and 1945, and to divert attention from studying that barbarity in its own—that is to say, its German—context. Thus, Nolte notes that in the 1960s, America "was compelled to take notice of the world-wide reproach that the United States was after all putting into practice, in Vietnam, nothing less than its essentially crueler version of Auschwitz—*ihre im Grunde noch grausamere Version von Auschwitz*" (p. 528). Since Nolte neither reveals the sources of these "world-wide" protests nor (a greater lapse) informs his readers whether he applauds or questions them, he makes, at least implicitly, light of the Nazi extermination camps; he has given these "reproaches" the imprimatur of his attention. Inflation devalues words as it does other currency. It has become fashionable in recent years to dilute the harrowing meaning and associations of terms coined for the Nazi nightmare by applying them, glibly and thoughtlessly, to lesser evil—to characterize, say, the deficiencies of school libraries in black neighborhoods as "genocide." Nolte here, by likening two very unlike events, shows himself a man—or possibly the victim—of fashion. Either he employs "Auschwitz" and "Vietnam" as metaphors for modern wickedness, or they stand in his mind for real events of recent history. If the first, he only demonstrates, once again, the damage that metaphors can do. If the second, they make it necessary to underscore what should be obvious to all, but is becoming, thanks to arguments like Nolte's, badly obscured: there is a world of difference between Nazi Germany's calculated policy of mass extermination and America's ill-conceived, persistent, often callous, prosecution of a foreign war.

Elsewhere (p. 160), Nolte minimizes the particular virulence of Nazi anti-Semitism by insinuating that it was, after all, largely a response to political and economic pressures—almost anyone, it seems, can be an anti-Semite if conditions are right: "How can one seriously doubt," he asks rhetorically, "that [Harry] Hopkins, too, and [Franklin D.] Roosevelt would have viewed an anti-Communist and anti-Semitic movement in the U.S.A. at least with sympathy, if the [Communist] Party . . . had played a role in American politics comparable to that of the KPD in Germany?" Such speculations even transcend comparative trivialization; they are a way of draining real experiences, real policies, in a word, real murders, of their terror. Indeed, Nolte finds it possible, mustering his sovereign philosophical distance, to describe the "destruction of the European Jews," if only "seen in the right perspective," as "nothing else" than a modern attempt to "solve problems connected with industrialization by means of disposing of a large group of human beings" (p. 159). True, Nolte qualifies such an attempt at problem-solving as irrational and dreadful, but the complacent abstractness of his language drapes a welcome haze of generalities over the cattle cars and the gas ovens, and thus materially advances the grubby enterprise of apologizing for acts that lie beyond all apology.

Techniques of this kind are, of course, particularly rewarding, and easy to apply, when the historian compares German with Soviet totalitarianism, though at one point (p. 360) Nolte's rhetoric reveals his preferences (or, I am charitably inclined to hope, his ignorance): after recounting stories of massive liquidations in the Soviet Union, he judges that "Compared to the conditions [under Soviet Communism], the National Socialist state down to 1939, in spite of the Roehm affair, must be practically called a constitutional and liberal idyll—*geradezu ein rechtsstaatliches und liberales Idyll genannt werden.*" I find it embarrassing to remind Nolte, a professor of history, that by 1939, the Nazis had tortured to death a number of victims in their concentration camps, though, of course, compared to the extermination camps, these earlier camps were practically constitutional and liberal idylls; that the Nürnberg laws of 1935 and, far worse, the Kristallnacht of November 1938 and the edicts that followed it, had legalized theft, fraud, mass persecutions and unbridled sadism, as long as they were practiced on Jewish Germans alone. After such statements, Nolte's placement of Zionism comes as no surprise. He graciously acknowledges that "in the framework of the world-revolutionary process," Jews, long persecuted, have particular significance, but the significance Nolte discerns from his world-historical perch is principally that modern Jewry demonstrates "the irony of history and the reversal of concepts." One such irony, one such reversal, is that, according to Nolte, National Socialism and Zionism are "such close neighbors—*zu sehr benachbart*"—that in the long run the attempt to see them as antitheses must fail (p. 607).

Nolte shows no awareness, at least in this book, of how offensive and (which for the historian is more unforgivable) how untenable his forays into comparative history are. He has no grasp of the essentially defensive nature of the Jewish drive for Palestine; no sense that Zionism is an ideal born amidst pogroms and matured amidst persecutions in which Nolte's countrymen particularly distinguished themselves. He reveals no trace, in his lofty obiter dicta, of the humane, wholly unideological position of Karl Dietrich Bracher that, Zionism or not, securing the survival of Israel is a moral obligation on the Western world since that world, after all, made that refuge, quite literally, a matter of life and death. I confess that I find these, and many similar passages in Nolte's book baffling because often I cannot decode their author's intentions. His tortuous syntax, his evasive conditional phrasing, his irresponsible thought experiments make it nearly impossible to penetrate to his own convictions. But such a way of writing is, and has long been, part of the German problem. Moreover, it helps to legitimize a very catalogue of unsavory notions. In Nolte's book, the true statement that we are all human is translated into the false statement that we are all alike.[3] And if we are, the Nazis were just like anybody else. Claims that Zionism is kin to Nazism, or that Vietnam was worse than Auschwitz, have long been staples of Arab and Soviet propaganda. They have nothing to do with the analytical rigor that the discipline of comparative history exacts.

It should be plain from my language that this collection of essays is a deeply personal book. And I would acknowledge that it is a piece of autobiography, part of reckoning with my origins and my changing life's experience. But I would reject the suggestion that it is a "merely" subjective report, claiming no greater authority than whatever authority my voice could muster. Just as, in *Style in History*, I took great historians as instances of my proposition that from subjectivity, objectivity can grow, I am using myself, in this book, as a guinea pig for the same proposition. I would like these essays to be read, and judged, as history.

Painful though it has been to dwell on some of these matters, working on this book has been an immense and prolonged pleasure to me, not least because institutions and individuals have been continuously kind to my enterprise. A generous research grant from the National Endowment for the Humanities (RO 7779 73 224) permitted me to take a year's leave from Yale in 1974–75 for work in Germany and in England, and to return to Germany in the summer of 1976, to call on some part-time research help, and to buy some needed books. Supplementary, repeated support from the Deutsche Akademische Austauschdienst and the Fritz Thyssen Stiftung enabled me to take several trips to archives in Germany, and to acquire some

3. I want to note that some of the passages that most disturbed me in Nolte's book also disturbed Felix Gilbert. See his impressive review of *Deutschland und der kalte Krieg* in the *American Historical Review*, LXXXI, No. 3 (June 1976), 618–20, and his reply to Nolte's protest in the same journal, LXXXII, No. 1 (February 1977), 235–36.

inaccessible publications. In addition, Yale assisted my researches in material ways: a grant-in-aid from the Council on West European Studies of the Concilium on International and Area Studies defrayed some extraordinary expenses, while an equally welcome grant from the A. Whitney Griswold Faculty Research Fund of the Yale Council on the Humanities eased my way in the German and the English archives, by supplying funds for photocopying manuscripts. Betty Paine and Florence Thomas did both heroic and speedy labor in transcribing my much-rewritten manuscripts; Joseph L. Koerner helped, effectively, when it counted, in preparing this manuscript for the press. I thank them all.

I also thank those archivists and librarians who, almost without exception, aided me beyond any reasonable interpretation of their duties. I am grateful to Herrn Professor Dr. Bernhard Zeller and Dr. Werner Volke for making me at home, in two extended visits, in their splendid repository of manuscripts, runs of periodicals, and collected works, the Schiller National-Museum, in Marbach a. N.; to the staff, both at the general library and in the Handschriften-Abteilung, of the Bayerische Staatsbibliothek in Munich, where I worked for nearly four months, with valuable local excursions to the Bayerische Hauptstaatsarchiv and the library as well as the Handschriftensammlung of the Stadtbibliothek; to the staffs of its various departments, including the music library and the several manuscript divisions of the Geheime Staatsarchiv gathered under the collective rubric of the Staatsbibliothek, Preussischer Kulturbesitz, as well as Dr. Walter Huder at the Akademie der Künste, and the staff of the Berlin-Abteilung at the Amerika-Gedenkbibliothek, all in Berlin, in each of which I had a number of enjoyable and profitable explorations; to Prof. Dr. Dietrich Kämper, of the Musikwissenschaftliches Institut at the University of Cologne; to Amtsrat Schroer at the Handschriftenabteilung of the Badische Landesbibliothek in Karlsruhe; to Frl. Diplom-Bibliothekarin Ilona Mandt-Merck of the Library at the Hamburger Kunsthalle as well as Dr. Rolf Burmeister at the Handschriftenabteilung of the Staats- und Universitätsbibliothek Hamburg. I owe particular thanks to Herrn Hans Joachim Mey, whose copious lists culled from the Zentralkartei der Autographen, Staatsbibliothek, Preussischer Kulturbesitz, Berlin, saved me untold hours tracking down elusive manuscripts.

I also gratefully acknowledge the help I received in a four-months' stay in Oxford, at the divisions of the Bodleian Library, particularly its music library; the help of the staff at the Cambridge University Library, and that of the Archives Department of the Manchester Public Library as well as the Henry Watson Music Library, also at Manchester; the Fine Arts Library in Glasgow; the Handschriftenabteilung of the Oesterreichische Nationalbibliothek in Vienna; and here at home, at the Leo Baeck Institute, New York, especially the late Mrs. Margaret T. Muehsam, the Sterling Library, the Manuscripts and Archives Division, and the Music Library, all at Yale. I want to add that I received a good deal of assistance by mail—from Dr. Manfred Eger at the Richard Wagner Gedenkstätte at Bayreuth, and from archivists in Giessen, Frankfurt a. M., Bonn, Nürnberg, Wiesbaden, Düsseldorf, and Basel.

Not all writing, of course, lives off reading; these essays, at least, have come out of a great deal of talk, including some pertinent comments and criticisms by my listeners. For many years, I have discussed these matters with friends, and much of our talk has clarified and sharpened my thinking even though, as is only natural, they have not always agreed with me. I am offering more than the conventional formula when I thank them warmly while, at the same time, absolving them of all responsibility for the views I have printed here. I am very much in debt to Karl Dietrich and Dorothee Bracher, and to Wolfram and Elisabeth Fischer, to whom I have dedicated this book, for reasons that the dedication only hints at. I am much indebted, also, to substantial and, to me, important discussions I have had across the years with Felix Gilbert and Sir Isaiah Berlin, with Henry Turner and, more recently, Henry Gibbons. The influence of Emil Busse on this work is both profound and intimate. Dr. Richard Newman persuaded me to correct a loose formulation in my essay on Freud, while Anna Freud graciously answered an inquiry about that mysterious mirror in the window of her father's study. A single, long talk with the late Heinz Hartmann continues to reverberate in these pages. My wife Ruth has read all these pages, more than twice; this book is part of an unending conversation between us—it was born, in its present form, from one of its fragments—and the contribution she has made to it, both in her private and in her professional capacity, is more decisive than even she could readily recognize.

New Haven, Conn.   P. G.
June 1977

ACKNOWLEDGMENTS

I want to acknowledge, with thanks, permission to reprint these essays; all of them, as I have noted, have been revised, often substantially. "Sigmund Freud: A German and His Discontents," appeared in its earlier form as "Introduction. Freud: For the Marble Tablet," in *Berggasse 19. Sigmund Freud's Home and Offices, Vienna 1938: The Photographs of Edmund Engelman* (Basic Books, New York, 1976). The first version of "Encounter with Modernism: German Jews in Wilhelminian Culture" appeared, under the title "Encounter with Modernism: German Jews in Wilhelminian Culture, 1888–1914," in *Midstream*, XXI, No. 2 (February 1975), 23–65; I particularly want to thank Mr. Ronald Sanders, former editor of *Midstream*, for many courtesies. My reason for writing this essay was to include it, in German, in a collective volume on German Jewry in the Wilhelminian age; it thus appeared, as "Begegnung mit der Moderne. Deutsche Juden in der deutschen Kultur," in *Juden im Wilhelminischen Deutschland 1890–1914*, ed. Werner E. Mosse, in collaboration with Arnold Paucker (J. C. B. Mohr [Paul Siebeck], Tübingen, 1976), 241–311. "The Berlin-Jewish Spirit: A Dogma in Search of Some Doubts" was published as a pamphlet under the same title, though in shorter form, as the fifteenth Leo Baeck Memorial Lecture (Leo Baeck Institute, New York, 1972); I am grateful to Dr. Fred Grubel for his active assistance. "Hermann Levi: A Study in Service and Self-Hatred" appeared as "Hermann Levi and the Cult of Wagner" in the *Times Literary Supplement*, No. 3814 (April 11, 1975), 402-4; my particular thanks go to John Gross, editor of the *T.L.S.* "Aimez-vous Brahms? On Polarities in Modernism" began as a lecture at Skidmore College, Saratoga Springs, New York, and was published in *Salmagundi*, No. 36 (Winter 1977), 16–35; Robert Boyers, editor and host, was most obliging. "For Beckmesser: Eduard Hanslick, Victim and Prophet" began as "For Beckmesser," published in *From Parnassus: Essays in Honor of Jacques Barzun*, ed. Dora B. Weiner and William R. Keylor (Harper & Row, New York, 1976), 42–54. Finally, I want to thank Dr. Friedrich Bohne, Director of the Wilhelm Busch Gesellschaft in Hannover, for granting permission to reproduce the two photographs on pp. 206 and 207.

CONTENTS

Freud, Jews and Other Germans

INTRODUCTION
German Questions

1. ON THE GERMAN TRAUMA

The calamitous history of modern Germany has propelled its students into anguished retrospection. That terrible question—How could it have happened?—weighs on them, a burden at once hard to bear and impossible to shake off. For the historian of the Nazi regime, I think, the melancholy mode is wholly appropriate. But it has also come to oppress the historian of the Weimar Republic and of the Wilhelminian Empire; not even students of those remote Germanic days of Martin Luther have been immune to it. Whether he is himself a German or a foreigner, the historian of Germany has found that the pressures of regret, even horror, contend with his need for discipline and distance. Even for Germans contemplating their past—especially for Germans—self-congratulation has yielded to self-laceration.

They look for, and debate over, continuities. The crimes of the Nazi era are beyond the doubts of reasonable men, but their historical origins remain mired in continuous, sometimes envenomed controversy. The distinguished intellectual historian Friedrich Meinecke, and some other representatives of the older generation, tried to enlist the prestige of tragedy, and searched for the tragic flaw that delivered their country, famed since Madame de Staël as the land of poets and thinkers, to its nightmare. But most other historians, painfully aware that Hitler's Reich was too obscene to reach the elevation of classical drama, instead evoke images of, or invite comparisons with, coroners performing autopsies on sordid corpses, or prosecuting attorneys lacerating the vicious criminal in the dock. Whatever their chosen vocabulary, whether sober or picturesque, clinical or vindictive, recent German historians normally treat the German past as a tale whose depressing end is known, and was implicit from the beginning. To write modern German history is, most of the time, to render a verdict, and the verdict of guilty is rarely in doubt.

In their search for the sources of Germany's mortal infection, German historians have identified such familiar social types as the authoritarian father or such long-lived habits as the political passivity presumably inherited from Martin Luther's religious thought. Or they have concentrated instead on more immediate causes, on more recent times, notably the German Empire founded in 1871: the profitable alliance between big agriculture and big business, the irresponsible adventurism of Wilhelm II's foreign policy, the adroitly manipulated fear of Red Revolution, the anachronistic revival of the feudal mentality exemplified by insolent Junker and arrogant bureaucrat, and, most of all, the stifling legacy left by that master politician, Bismarck, who (in Theodor Mommsen's memorable assessment) broke the back of the German people.

Diverse as these explanations for the course of modern German history may be, they all incorporate as a central ingredient that hapless figure, the unpolitical German. And to introduce him is to propel *Kultur* to center stage, for the unpolitical German is the burgher who infinitely prefers the ideal realm of high culture to the mundane realm of low politics. "Do not waste faith and love on the political world," Friedrich Schlegel wrote as long ago as 1800, "but offer up your innermost being to the divine world of scholarship and art, in the sacred fire of eternal *Bildung.*" When Schlegel offered this escape from politics, his attitude was not wholly unprecedented; when, during the first World War, in his notorious *Betrachtungen eines Unpolitischen,* Thomas Mann further elaborated this cult of personal culture with its corresponding denigration of public life, he could draw on a rich and solid tradition. For well over a century, cultivated

Germans had been wrinkling their noses at the dunghill of politics.[1]

Not surprisingly, the unpolitical German has become a staple in recent historical and sociological literature.[2] Though he has many guises, he is always recognizable. He is the self-confident Weimar *Literat* around 1800, cheerfully renouncing the right to mix in public affairs in exchange for literary and sexual license. On a rather lower level he appears as the Biedermeier philistine who submits to authority without question that he may enjoy his domestic peace and pursue his innocent pleasures. A later version of this happy mediocrity is the half-educated bourgeois of the Second Empire who makes a fetish of his *Bildung*, celebrating intimate virtues and fleeing larger responsibilities. But the archetype of the unpolitical German, at least in the polemical literature, is the liberal forty-eighter who has become disillusioned with liberalism, chosen national greatness over civic freedom, and made his peace with Bismarck's authoritarian Germany, conveniently adjusting his ideals that he may share in the profits of imperialism. Whatever his face, for a century and more, we are told, the unpolitical German has rationalized his impotence and shifted the burden of shame so that, instead of despising himself, he can despise others.

It would be practicing revisionism for its own sake to dismiss the diagnostic value of this construct. There is a massive literature of German self-appraisal dating back to Goethe and Schiller, part self-criticism and part self-advertisement, which supports the

1. Friedrich Schlegel, Fragment No. 106, "Ideen" (1800). *Schriften und Fragmente*, ed. Ernst Behler (1956), 111. Quoted, among many other books, in W. H. Bruford, *Culture and Society in Classical Weimar, 1775–1806* (1962), 412. Thomas Mann's polemic was published in 1918.
2. The classic source from which others have drawn is Hajo Holborn, "Der deutsche Idealismus in sozialgeschichtlicher Beleuchtung," *Historische Zeitschrift*, CLXXIV (1952), 359–84. See also Leonard Krieger, *The German Idea of Freedom: History of a Political Tradition* (1957); Ralf Dahrendorf, *Gesellschaft und Demokratie in Deutschland* (1965), tr. by the author, *Society and Democracy in Germany* (1967); and Fritz Stern, "The Political Consequences of the Unpolitical German," *History*, No. 3 (1960), now in Stern, *The Failure of Illiberalism: Essays on the Political Culture of Modern Germany* (1972), 3–25.

proposition that, while other nations acted politically, Germans (in Karl Marx's acid phrase) only thought about politics. In a cultural history of Imperial Germany on which I am now engaged, I intend to investigate the hold of what Schiller once called, in a famous poem, the "realm of dreams" on German perceptions of reality.[3] What will emerge, I think, is that Germans were in fact strenuously political throughout the nineteenth century. They did not merely theorize, but actively engaged in efforts to translate ideals and interests into reality. It was a kind of politics, to be sure, of which observers trained in the Anglo-American tradition are thoroughly suspicious: a politics of extreme engagement in both its early "idealistic" and later "realistic" phases. Before the disappointments of 1848–49, Germans forged grand plans for political reorganization, plans in which the achievement of nationhood and freedom were happily joined. After 1849, dismayed forty-eighters turned to what they liked to call *Realpolitik*, a politics which, by reaction to the earlier naïveté, would concentrate on the possible in a hard, often brutal world. The politics of compromise, with its emphasis on means, its patience with imperfection, and its intelligence about institutions, was a relative rarity in Germany: even the "realists" were, in the accustomed fashion, ideological about their superiority to ideology. But all this means is that politics is a plural, not a singular term. The cherished figure of the unpolitical German, then, is far less representative than his detractors, and his admirers, claimed him to be: the historian must be as skeptical of him as he must be of all convenient self-appraisals. And his current popularity derives mainly from his utility to those historians intent on discovering continuities between nineteenth- and twentieth-century Germany. He is the product less of insight than of hindsight.

Of course, hindsight is the historian's professional condition. He studies what life has, as it were, done with, frozen for permanent display, and he can never muster the judicious ignorance of the juror or recapture the open-eyed naïveté of the child. Nor is ancestor-hunting, for him, a form of snobbery; it is a central

3. As presently planned, the work will be called "Imperial Culture," and consist of three parts (or volumes), of which "The Realm of Dreams" will be the first.

assignment. Yet the clarity that hindsight provides is, though often dazzling, sometimes specious, and for the historian of modern Germany, the search for damaging, even deadly, causes has become something more problematic than an occupational hazard: it has become an obsession. He has come to see all past as prologue—to Hitler. He has come to appraise every presumed German trait as one more brick for that hideous edifice, the Third Reich. And he has learned to live with the irony that the history of Ranke's own country is peculiarly resistant to Ranke's much-invoked appeal to treat the past, all the past, with even-handed generosity.[4]

This anguish is commendable, infinitely preferable to evasion or lofty indifference. Other countries, other cultures, also have much to answer for; they too have professed ideals and committed acts they would rather deny, or disguise, than face in the cold light of historical inquiry. But modern Germany, with its calculated and massive barbarity, has been uniquely inhuman; its recent history virtually exacts a certain preoccupation with the causes of the calamity. To repress the question—How could it have happened?—calls for a determination to flee the truth that is far worse, in motives and consequences, than a morose preoccupation with Germany's crimes.

I have no intention of discounting the urgency of that question, or of minimizing the historian's responsibility for finding answers to it. A refusal to confront it would be to betray the historian's exacting vocation, which includes the obligation to testify, not to prettify; to remember what others would just as soon forget.[5] And it would be to betray the victims the Third Reich claimed in vast and undetermined numbers, gassed, shot, starved to death, driven to ineradicable feelings of guilt for surviving, to madness or suicide, often with a smiling and sadistic

4. See Thomas Nipperdey, "Wehlers 'Kaiserreich.' Eine Kritische Auseinandersetzung," first published in *Geschichte und Gesellschaft*, I (1975), 539–55; now enlarged in Nipperdey, *Gesellschaft, Kultur, Theorie* (1976), 360–89. The essay is a powerful and, to my mind, persuasive refutation of Hans-Ulrich Wehler's *Das deutsche Kaiserreich, 1871–1918* (1973), the leading text in the prosecutorial style.

5. For one instance of such denial, see my Preface above, xi–xiv.

ingenuity that must forever haunt even those who did not experience any of it and know it only from the feeble echo that memoirs and photographs supply. Nor can I muster the slightest degree of patience with apologists who disguise the Third Reich as an alien import or encapsulate it as a grotesque interlude, with no substantial ties to the German past. Hitler was neither an unwelcome invader nor an uncaused accident. Much in the German situation of the nineteenth and early twentieth centuries pointed to him, or to someone like him. Doctrinaire anti-Semites, impassioned eugenicists, fanatical ideologues for the *Volk*, smug advocates of a German mission in the world struck postures and used words that were not out of place in *Mein Kampf*. Some of the private attitudes, political perceptions, and social habits prevalent in nineteenth-century Germany, each with a pre-history of its own, were deplorable in themselves and portentous as a legacy. To strike a balance soberly, to reject the dubious advantage of belated wisdom, in no way requires the historian to forget such symptoms, or to conceal their repulsiveness. There is no need to exchange the tendentious condemnation of the whole German past for an equally tendentious denial of all antecedents, in that past, for the Nazi trauma. There was significant continuity between the Germany of the nineteenth and that of the twentieth centuries, but there was equally significant discontinuity. These essays will exhibit instances of both without offering a conclusive appraisal of how much there was of the one, how much of the other. The issues remain too tangled, the evidence too confusing, and the warring factions too well-provided with arguments, to permit such conclusions.

This much, though, is I think beyond dispute: however many hints the historian may detect in the Second Reich for the thesis that it was a pestilential breeding ground for the Third, it remains true that his preoccupation with 1933 and later, when he is writing about 1890 and earlier, has served to limit and to distort his vision. By treating nineteenth-century ideas and institutions as clues of crimes to come, he has torn them from their living context and concentrated on the vertical connections of passing time at the expense of the horizontal connections of lived experience. And this skewed perspective has imposed on him a false determinism, amounting to fatalism, which draws strength from the plausible but circular argument that what happened is proof that it had to happen because, after all, it happened. To read history in this way is to slight the ubiquitous, often subterranean work of contingency. Most events are the vectors of competing, irreconcilable forces which might well have issued in other, often far different consequences, or in no consequences at all. History is the actualization of the potential. Compared to the mass of possibilities inherent in any situation, the number of possibilities realized is small. Modern historians like to complain that they are overwhelmed by the crowding of clamorous events; yet when one reflects how much might have happened, the texture of what actually did happen proves to be remarkably thin. While the modern historian selects among surviving evidences of the past, history itself, as it were, has already done much of his work for him. In this sense, history is an implacable Darwinian battle, in which few aspirants succeed in fighting their way into the permanent record.

Not all history, to be sure, is equally unpredictable—or predictable: the events that resulted in Hitler's accession to power moved in an ever-narrowing corridor of shrinking alternatives. By September 1930, when the national elections gave the Nazi party a stranglehold on the Reichstag, Germany's experiment in parliamentary democracy was moribund. But as late as December 1932, when some authoritarian regime seemed unavoidable in Germany, the Nazi regime was no more than a prominent, and by no means the sole, prospect. To say that the Third Reich was grounded in the German past is true enough; to say that it was the inescapable result of that past, the only fruit that the German tree would grow, is false.

And to slight contingency is to drain all vitality from the course of events. After all, what is past to us, and material for analysis, was future to those living only two generations before us, an often improbable, perhaps inconceivable future. Their present—the decades of the late nineteenth and early twentieth centuries—was, to them, anything but a chamber of potential horrors. It was a blooming buzzing confusion alive with conflicts and uncertainties and gratifications. Their present was what the present always is: bewildering, luxuriant in illegible, often contradictory clues. To establish what I have called the vertical connections—to write the narrative sequence moving from earlier to later events and to forge the analytic chain linking effects with causes—remains high on the historian's professional agenda. But to retrace the horizontal connections, to rediscover men and ideas at work in the world from which they came and on which they acted, is to breathe life into narrative and analysis alike.

I am aware that to preach all this is to preach the obvious; every apprentice historian has to learn, and most practicing historians like to profess, this historicist ideal. It is a wry, and appalling, tribute to the hold of the Nazi experience on German historians that when they come to write their history, they are moved to set the obvious aside. There was much within the circle of nineteenth-century German culture that was anything but admirable: a streak of arrogance and complacency, a humorless overvaluation of ideas at the expense of experience, a strident, almost comical assertion of superior cultivation combined with the crassest materialism. But, hard as it may be to come to terms with the Germany of the late nineteenth century, the terms in which we see it must be its own. This, at all events, is the conviction that informs these essays.

2. GERMAN BOUNDARIES

There are many ways of asking the German questions. Even without squinting at their future, at traumas of more recent vintage, the historian finds the years of Bismarck and of Wilhelm II pervaded by conundrums of their own. They were geographic, ethnic, I am tempted to call them tribal conundrums. Were German-speaking Austrians real Germans? Were German-born Jews German Jews or Jewish Germans? Questions such as these were not academic, for the answers to them had psychological, social, and political consequences. Nor were they easy, for, as everyone knows, the proffered answers diverged radically from one another, and were often energetically debated. To increase the general disquiet: not even the self-appraisals that these problematic populations proposed for themselves ever added up to a serene consensus. Among Austrians, unsatisfied *Grossdeutsche* confronted loyal supporters of the Hapsburg dynasty; among Jews, in these very years, the spectrum of self-identification ranged all the way from total assimilation to a new version of total rejection of German identity: Zionism.

The German Reich founded in January 1871 muted some of the debates through the irrefutable, pragmatic argument of success. Most Germans celebrated it as a consummation they had almost despaired of ever obtaining; the unification provided, quite apart from obvious strategic, political, and economic rewards, enormous, indeed inestimable emotional satisfactions. At the same time, the Empire was not a source of relief and profit alone; it generated much regret and a persistent uneasiness. Certainly, neither the boundaries nor the structure of the Reich proclaimed at Versailles followed the contours of some ideal Platonic pattern; both had been dictated, only too patently, by historical accidents, political calculations, necessary compromises. And because the new Germany seemed like a practical application of Bismarck's famous *bon mot* that politics is the art of the possible, political fanatics and cultural ideologues—servants of the impossible—continued to spin their fantasies of a mighty Central European empire under German domination. They wanted an empire embracing all persons of German speech and German culture in a single sovereign realm, which would at the same time exclude "unassimilable" elements—Jews, or Poles—from the conduct of the great nation's business. Expansionists claimed related ethnic populations, like the Dutch, for the German *Volk*. Julius Langbehn's widely discussed lament of 1890, *Rembrandt als Erzieher*, which insolently kidnapped Rembrandt to serve, incongruously, as the bearer of an anti-materialist, anti-Modernist Germanic ideal, was only the most notorious instance of such cultural imperialism.[6] The enormous and enduring popularity of that book testifies, among other things, to dissatisfaction with Bis-

6. For this book, see Fritz Stern, *The Politics of Cultural Despair: A Study in the Rise of the Germanic Ideology* (1961), 97–180.

marck's solution and with his implicit definition of what it meant to be a German in the late nineteenth century.

To most, if not to all, it was perfectly transparent at the time that this cultural polemic was hysterical and Utopian, the bastard offspring of specious biological theories and untenable historical claims. Yet this much was true, and equally transparent: the boundaries of German culture were wider than the boundaries of the German Reich. There were marked distinctions among the social climates and political habits of the diverse regions which, together, made up the German cultural terrain. The history of Jewish integration in Prussia—to take an example with which I will be concerned—differed radically from that in Austria: while in the first it seemed to follow the curves of economic prosperity and depression, in the second it was apparently governed by the fortunes of political liberalism. To write the history of German culture, in short, is to write comparative history. And yet, what tied all these regions to one another was more important than what divided them. Language was the great unifier, language and the free migration of writers, artists, composers, and performers from court to court, city to city. Whatever local and regional peculiarities might persist—and there were many—German culture enjoyed the benefits of a *Zollverein* of the mind, a free traffic of masters and masterpieces across political frontiers. Johannes Brahms was, and remained, an unreconstructed North German, a loyal child of Hamburg, who moved to Vienna mainly because he could not obtain a post in his native city; but once established, he made himself fully at home in the musical capital of German-speaking Europe. And his slow conquest of the concert and recital hall requires a study, not merely of taste in Vienna, but of taste in Munich, and Frankfurt, and Berlin. Eduard Hanslick, born in Prague but a permanent resident of Vienna, poured out his periodical reviews and critical essays for the Viennese press and, when he turned cultural historian, wrote about the history of music in his adopted city; but his influence— much enhanced by his many volumes of collected criticism, all of them published in Berlin and all of them popular as well as critical triumphs—extended throughout the German-speaking reaches of Europe. Though a lifelong resident of the Hapsburg monarchy, Hanslick was a fierce German patriot who welcomed the military triumphs of Prussian arms in 1870–71 as though he came from some Junker house. Moreover, his most implacable and most important adversary was a German—a professional German—from Saxony, Richard Wagner. As for Sigmund Freud: I will have occasion to insist that he also, with all his discontents, was a German.

To place Freud in the German ambiance is doubly problematic, for he was, of course, doubly marginal, both as an Austrian and as a Jew. And the place of Germany's Jews in German culture was then a vexed, and has since become a tragic matter. Marc Bloch, that consummate French medievalist who fell victim to the Nazis in 1944, says somewhere that the way a society treats its criminals tells the historian much about its character. Considering the share of anti-Semitism in the trauma of the recent German past, the historian of German may substitute its treatment of Jews as a peculiarly sensitive test of the changing character, the underlying intentions, the dominant pressures of modern German culture. "The image of the Jew which had formed in many German minds," writes George Mosse about the late nineteenth century, "goes far to explain the surrender to National Socialism's anti-Semitism by even the more respectable elements of the population."[7] And he contends that this image was made, in large part, by popular novels like Gustav Freytag's *Soll und Haben* and Wilhelm Raabe's *Hungerpastor*, which both draw acidulous and, alas, memorable caricatures of Jews. I am inclined to think that Mosse's somber assertion does less than justice to a phenomenon only apparently monolithic, only apparently one-dimensional. German anti-Semitism issued from cross-currents to which I have devoted a good deal of space in the essays that follow. Here I want to note only that anti-Semitism is a cluster of behaviors with a single name. It ranges from social snobbery to a program for systematic extermination: some of its carriers

7. George L. Mosse, *Germans and Jews: The Right, the Left, and the Search for a "Third Force" in Pre-Nazi Germany* (1970), 34.

would merely stop short of welcoming a Jew to their families or their clubs, while others would exclude all Jews from the human race. The identity of the Jew under attack varied from place to place, time to time, purpose to purpose: in Imperial Germany, many anti-Semites concentrated their venom on immigrant East European Jews, while others professed to see in every Jew, including the most completely assimilated, unpalatable characteristics that, they thought, marked *Ostjuden* most prominently, and most distastefully.[8] And the sources of the anti-Semitic infection varied as much as its diagnoses or prescriptions which, with anti-Semites, were never in short supply. Some disliked Jews in conformity with family tradition or caste prejudice; others discovered reasons for bigotry in the biological speculations so widely current in the late nineteenth century; many found anti-Semitic arguments persuasive only in times of social dislocation or economic misery. Radical anti-Semites saw Jews as a bulwark of capitalism; liberal anti-Semites saw them mired in tribal exclusiveness; conservative anti-Semites saw them as a rootless people bereft of tradition. To complicate the definition further: the intensity, rhythm, and outcome of the malady varied from individual to individual. Richard Wagner's anti-Jewish diatribes, though a consistent outgrowth of prejudices early acquired and shamelessly broadcast, grew more all-embracing and more bloodthirsty with age. In sharp contrast, Heinrich von Bülow, distinguished pianist, unexcelled conductor, and sardonic letter-writer, outgrew in his mature years what he came to consider the infectious illness of anti-Semitism. As a young virtuoso, he peppered his voluminous correspondence with inventive and malicious epithets against "the circumcised"; in 1880, he lent his name to the notorious "anti-Semitic petition," which asked Bismarck to restrict Jewish activities within Germany. Yet at this very time he allowed his gratifying experiences with Jewish musicians to influence and correct his facile set of prejudgments. By 1889, he publicly described those prejudgments as the "*cholera morbus antisemiticus*" from which he had been freed (typically enough for Bülow) by the counter-productive ministrations of anti-Semites: the "in-

8. For details see below, "The Berlin-Jewish Spirit."

voluntary homeopaths Liebermann von Sonnenberg and Wilhelm Marr had brought improvement, and court preacher Dr. Adolf Stöcker effected a complete cure."[9]

The perception of anti-Semitism as a disease, soothing in an age of impressive medical advances, had wide currency in the Empire, especially, but not only, among those who had been cured and thought themselves now immune to infection. Hellmut von Gerlach, who moved from Stöcker's anti-Semitic Christian Social party to the philo-Semitic Social Democrats, spoke in 1904 of his youthful dislike of Jews as a "childhood illness—*Kinderkrankheit.*"[10] This was also the reassuring metaphor to which the liberal politician Eduard Lasker resorted around 1880 in consoling his fellow-Jew, the Ur-German writer Berthold Auerbach, who had expressed his dismay at witnessing an anti-Jewish demonstration in Berlin: "What do you want? Would you reproach a sick man for having the cholera?"[11] For Lasker, as for many Germans, Jewish and gentile alike, anti-Semitism was a recurrent epidemic that better sanitation would make obsolete.

It follows that nineteenth-century German anti-Semitism, however unpalatable even at the time, however pregnant with a terrifying future, was different in kind from the twentieth-century variety. It belonged in a coarse, remarkably crude culture, a culture in which cruel ethnic jokes—jokes that would make us cringe today—formed the staple of innocuous, even benign humor, and unfeeling ethnic caricatures—caricatures we have learned to identify with the lethal stereotyping of the Nazis—were common coin; both the jokes and the caricatures, indeed, seem to have amused its targets as much as its retailers.[12] It was a culture in which clusters of ideas we would regard as grossly contradictory coexisted without strain in the same person. It is true that Gustav

9. Hans von Bülow, *Briefe*, ed. Marie von Bülow, VII (1907), 33.
10. Quoted in Richard S. Levy, *The Downfall of the Antisemitic Political Parties in Imperial Germany* (1975), 90. I am much indebted to Levy's book, an important monograph.
11. Theodor Mommsen, though more pessimistic, used the same language: "Antisemitism," he wrote to a friend, "is the mentality of the canaille. It is like a gruesome epidemic, like the cholera." Quoted in Wehler, *Das Deutsche Kaiserreich*, 113.
12. See below, "Hermann Levi: A Study in Service and Self-Hatred."

Freytag, once a famous publicist, politician, and novelist, invented for his novel, *Soll und Haben,* a Jewish villain laden with all the fabled vices of "the" Jew. But Freytag could, only a few years later, repudiate Richard Wagner's anti-Semitism in music as absurd and "offensive to our fellow citizens of the Israelitic faith," join an association founded to combat anti-Semitism, and polemicize against what he, too, called the anti-Semitic disease.[13] For his part, Theodor Fontane, the most distinguished novelist of the Empire, flattered his Jewish friends one day and snidely denigrated Jews on the next.[14] And Friedrich Nietzsche over and over again denounced German political anti-Semites as rabble, but could endorse, with no sense of inconsistency, some of the condescending commonplaces borrowed from the repertory of those very anti-Semites. In the grip of his mental breakdown, in January 1889, he dashed off, with a last glimmer of prophetic sanity, a letter to his old colleague, Jacob Burckhardt: "Have abolished Wilhelm, Bismarck, and all anti-Semites." Yet only a short time before, in *Anti-Christ,* he had been able to say, in his aphoristic manner: "We would choose for company the 'early Christians' as little as we would Polish Jews: . . . both of them smell bad."[15] It would be futile to single out one strand—the anti- or the philo-Semitic strand—as constituting the "real" Freytag, Fontane, or Nietzsche; each of them, like most other Germans, was made up of both.

Germany's Jews, then, had to navigate among conflicting, often bewildering social signals. In the company of all Germans, they lived in the midst of drastic upheavals, and the array of public and private attitudes toward them were visible traces of unconscious responses to these fundamental transformations. Jewish

13. See Freytag, "Der Streit über das Judentum in der Musik," first in *Grenzboten* (1869), reprinted in *Gesammelte Werke,* series I, vol. VIII, 325–30. See also Ismar Schorsch, *Jewish Reactions to German Anti-Semitism, 1870–1914* (1972), 82.
14. See below, 111–13.
15. Nietzsche to Burckhardt, January 6, 1889. In Friedrich Nietzsche, *Werke,* ed. Karl Schlechta, 5 vols. (1972), IV, 944. On Polish Jews, see *Anti-Christ,* ibid., III, 656. For some sensible comments on Nietzsche's inconsistent attitude toward Jews, see Henry Hatfield, *Clashing Myths in German Literature: From Heine to Rilke* (1974), ch. 5.

assimilation, and resistance to it, were, after all, only two elements, and scarcely the most important, in the revolutions that Germany experienced in the second half of the nineteenth century. In its relentless ascendancy, Prussia had subjugated many political entities and destroyed others; naturally the unification of 1871 further compromised whatever autonomy such surviving kingdoms as Bavaria had earlier retained. And these political changes, far-reaching as they were, shrink into relative insignificance compared to massive economic and social changes: urbanization and industrialization, with their myriad companions, were notably reducing rural isolation, creating an industrial proletariat, threatening traditional religious and cultural values, and posing unprecedented social problems. There was much tough, admiring talk about Bismarck, especially among his former liberal adversaries: Germans liked to acknowledge, with their newly discovered realism, that Bismarck had been right all along because he had won. And indeed, he had wrought well. The trappings of federalism, carefully embalmed in the new constitution, preserved emblems of valued old identities: separate stamps, flags, kings, and residual powers over taxation and education. Yet, at the same time, however respectful of tradition, Bismarck's Reich was bracingly modern, giving Germans a Germany that was moving with the times, capable of competing on the world market, and in world diplomacy, with older, more experienced rivals.

Jews and other Germans had then, as I have suggested before, ample grounds for greeting the new Reich with much satisfaction and some prudent reserve. And I submit that it was this very compound of acceptance and anxiety that fed the forces of political paranoia of which anti-Semitism was one, but only one, manifestation. I do not mean to suggest that irrational fears can provide an exhaustive explanation for the anti-Semitic movement. As professional demagogues and Conservative politicians alike discovered, there were calculable rewards in fishing in troubled waters and, indeed, in deliberately troubling those waters for the sake of political profit. Manipulation of public opinion was part, and a far from insignificant part, of the story. But the irrational, often unconscious element was another, less familiar, part. Bismarck's elaborate political structure seemed precarious, endangered from without as from within by elements hostile to wholeness. And these forces seemed particularly threatening because they were so intimately intertwined with the organism they appeared determined to destroy. In recent years, psychoanalysts and ethologists have adduced impressive evidence in behalf of the old observation, common among political theorists and diplomats, that one's closest neighbor is one's most dangerous enemy. Anxiety, and with anxiety, hostility, arise most infallibly when the familiar appears in an unfamiliar shape: a beloved maternal figure in a new dress, a life-size or life-like doll, are far more menacing than a stranger or a little stick-figure. "Even the smallest difference can be stressed and overstressed and may become a focal point around which prejudice may crystallize," Ernst Kris has written. "One can go even further: propinquity seems to invite such overemphasis." And that overemphasis, he adds, "serves mainly the purpose of maintaining" the "integrity of the group." If "one difference tends to disappear or to lose its importance," then "another one is called upon to take its place."[16] Familiarity, slightly modified, breeds anxiety.

The political rhetoric and political action of Germany's governors in the 1870s and 1880s support this diagnosis. Critics were stamped with the name "Reichsfeind," a convenient epithet but one that expressed a widespread perception. Enemies of the Reich were enemies of wholeness; they were, in the instructive phrase of the day, "disintegrating—*zersetzende*" forces. Particularists were trying to dissolve, or decisively weaken, the just-born organism by restoring earlier, smaller units. Roman Catholics were employing their massive numbers and clerical discipline to undermine the unity so ardently desired and so recently secured. Social Democrats threatened to tear apart the new, still-delicate fabric by seducing workers into atheism and rebellious conduct in the factory.

The Jew was a peculiarly suitable victim of this anxious scheme

16. Ernst Kris, "Notes on the Psychology of Prejudice" (1946), in *The Selected Papers of Ernst Kris* (1975), 465–72, esp. 467–68. Freud speaks of "The Narcissism of Small Differences," *Civilization and Its Discontents*, S.E., XXI, 114; G. W., XIV, 474. (For full references to Freud's works see p. 41, note 20.)

of perceptions. He was the most insidious enemy because he was the most insinuating. The psychological mechanisms of anti-Jewish sentiment were far from simple; psychological mechanisms rarely are. Many German anti-Semites feared and detested the Jew because, they said, he insisted on retaining, and parading, his differences; Heinrich von Treitschke, who around 1880 lent anti-Semitism his enormous prestige, was not alone in hoping that his "Israelitic fellow-citizens" would become fully Germans.[17] For such as Treitschke, anti-Semitism was a response to disappointment: those he had invited to be like himself persisted in being themselves. But other anti-Semites disliked the Jew for precisely the opposite reason: for making such strenuous efforts to erase all boundaries between themselves and their gentile fellow-citizens. For these haters of Jews, it was proximity, the narrowing gap, that moved them to exaggerate, or to invent, stigmas of difference. But there were also many Germans who had outgrown both varieties of Teutonic tribalism; in fact, toward the end of the nineteenth century it seemed that they were increasing, in gratifying numbers. Germany's Jews had therefore good reason to feel themselves, or to aspire to feel themselves, to be Jewish Germans. They indignantly rejected all talk of a "Jewish question" as a survival of primitive politics. In retrospect we know that in a sense, a sense they did not intend, they were right: the so-called Jewish question had no reality in isolation. It was part of, and clue to, that larger question, the German question.

3. GERMANS AMONG THE MODERNS

The uses of the Jewish question as a cultural clue do not end here; it points to an even larger theatre than Germany, to that international movement that came to dominate European culture in the late nineteenth century: Modernism. The question will prove to be instructive, paradoxically not in what it was, but in what it was perceived to be—and was not.

17. See below, "The Berlin-Jewish Spirit."

In recent years, historians of anti-Semitism have refined earlier political and economic diagnoses by adding a subtle psychological dimension; they have perceived the malady as exhibiting a particularly virulent strain of cultural nostalgia. They have suggested that for anti-Semites, the Jew appeared to concentrate, in his character and conduct, all the qualities that they, as anxious, tradition-ridden Germans, found most unmanageable and most unsettling. He seemed to them clever, rootless, physically and psychologically mobile—a provocative assailant, the unpalatable antithesis, of their cherished Teutonic ideals. The Jew was the parvenu adept at mimicry, the pushy migrant elbowing his way up the social ladder or clambering across political frontiers, carrying, for either journey, precious little moral baggage. He stood, in short, for all the forces the anti-Semite felt powerless to prevent from taking over his world.[18]

The myth of the mobile, the intolerably modern Jew was not the monopoly of village philosophers or political demagogues; it found respectable support in treatises by sociologists like Werner Sombart and rather less respectable, hence far weightier, support in satirical periodicals like *Simplicissimus*. It was really no accident, these tendentious observers would insist, that Jews should have "invaded," in unprecedented, almost uncanny numbers, the very pursuits that offered easy and substantial rewards to quickness of mind and absence of scruples: wholesale trade, stock market speculation, periodical journalism, radical politics— and avant-garde art, theatre, and literature. It mattered not at all that many Jews stood as living refutations to this cluster of stereotypes, that many of them were upright and cultivated, conservative in their politics and conventional in their tastes, patriotic and sometimes downright chauvinist Germans: the point of caricature was, after all, not to sum up actual characteristics, but to identify a convenient target for inconvenient emotions. It permitted the projection of feelings that anti-Semites found in themselves but thought dishonorable, and it licensed aggression against easily recognizable and often helpless "outsiders." Whatever else it was, German anti-Semitism was a way of confronting—or,

18. See among others, Stern, *Politics of Cultural Despair*.

rather, not confronting—the pressures of contemporary life, which were remaking Germany as they were other industrial nations in the nineteenth century: specialization, mechanization, the crowding in of impulses and the speeding up of existence, the burgeoning threats posed by Godless morality, Socialist revolution, and cultural nihilism; anti-Semitisim was, in short, an irrational protest against the modern world.

Threatening modernity pervaded all of life—work, play, morals, religion. But its most conspicuous manifestations clustered in high culture: in the arts, in literature, and in the domain of ideas—philosophy, psychology, the social sciences. It became almost a ritual (among proud Jews and nervous anti-Semites alike) to invoke the magical names of Marx, Freud, and Einstein to demonstrate the disproportionate share and dramatic influence of Jews in changing culture; names of only slightly lesser luster like Max Liebermann or Max Reinhardt or Georg Simmel only rounded out the picture of the Jew as the great innovator—or great subverter. Perceived as the archetypal modern in society, he also appeared as the archetypal Modernist in culture.

I will argue in this book that this reading of Modernism is grossly inaccurate. It gives Jews more publicity than they deserve—whether favorable or unfavorable. There were many Modernists who were not Jews, many Jews who were not Modernists. And many of the Jews who were Modernists were so not because they were Jews.[19] It is sheer anti-Semitic tendentiousness, or philo-Semitic parochialism, to canvass the great phenomenon of Modernism from the vantage point of the Jewish question. That perspective may illuminate some aspects of the cultural upheavals that made us what we are today; on most aspects it can throw no light whatever.

Modernism was a pervasive cultural revolution, a second Renaissance. Whether it had its inception with the German Romantics, with the intense artistic and literary atmosphere of Paris in the days of Baudelaire and Daumier, or with the informal alliance of French Impressionists, Modernism transformed culture in all its branches. It utterly changed painting, sculpture, and music;

19. See below, "Encounter with Modernism."

the dance, the novel, and the drama; architecture, poetry, and thought. And its ventures into unknown territory percolated from the rarefied regions of high culture to general ways of thinking, feeling, and seeing. A very troop of masters compelled Western civilization to alter its angle of vision, and to adopt a new aesthetic sensibility, a new philosophical style, a new mode of understanding social life and human nature.

The literary critics and literary historians who have by and large engrossed the inquiry into Modernism have, with rare unanimity, stressed its destructive energies, the invincible aversion of their favorite witnesses—Eliot, Pound, Yeats—to industrial civilization. With no hesitation, they have taken for the motto of this revolution Paul Claudel's outburst to Mallarmé: "I hold modern civilization in horror, and have always felt a stranger in it."[20] Modernism, it would seem, was the work of aliens, of exacerbated civilized exiles in a world dominated, and disfigured, by complacent philistines. At its very heart stood a curious verbal paradox: Modernists hated modernity—they hated, in other words, the rule of the machine, the vulgarity of bourgeois society, the pretensions of parvenus, the waning of community. In his felicitous and influential essay "The Modern Element in Modern Literature," the late Lionel Trilling characterized that modern element as "hostility to civilization," as the "canonization of the primal, non-ethical energies," as "the disenchantment of our culture with culture itself."[21] Other historians of Modernism have filled out Trilling's stark sketch of a duel to the death in Western culture by underscoring its combative posture. "The modern," writes Irving Howe, for one, "must be defined in terms of what it is not: the embodiment of a tacit polemic, an inclusive negative."[22] And these historians have carefully differentiated the Modern from the moderate, rational impulse for reform, or from the private ambition for achieving fame by asserting individuality;

20. Robert D. D. Gibson, *Modern French Poets on Poetry: An Anthology*, 43.
21. (1961). Reprinted as "On the Teaching of Modern Literature," in Trilling, *Beyond Culture* (1965), 19.
22. "The Idea of the Modern," Introduction to Howe, ed., *Literary Modernism* (1967), 13.

their Modernists live by passionate acts of sweeping rejection, with strenuous pessimism and muscular nihilism.

To be sure, historians and practitioners of Modernism alike have recognized that the movement was something other, something more, than reaction. Friedrich Nietzsche, victim of the modern and prophet of Modernism, appraised one of his own central texts, *Beyond Good and Evil*, as "in all essentials *a critique of modernity*, not excluding the modern sciences, the modern arts, even modern politics, and complete with hints for a counter-type which is as unmodern as possible: an aristocratic, a yea-saying type. In the final analysis, the book is a school of the gentleman." But then he added—and it is this proviso that lends the passage its significance—that he wanted the term "gentleman" to be taken "in a more spiritual and more radical fashion than ever in the past."[23] When Modernists turned to the classical tradition—witness Nietzsche late in the nineteenth century, and Joyce, Picasso, Stravinsky, Eliot, and others some decades later— they did so to exploit rather than to embrace it. Their classicism was ironic, manipulative, almost cannibalistic. This was the exploitation that T. S. Eliot professed to see in James Joyce's *Ulysses*, a work which, as he wrote in his famous review, used the myth of Odysseus to lay bare "the immense panorama of futility and anarchy which is contemporary history."[24] Even when they resorted to the old, the Modernists wanted, in Ezra Pound's much-quoted phrase, to make it new.

The dominant reading of Modernism, in sum, sees it as a confluence of anti-rationalism, experimentalism, and alienation. As anti-rationalists, the Modernists rejected what they disdained as mere surface knowledge, as shallow and positivist science, in favor of a deeper, more penetrating and more expressive radical subjectivity which would give access to the causes of conduct, the springs of imagination, the grounds of being. This anti-rationalism was necessarily embodied in experiments, bold departures in style and substance, which the historian must read as devastating reflections on the bankruptcy of nineteenth-century academic art

23. *Ecce Homo, Werke*, III, 587.
24. See Stephen Spender, *The Struggle of the Modern* (1963), 208.

and science, and of respectable ways of doing literature or architecture or music, and read also, more positively, as reflecting invincible pressures for new approaches to old aesthetic and philosophical verities. And both anti-rationalism and experimentalism
were in turn embodied in the posture of alienation, a stance not
freely chosen but forced on all creative persons by the triumphant
and barbaric reign of the philistine, and the stupidity of prevailing norms in art and life: Jean-Paul Sartre speaks for this view
when he accepts the Symbolists' verdict that "from 1850 on, one
had to be insane to be a writer," and adds that "from 1830 onward, a neurosis was the royal road to a masterpiece."[25] This
alienation was unprecedented, different in kind from the splendid
isolation of a Michelangelo or a Leonardo; it generated a receptive, if rather exclusive, public for what was valid and enduring
in art and thought by forming social groupings unknown to earlier
ages, the avant-garde, which produced the unmistakable emblem
of Modernism: the adversary culture.

The evidence supporting this interpretation of modern culture,
whether drawn from poets or novelists, composers or critics, is
voluminous and seems conclusive. Not without reason, studies
and anthologies of Modernism fairly burst with texts amounting
to declarations of war on the vile bourgeoisie, texts dating back
to Flaubert, that great *bourgeoisophobus*, to Stendhal, to the
German Romantics, and back even, in rudimentary yet recognizable form, to Goethe's Werther: expressions of disgust with
the stuffy Academy or the vulgar patron, laments for the decay of
creative vigor in a sea of mediocrity, claims for the heroic artist
and embattled thinker, elevated into guide, prophet, or martyr.
Whether dandy, Bohemian, failure, madman, or cult hero, the
Modernist appears in modern society as a rebel, as the unappeasable adversary of accepted pieties, looking down on his contemporaries from the lofty height of his mission, and across an
unbridgeable gulf of disdain, not unmixed with despair. Lionel
Trilling notes that Thomas Mann "once said that all his work
could be understood as an effort to free himself from the middle

25. *L'Idiot de la famille: Gustave Flaubert de 1821 à 1857*, 3 vols. so far,
III (1972), 41.

class," and, Trilling comments, "this, of course, will serve to describe the chief intention of modern literature."[26] Mann's observation, and Trilling's gloss, reverberate with the authentic accents of the adversary culture.

It is hard to know which is more astonishing: Mann's self-appraisal or Trilling's unhesitating acceptance of it; Trilling's "of course" especially must engage our skeptical attention. For, while the prevailing view of Modernism can claim a measure of validity, its confident generalities are at the least too sweeping and in many instances false. It is not just because we can find exceptions—there are always exceptions to comprehensive periodic terms or cultural definitions—but rather because these presumed exceptions are almost as numerous and, I want to argue, almost as characteristic of Modernism as the voices of rejection that are so often, and so affectionately, adduced as truly representative of its work and our age. By no means every innovator was a *poète maudit*, or a poverty-stricken, misunderstood eccentric, or a philosophical nihilist in love with prostitutes, or with death. There were Modernists, radicals in their craft yet eminently sane in their private being and at home in respectable circles; there were other Modernists who made their revolutions quietly, by returning again and again to the very tradition that nourished them and that they were, quite unconsciously, subverting forever. If Baudelaire was an outsider, unpredictable, unique on principle, a taker of drugs and a seeker of sensations, he was also a disciplined poet, a tough-minded critic of art and literature, an appreciative Parisian, a social observer who could celebrate, with benign irony and genuine affection, the "heroism of modern life." Edouard Manet, who more than any other painter deserves the title Father of the Moderns, persisted in submitting his shocking, "unfinished" canvases to the Salons to cajole and persuade the unadventurous public that attended them; he craved no recognition more than the ribbon of the *Légion d'Honneur*—the very emblem, to fellow-rebels, of the hated bourgeoisie. And Baudelaire and Manet are as authentic Modernists as Van Gogh, pariah and suicide, or Gauguin, iconoclast and primitive. The historians of Modernism have

26. "On the Teaching of Modern Literature," *Beyond Culture*, 30.

fastened on the disdain and despair of Modernists at the expense of their frequent conformism and their equally frequent exhilaration.[27]

Moreover, the avant-gardes which, together, made Modernist culture were no more monolithic than the Establishment that they were, according to common report, committed to destroying; there was civil war in both camps. Indeed, my military metaphor, designed to complicate the picture, still leaves it too simple, for there were more than two camps, however disunited, and there were shifting alliances, cordial exchanges, across what we have been taught to regard as permanent battle lines. Whatever T. S. Eliot might have believed, James Joyce did not write *Ulysses* to pillory contemporary life as an immense panorama of futility and anarchy; Joyce chose "yes," that memorable last word of *Ulysses*, emphatically, rhythmically reiterated, with as much deliberation as he chose anything else in this sprawling and controlled masterpiece: he wanted, as he explicitly said, to end his novel with the most positive word in the English language.[28] *Ulysses* was an act of affirmation, not of alienation. So were other monuments of Modernism.

I am not denying the prominent place of irony, of impudence, of unconventionality, of imaginative freedom in the Modernist movement. But its bursting of boundaries did not imply hostility to discipline; its vigorous aesthetic and social criticism did not involve a yielding to depression; its profound exploration of unreason was not a celebration of irrationality.[29] The Modernists found almost as many ways of affirming life as they did of rejecting it, and they were equally modern in each of these postures.

It follows from these reflections that the historian of Modernist culture may best begin his revision of current, clearly inadequate interpretations by enlarging the territory of Modernism. He is taking risks, the risk of smuggling preferences into a descriptive term, making "Modernism" a synonym for everything

27. I have discussed the more positive element in Modernism in my *Art and Act: On Causes in History—Manet, Gropius, Mondrian* (1976).
28. The details are lucidly, if briefly, laid out in Richard Ellmann, *James Joyce* (1959), 536.
29. See below, 70.

he likes, or dislikes, or the even greater risk of diluting the capacity of the term to discriminate by calling "Modernist" every idea, every artifact, made since 1850. But these are risks worth taking; once noted, the historian may evade them. At all events, he is compelled to raise the most far-reaching doubts about the accepted polarities that constrict the meaning of "Modernism," apparent opposites like spontaneity versus form, unreason versus reason, experiment versus conformism, future versus past. By questioning these polarities, which are willed inventions rather than observed realities, he will see this great cultural upheaval freed from prejudgments, with a new responsiveness, and thus be able to accommodate the varieties of the Modernist impulse.

Several of the essays that follow address themselves to such a re-evaluation, but I know that more, much more, needs to be done. This injunction holds for the historian of Germany as forcefully as it does for the historian of other cultures. Indeed, Modernism was an incurably international movement; it subsisted on a network of exchange, a trading of ideas, innovations, techniques, far more extensive, and intensive, than most observers then, living in an increasingly chauvinist atmosphere, were ready, or even able, to recognize. After all, even chauvinists borrowed many of their most telling epithets, some of their most exclusive claims, from abroad. And Germans were actively and continuously trading in that enormous cultural bazaar that constituted nineteenth-century Western civilization, trading not as consumers alone, but as producers. The historian of Modernist culture who does not know German culture does not know Modernist culture. And the obverse is equally true: the historian of German culture who knows German culture alone does not know that culture.

But while the history of Modernism is pre-eminently international history, history without frontiers, it is also, and significantly, comparative history. For each cultural region generated, received, and transmitted the innovations of the day in its fashion, and developed particular institutions to foster, or stifle, the new impulses. Germany had its Bohemia, in Munich and in Berlin, in imitation of the French original, but forty years later and with characteristics of its own. Germany had its select coterie of poets and cultural critics, the Stefan George *Kreis*, on the Parisian model, but with a mystique and with political implications that were unique. Germany, much earlier, had had its circle of religious painters, the Nazarenes, whom the English in the 1830s and 1840s devoutly admired but whose style they, in receiving it, adapted to their domestic needs. Germany both changed, and was changed by, such temporary visitors, such magnificent exiles, as Ibsen, Strindberg, and Munch. The German cultural historian, in short, still has much to do; my essays are first attempts at doing some of the work still required. That so much should still remain undone is perfectly understandable: German questions, it would appear, are not German questions alone.

I

SIGMUND FREUD
A German and His Discontents

1. CANDOR AND CONCEALMENT

Anyone who knows just one thing about Freud knows something
that is not so. He knows that Sigmund Freud wholly derived his
theory, and developed his therapy, from his work with neurotic,
middle-class, Jewish, Viennese women, and that both theory and
therapy therefore are valid for them alone—if for them. In reality,
Freud's exposure to the varieties of mental stress was far more
differentiated than this: if all his patients were, by definition,
neurotic, many of them were aristocrats or Christians or foreigners or men. Freud's most historic analysand, himself, constitutes a catalogue of exceptions; he was, of course, no woman, a
most indifferent Jew, and a Viennese only by adoption. After
World War I, in fact, Freud conducted more analyses in English
than in German, and while he did so more from necessity than
choice—in the midst of Austria's postwar economic distress, and
his own, he desperately wanted hard currency—this says something about the possible application of psychoanalysis beyond
that highly selected, narrowly specialized circle—bourgeois, Jewish, female, Viennese—that legend has foisted on it.[1] The rich

1. Hanns Sachs, *Freud: Master and Friend* (1945), passim; Ernest Jones,
The Life and Work of Sigmund Freud, 3 vols. (1953–57), III, ch. 1 passim.
While often gracelessly written and lacking distance from the master, Jones's
Freud remains indispensable for massive material unavailable elsewhere and
for superb inside information.

and varied repertory of Freud's cases matters; it matters not merely because it lends support to his claim that he was propounding a general psychology, but also because it helps to place Freud in that sprawling, familiar, yet often surprising terrain we call German culture.

The most misleading implication commonly drawn from the misinformed myth about Freud's cases is the conviction that psychoanalysis is somehow characteristically, inescapably, Viennese—as though Freud could never have made his discoveries in Munich, let alone Berlin. Vienna, we are told, was a city vibrant with intellect and sex, and Freud, seizing his unique opportunity, used the first to explore the second. "Vienna of the late nineteenth century," A. J. P. Taylor, for one, has written, "was an exciting creative city. Quite apart from the new movements in art and music, Freud was working out a new approach to psychology that would rock the foundations of established morality," and he goes on to list, as proof of Vienna's creativity, Brentano's philosophizing, Boehm-Bawerk's economic thought, and the pioneering studies by Austrian sociologists. "Wits were quicker in Vienna than in Germany, ideas more novel, and spirits less restricted." And sexual frivolity had a conspicuous part in the atmosphere: love affairs, quickly consummated and just as quickly abandoned, were, as Taylor puts it, "something of a Viennese speciality. Sentiment had to come into them as well as bed. Love affairs were as light as most Viennese emotions. The male partner was always aware that that affair would end and was usually relieved when it did." What made these affairs so easy to begin and to break off was that the girls were normally of a lower social class than their lovers, "barmaids, shopgirls, dressmakers, amateurs who were readily available," glad, the young men about town thought, to be seduced and grateful to have such distinguished company. Yet "ultimately," Taylor concludes, "the men would settle down and become patriarchs, tyrannizing over their wives and children. Freud," he notes in his parting shot, "assumed too readily that all men were like the Viennese."[2] It hardly sounds like a reliable foundation for a general science of the mind.

2. "Foreword" to Arthur Schnitzler, *My Youth in Vienna*, tr. Catherine Hutter (1970), xii, xiii.

These passages are representative of a large literature. Taylor, one might object, is a political historian who has exhibited an almost hilarious ignorance of psychoanalysis,[3] but other writers, better informed, have been equally insistent on the essentially Viennese character of Freud's mind. Thus, in his obese history of dynamic psychology, Henri Ellenberger says flatly, though without offering much evidence, that "Freud was Viennese to his fingertips"; to call him "un-Viennese shows a confusion between the stereotype of a Viennese operetta and the historical reality."[4] And at the beginning of his much-cited article "Politics and Patricide in Freud's *Interpretation of Dreams*," Carl Schorske reports Freud's witty response to the news that he had just been made an *Ausserordentlicher Professor* at the University of Vienna: writing to his friend Wilhelm Fliess in Berlin, Freud describes his "promotion as a political triumph," and fantasizes about immense public enthusiasm, about a steady flow of bouquets and congratulations, as though His Majesty the Emperor had just

3. "Freud," wrote Taylor, reviewing that controversial "psychobiography" of Woodrow Wilson by William Bullitt in which Freud had a hand, *Thomas Woodrow Wilson: A Psychological Study* (1967), "Freud had some bright ideas, which he called 'laws.' They applied to every human being, dead or alive, and did not go far to explain why one individual differed from another. The starting point was the Oedipus complex. This lays down that, by the nature of things, all young men love their mothers and hate their fathers. Incidentally Oedipus was remarkably free from this complex. No man took more trouble to avoid killing his father, and he so disliked his mother that he tore his eyes out when he discovered that he was married to her. This faulty analogy was characteristic of the slapdash way in which Freud operated. However, here we are with the Oedipus complex. Unfortunately many men like their fathers or even love them. This does not seem surprising if the father is likable, as fathers often are. However, according to Freud, it has appalling results. . . ." *Thomas Woodrow Wilson*, Taylor concludes, "quite funny when read in small doses" but "boring after a time," leaves the historian with only one question: "How did anyone ever manage to take Freud seriously?" "Silliness in Excelsis," *The New Statesman and Nation*, May 12, 1967, pp. 653–54.

4. Henri F. Ellenberger, *The Discovery of the Unconscious: The History and Evolution of Dynamic Psychiatry* (1970), 465, 463. Self-important and opinionated, the book dishes out verdicts of approval and disapproval much like an old-fashioned schoolmaster, though it is, necessarily, full of historical information.

recognized the role of sexuality, the Council of Ministers confirmed the interpretation of dreams, and parliament voted, by a two-thirds majority, the need for the psychoanalytic treatment of hysteria. "It is a cheerful fantasy," Schorske comments, "very Viennese: political authority bends the knee to Eros and to dreams."[5] The nexus between psychoanalysis and Vienna seems, in a word, beyond need for discussion. But there is one matter on which historians linking Freud with Vienna divide, and their conflict of opinion constitutes, as it often does, an invitation to skepticism and the road to interpretative freedom. Some have suggested that psychoanalysis had to emerge in Vienna, and nowhere else, because prevalent sexual hypocrisy virtually cried out for someone to probe the dominant, though hidden, preoccupation that marked all of Vienna's inner life; others, in contrast, that psychoanalysis was Viennese because sexual candor provided the inquisitive psychologist with ample materials, materials more abundant and more freely displayed here than in other cities.[6] Both of

5. Carl E. Schorske, "Politics and Patricide in Freud's *Interpretation of Dreams*," *American Historical Review*, LXXVIII (1973), 328–47, at 328. While I do not accept its conclusion, I have learned much from this subtle essay, as well as two others by Schorske, "Politics and the Psyche in *fin-de-siècle* Vienna: Schnitzler and Hofmannsthal," *American Historical Review*, LXVI (1961), 930–46; and "Politics in a New Key: An Austrian Triptych," *Journal of Modern History*, XXXIV (1967), 343–86. For a recent expression of the thesis that Freud was essentially Viennese, see Jerome Bruner, "Psychology and the Image of Man," a Herbert Spencer Lecture at Oxford: "Freud's scripts may have been culture-bound projections of *fin-de-siècle* Vienna. But for him they served as the cognitive systems in terms of which the symbolic significance of events could be understood." (*The Times Literary Supplement*, December 17, 1976, p. 1591.)

6. The *locus classicus* for a description of Viennese sexuality and hypocrisy is Stefan Zweig, *Die Welt von Gestern: Erinnerungen eines Europäers* (1944), which is more excited than analytical. Another presumed link is equally tenuous: Hugo von Hofmannsthal's dramas have sometimes been placed in the Freudian tradition. And it is true that Hofmannsthal had the first editions of Breuer and Freud, *Studien über Hysterie*, and Freud's *Traumdeutung* in his library. But, writes Michael Hamburger, who records this biographical detail, as a poet Hofmannsthal had access to the regions of unconscious impulses in ways other than studying Freud, and that, at most, Freud was one of many guides. Freud himself would have said the

these assertions cannot be true at the same time, but all agree that Vienna at the turn of the century boasted a disparate yet closely associated army of freedom fighters, of liberators who must have inspired one another in important ways: Arthur Schnitzler, Karl Kraus, Ludwig Wittgenstein—and Sigmund Freud.

It is certain that Freud was very much aware of Vienna and that (though to a much smaller degree) Vienna was aware of Freud. He conducted many of his scientific skirmishes here; his earliest detractors, though not his earliest admirers, were Viennese. He admired Schnitzler—his tribute to Schnitzler as a "colleague" in the investigation of the "underestimated and much-maligned erotic" has often been quoted[7]—was in turn derided by Kraus, and gave Wittgenstein food for tortured reflections.[8] But it would be rash, and I think wrong, to conclude that the boldness of his fellow-Viennese somehow infected Freud with a boldness of his own, or that their observations shortened or in any way eased his own laborious descent to the foundations of human behavior. I want to argue that Freud lived far less in Austrian Vienna than in his own mind; he lived with the international positivist tradition, with the tantalizing triumphs of classical archeologists, with the admirable and moving model provided by that

same thing. (Hamburger, *Hugo von Hofmannsthal: Zwei Studien* [tr. into German by Klaus Reichert, 1964], 87.)

7. Schorske, "Politics and the Psyche," 936.

8. See, for details, William M. Johnston, *The Austrian Mind: An Intellectual and Social History 1848–1938* (1972), especially chs. 15–17; and Allan Janik and Stephen Toulmin, *Wittgenstein's Vienna* (1973), 62, 64, 75–77. As will emerge in my text, I reject their construction of "Vienna." Soberer is the pioneering effort at debunking, Ilsa Barea, *Vienna* (1966). A most useful general study of the crucially important clash and cooperation of nations in the Hapsburg domains is Robert A. Kann, *The Multinational Empire* (1950). The measure of Freud's isolation in the academic world of Vienna remains controversial, though K. R. Eissler's bellicose *Sigmund Freud und die Wiener Universität* (1966) shows pretty convincingly that Freud's career was slower than that of others. This does not mean, however, that he had no influential sponsors among physicians who rejected his psychoanalytic ideas—he did. Erna Lesky, *Die Wiener medizinische Schule im 19. Jahrhundert* (1965), is indispensable.

great French scientist of the mind, Jean-Martin Charcot, with the consolations of his far-flung correspondence, and with the infinitely instructive surprises of systematic introspection. Naturally, his introspection fed, often casually and quite unconsciously, on materials Freud gathered up in Vienna, on visits to his cigar merchant or during his regular card game, in the slow progress up the academic ladder and with his experience of Austrian anti-Semitism. After all, like many of his early patients, Freud was brought up in Vienna and permanently settled there; Vienna's often bizarre politics impinged on his awareness daily, with his reading of the newspaper.

Yet it is, I think, scarcely claiming too much to say that "Vienna," that distinctive, impalpable, all-pervasive, electric atmosphere in which everyone knew everyone who counted, and everyone who was anyone acted both as teacher and pupil in an intense, continuing seminar on Modernist culture—*that* Vienna is an invention of cultural historians in search of quick explanations. There were indeed opulent salons in Vienna, fostering surroundings for new poems, new ideas, new compositions. Poets recited to each other, composers visited their rivals' concerts, philosophers formed working circles. And some of the physicians with whom the young Freud worked attended these schools for culture. Yet Freud himself went to the theatre less and less, and never became a habitué of Viennese salon life; his Vienna was medical Vienna, and *that* city rarely frequented the hospitable mansions of Vienna's patrons.[9] Besides, that medical Vienna was only partially Austrian; instead it represented, late in the nineteenth century, a microcosm of German scientific talent: the physiologist Ernst Brücke and the clinician Hermann Nothnagel, two distinguished medical men whose influence on Freud's scien-

9. George Rosen is almost alone to have noticed this; see his perceptive essay, "Freud and Medicine in Vienna," in Jonathan Miller, ed., *Freud: The Man, His World, His Influence* (1972), 21–39; esp. at 23. Most instructive for glimpses of that world are the study by Meynert's daughter, Dora Stockert-Meynert, *Theodor Meynert und seine Zeit: Zur Geistesgeschichte Österreichs in der zweiten Hälfte des 19. Jahrhunderts* (1930); Ernst Theodor Brücke, *Ernst Brücke* (1928); and Siegfried Bernfeld, "Freud's Scientific Beginnings," *American Imago*, VI (1949), 163–88.

tific mode of thinking was decisive, were both Germans who had assumed their posts in Vienna after training and working in the "north." Freud, then, had relatively little to do with the "prison"[10] he sometimes loved and often hated, and reached out beyond it. His mind, it will emerge, was as large, as free, as his physical habitat was constricted.

Berggasse 19, where Freud lived for nearly half a century, is an unpretentious apartment house on a respectable residential street in northern Vienna. When he moved there in the summer of 1891 to take a small apartment, Freud was a promising young neurologist with unorthodox ideas and a future to make; when he left the house and Nazi-occupied Austria in June 1938 "to die in freedom,"[11] he was a world-famous old man, founder of a science as pervasive in its influence as it was controversial in its claims. He enacted much quiet drama in this building; the silent struggles and private triumphs that mark the lives of all intellectual innovators marked this innovator more than others. Here, at Berggasse 19, Freud wrote most of his books and analyzed most of his patients; here he gathered his library, collected his art, met his associates, raised his children, and conducted a voluminous correspondence in which he rehearsed his momentous ideas and kept the threads of the psychoanalytic movement from twisting or from disintegrating altogether. His apartment is now a museum, and a plaque informs the passer-by that Sigmund Freud "lived and worked" here. The celebration seems modest enough for one of the decisive discoverers in history, for the Columbus of the mind. Nor does the plaque represent an effusion of local pride: it was put up in 1953 by the World Federation for Mental Health. In fact, most of the recognition Freud has received in Vienna has been the work of foreigners: his bust, which now stands in the University, was presented by Ernest Jones. There is in Vi-

10. Freud to Max Eitingon from London, June 8, 1938; quoted in Jones, *Freud*, III, 230.
11. Sigmund Freud to his son Ernst, May 12, 1938, in English. *Sigmund Freud, Briefe 1873–1939*, selected and edited by Ernst L. Freud (1960), 435.

enna, crisscrossed with streets named after its great, or at least prominent, residents, no Freudgasse.[12] Guidebooks and leaflets advertising the city, though in their accustomed way assiduous in rescuing once-famous Viennese from oblivion, barely mention his name. The public indifference, the latent hostility, are chilling. Freud, the first psychologist to chart the workings of ambivalence, had in this city abundant materials for the exercise of mixed feelings. Vienna, it seems, has largely repressed Freud.

But Freud is irrepressible. He has scattered rich and rewarding clues to himself, to his way of thinking and his mode of working, to his habits and his aversions. His living quarters were a museum in the figurative sense—a crammed, instructive storehouse of ideas, tastes, and convictions—long before they were elevated into an official place of pilgrimage for foreign psychoanalysts and foreign analysands. His autobiographical writings are terse but informative. His letters are abundant, energetic, and wholly characteristic. Best of all, his scientific works provide sketch maps to his innermost nature. Considering the kind of science he founded, they could not do anything less: psychoanalysis is controlled and deep autobiography, and as the first psychoanalyst, compelled as he was to use himself as material, Freud found it necessary to publish some of his most private fantasies. His life was among his best documents.

Yet Freud presents himself to the world not without masks—some of them deliberate strategies of self-protection, others unconscious devices. It is true, and helpful, that Freud was not afflicted with the vice of modesty. He spoke and wrote of his discoveries and accomplishments with an engaging absence of coyness; having been a well-loved child, he always retained a firm sense of his gifts. But he failed, for all his confidence, to recognize the full measure of his qualities and of his historic stature. In a famous autobiographical summing up, he told Wilhelm Fliess in February 1900, "I am actually not a man of science at all, not

12. It is fair to note that for a time during the 1930s the City Council of Vienna proposed to name Berggasse after Freud, a suggestion that Freud found objectionable and that political events made impossible. And there is now a block of apartments named after Freud in the district of Vienna, the Ninth, in which he lived for so long. Jones, *Freud*, II, 14, 380.

an observer, not an experimenter, not a thinker. I am nothing but a conquistador by temperament, an adventurer, if you want to translate this term, with all the inquisitiveness, daring and tenacity of such a man."[13] The passage is candid and sincere. Fliess was a prominent ear, nose, and throat specialist with a lucrative practice in Berlin, a man of charismatic presence and with scientific ambitions second only to Freud's own; during the 1890s, the lonely decade of Freud's discoveries, he was Freud's closest friend, probably his only friend. But while we may accept Freud's denials as a serious attempt at self-appraisal, we must reject their pretensions to being an accurate self-portrait. It suggests the solidity of his self-regard, the strength of his ego; it exemplifies his readiness to speak of himself with large, sweeping gestures. But it displays, too, a certain myopia, and a reductionism rare in Freud's thinking. Freud was in many respects unique, but in this he was like other humans: he was not his own best judge.

His misjudgment, coupled as it was with a fierce desire to guard his privacy, has generated a contradiction which every student of Freud must confront. Freud's science was, above all, the science of candor. The technique of psychoanalysis depends, as everyone knows, on the uninhibited freedom with which the analysand produces his associations, without fear and without reserve; his most illogical notions and most forbidden desires must come out, and be recorded, in the apparent disorder in which they emerge into his awareness—that is, as much as his ever-alert defenses will let him. He must arrange nothing, conceal nothing: the psychoanalyst and the censor are sworn enemies. The candor is, to be sure, one-sided; Freud said more than once that for the sake of the patient the psychoanalyst must remain a stranger, keeping himself to himself, a blank sheet on which the analysand inscribes his transferences. But Freud stands in history as analyst and as analysand, and we must see him in both capacities to see him at all, as Freud himself did in the course of his self-analysis. Yet here he fails his historian, at least partially. His confessions in *The Interpretation of Dreams* and elsewhere, intimate and copi-

13. February 1, 1900. From the German text printed in Max Schur, *Freud: Living and Dying* (1972), 547. Schur's intimate biography adds much valuable unpublished material.

ous as they are, require elucidation, enlargement, correction—in short, interpretation. They often sound grudging, almost extorted. Max Schur, Freud's physician and friend, notes the reluctance with which Freud saw the forthcoming publication of his letters to Fliess, the most revealing and intimate letters he ever wrote. And his confessions are, and will always remain, fragmentary: in April 1885, Freud told his fiancée, Martha Bernays, "I have almost completed an undertaking which a number of people, still unborn but fated to misfortune, will feel severely. Since, after all, you can't guess what sort of people I mean, I will tell you right off: they're my biographers. I have destroyed all my notes of the last fourteen years, as well as letters, scientific extracts, and manuscripts of my works. Among letters, only family letters have been spared."[14] When he wrote these lines, Freud clearly had some intimation of his possible importance; he was writing lightheartedly, but then, Freud has taught us to take all expressions seriously. We are therefore entitled to conclude that as early as 1885, when he was twenty-eight and wholly unknown, he had fantasies of biographers in his future. Fifteen years later, after he had made his discoveries, he wondered to Fliess whether one day there might be a "marble tablet" at the house in Bellevue where he had dreamt the "Irma" dream: "Here, on July 24, 1895, the Secret of Dreams was revealed to Dr. Sigm. Freud."[15] It is doubtless an appealing trait in Freud that he did not permit himself to posture either as a poor, worthless creature, or, conversely, as a monument before his time; his ironic informality even in moments of exaltation, his unvarying stoicism in days of disappointment, lend the evidence he chose to preserve an authority it would not have were it artfully, self-consciously, squinting at the biographer. Yet by disguising some of that evidence and destroy-

---

14. April 28, 1885. Freud, *Briefe*, 136. See also Jones, *Freud*, I, xii.
15. Sigmund Freud, *The Origins of Psychoanalysis. Letters to Wilhelm Fliess, Drafts and Notes: 1887–1902*, ed. Marie Bonaparte, Anna Freud, Ernst Kris; tr. Eric Mosbacher and James Strachey (1954), 322; Sigmund Freud, *Aus den Anfängen der Psychoanalyse. Briefe an Wilhelm Fliess, Abhandlungen und Notizen aus den Jahren 1887–1902* (1950), 344. (For this and other dual citation, see below, footnote 20.)

ing some of the rest, Freud did not act as a man seriously expecting that marble tablet ever to be put up.

There is much, then, that Freud has not allowed posterity to know about him. Face to face with this selective—from the inquirer's vantage point, most thoughtless—discretion, the historian is compelled to explore the clues that Freud did permit to survive. He can interrogate Freud's writings, noting his deliberate stylistic strategies and unconscious literary habits; he can profitably juxtapose the radicalism of Freud's ideas with the conservatism of his social posture; he can pursue Freud's commitment to science to its intellectual and emotional roots. I intend to follow all three of these paths of inquiry, but I want to begin by surprising Freud at home, in his consulting room, his study, his larger apartment, and to discover what this historic laboratory reveals about Freud, that puzzle from which too many pieces are missing. He lived, after all, surrounded by objects he cherished—books, photographs, sculptures—and these objects testify, reluctantly and eloquently, like a dream, to the mind of their owner.[16] To see how he lived is the first step toward resolving the tension in Freud between candor and concealment, a tension which his ideas amply explain and his character imperiously exacted.

2. A PARTIALITY FOR THE PREHISTORIC

The first and overpowering impression that Freud's habitat made on the visitor was the profusion of things. The books were neatly arranged, the pictures neatly hung, the rugs neatly spread over wall, couch, and floor, the sculptures neatly placed facing forward in close-packed ranks like soldiers on parade. The books alone did not invite comment; they seemed wholly right for a learned professor and prolific writer. But the pictures were crowded together

16. For a pictorial account of Freud's apartment in Vienna in 1938, see *Berggasse 19: Sigmund Freud's Home and Offices, Vienna 1938, The Photographs of Edmund Engelman* (1976), to which an earlier version of this essay served as an introduction.

as if imitating the hanging arrangements of some old-fashioned museum, and there were, even so, too many of them for the available space: some framed photographs obstructed and obscured the books behind them. And the rugs encroached on each other's visual field, literally overlapping; handsome orientals of varying provenance, they did not complement but almost canceled one another with their clashing patterns. The sculptures, finally, had their assigned shelves and their glass cases, but they intrusively invaded surfaces intended for other purposes: bookshelves, tops of cabinets, writing tables, even Freud's much-used desk. The whole was an embarrassment of objects.

It was the pieces of sculpture that advanced the most irresistible claim to attention. When, in 1909, the psychoanalyst Hanns Sachs, who came to know Freud well, first visited Berggasse 19, he observed that while Freud's collection of antiquities was "still in its initial stages, some of the objects at once attracted the visitor's eye."[17] They were to become more conspicuous, more eye-catching, with the passage of years. Summoning up his memories a few days after Freud's death, the German psychoanalyst Victor von Weizsäcker could recall, of the consulting room at Freud's study, "only the long gallery of antique statuettes, bronzes, terracottas on his desk. Thus, when he looked up, the eye of the professor viewed these satyrs and goddesses."[18] But what did he see?

To pursue these antiquities to their points of departure is to travel among the remote roots of Western culture in the Mediterranean world: in Egypt, Cyprus, Pompeii, Greece, and Rome. It was only in his later years that Freud added objects from China to this rather concentrated collection. His pieces were reminders of the South, that place of warmth, of uninhibited freedom and cherished schoolboy tales, which has for centuries exercised its irresistible attraction on Northerners, including Freud's beloved Goethe, and on Freud himself. "A basket of orchids," he told Fliess on the occasion of his forty-fifth birthday, "shams splendor

17. Sachs, *Freud*, 49. Sachs's reminiscences are economical, admiring, and wise. Ch. II, "Vienna," provides some important insights.
18. "Reminiscences of Freud and Jung," in Benjamin Nelson, ed., *Freud and the 20th Century* (1957), 60.

and the blazing sun, a piece of a Pompeiian wall with a centaur and faun translates me to longed-for Italy."[19] Collecting was for Freud the passion of his life: Max Schur records that he called it "an addiction second in intensity only to his nicotine addiction."[20] In the last year of his life, eighty-two and dying painfully of cancer, he still corresponded with Princess Marie Bonaparte, who had helped to rescue him and most of his family from the Nazis, about his beloved statuettes.

It was a well-informed addiction. Freud liked to read in the relevant literature, and followed excavations, though when he told Stefan Zweig in 1931 that he had "made many sacrifices for my collection of Greek, Roman, and Egyptian antiquities and actually have read more archeology than psychology,"[21] the first half of the statement is more credible than the second. Doubtless Freud knew his ancient history and his archeology exceedingly

19. May 8, 1901. Freud, *Origins of Psychoanalysis*, 330; *Aus den Anfängen*, 354.

20. Schur, *Freud*, 247. Not long after 1900, Freud publicly referred to his antiquities as a "small collection." *The Psychopathology of Everyday Life*, in *Standard Edition of the Complete Psychological Works of Sigmund Freud*, translated under the general editorship of James Strachey in collaboration with Anna Freud, assisted by Alix Strachey and Alan Tyson, 24 vols. (1953–75), VI, 167 (henceforth S.E.); *Zur Psychopathologie des Alltaglebens*, in Sigmund Freud, *Gesammelte Werke*, ed. Anna Freud, E. Bibring, W. Hoffer, E. Kris, and O. Isakower in collaboration with Marie Bonaparte, 18 vols. (1940–68), IV, 186 (henceforth G.W.). While it is fair to say that Freud's translators (of his works and the various volumes of his letters) have done a heroic job in rendering his vigorous and supple German into English and normalizing his language across a lifetime of writing, they have often failed to convey Freud's economy of expression or capture the felicity of his formulations. Hence, while I have consulted the S.E. and the English versions of Freud's letters regularly, I have retranslated all passages from Freud myself. At the same time, for ease of reference, I have cited the English translation every time as well. The translators have done Freud two kinds of injustice: they have made him both more prolix and more genteel than he really was. They have rendered such an ordinary and suggestive German word as *Besetzung* with the formidable neologism "cathexis." (See, for a justification, S.E., III, 63n.) And they have rendered Freud's blunt word *Dukatenscheisser*, which is to say, "Ducat-shitter," as "one who excretes ducats." (See *Origins*, 189.) Actually, in a rare instance of inconsistency, they render this word as "shitter of ducats" in *Character and Anal Erotism*, S.E., IX, 174.

21. February 7, 1931. *Freud, Briefe*, 398–99.

well, but the books on his shelves—the bound volumes of journals he helped to edit, the books he read, and the books he wrote—reaffirm that the center of his attention was always the human mind, a dominant concern to which all the others, including his collecting, were tributaries. But the ancient world was a privileged tributary: some of the most prominent pictures on his walls, like that of Abu Simbel over the analytic couch, are commentaries on an inexhaustible interest. And it is certain that he made sacrifices to his addiction, especially in his earlier years, when he was an impecunious, struggling innovator in mental medicine. His letters to his family and to his friends are punctuated with reports of purchases he could not resist, bargains he could not pass by. "The ancient gods still exist," he wrote to Fliess in the summer of 1899, "for I have bought one or two lately, among them a stone Janus, who looks down on me with his two faces in very superior fashion."[22]

Beyond the sheer pleasure in collecting, Freud's acquisitions meant much to him. Like other mental events, his addiction, too, was overdetermined.[23] His letters suggest that what he called his "partiality for the prehistoric"[24] had several animating causes. "I have now adorned my room with plaster casts of the Florentine statues," he wrote to Fliess in December 1896. "It was a source of extraordinary refreshment for me; I am thinking of getting rich, in order to repeat these trips. A congress on Italian soil! (Naples, Pompeii)."[25] For one thing, then, Freud's Janus heads and terracotta statuettes were simply gratifying, pleasing to the senses of sight and touch. For another, they took him out of his daily routine and, even better, the often contemptible present. When he was young and poor, Freud had felt alone and embattled; after

22. July 17, 1899. *Origins*, 286; *Anfänge*, 305.
23. "Overdetermination" is a most useful, if perhaps infelicitously named, Freudian category. Freud first formulated it in the mid-1890s, in the years of his collaboration with Breuer, to emphasize that mental events must be traced to several regions of human psychology. The stress on the multiple causation of all events was, and remains, a salutary caution against dogmatism or reductionism.
24. January 30, 1899. *Origins*, 275; *Anfänge*, 293.
25. December 6, 1896. *Origins*, 181; *Anfänge*, 192. On Freud's longing for Rome, see the sensitive treatment by Schorske, "Politics and Patricide."

he became something of a celebrity and, though not rich, prosperous, he retained an ironic distance from his fame and a deep skepticism about human motives in general. For a healer, it has been justly observed, Freud had a strikingly low opinion of the human animal. Much happened to him across the years, much happened that pleased him. But the unreceptive world of Vienna never changed; neither did the hatred the educated mob felt for Freud the indiscreet discoverer, nor the hatred of that larger mob, educated and uneducated, for Freud the unrepentant Jew. "Something in me rebels against the compulsion to go on earning money which is never enough," he wrote glumly to his trusted Sàndor Ferenczi in early 1922, "and to continue with the same psychological devices that for thirty years have kept me upright in the face of my contempt for people and the detestable world. Strange secret yearnings rise in me—perhaps from my ancestral heritage—for the East and the Mediterranean and for a life of quite another kind: wishes from late childhood never to be fulfilled."[26] To contemplate his antiquities was to conjure up, in cheerful moods, trips taken and trips yet to be taken, and, in moments of discouragement, a world he liked better than his own. Writing to Fliess from Berchtesgaden in August 1899, he announced that on the next rainy day he planned to walk to his "beloved Salzburg," where he had recently "picked up a few Egyptian antiquities. These things put me in a good mood and speak to me of distant times and lands."[27]

But Freud was a psychoanalyst first and last; he would have permitted no obsession to dominate him so completely for so many years if it had not been somehow relevant to the science that was his life. Collecting antiquities both freed him from his work and brought him back to it. It is striking, and has not gone unnoticed, that Freud liked to draw on archeology for his metaphors. In the early *Studies on Hysteria*, which he wrote with Josef Breuer, Freud still employs such metaphors a little self-consciously: "In this, the first complete analysis of a hysteria that I undertook"—the analysis of Fräulein Elisabeth von R.—"I arrived at a

26. Quoted in Jones, *Freud*, III, 83–84.
27. August 6, 1899. *Origins*, 291; *Anfänge*, 310.

procedure which I later elevated to a method and deliberately employed: the procedure of clearing away, layer by layer, the pathogenic psychical material which we liked to compare with the technique of excavating a buried city."[28] And in *Civilization and Its Discontents*, one of his last and richest essays, Freud illustrates the "general problem of preservation in the mental sphere" by means of an analogy: the "growth of the Eternal City," which is really a series of cities, of which some of the earliest fragments survive—or, rather, have been recovered through excavations—side by side with ruins of later buildings. The human mind bears some resemblance to this evolution of many-layered Rome. But only some: Freud, having drawn the archeological analogy at length, nimbly abandons it before the difficulties of representing historical succession by spatial pictures.[29] Freud is always willing to play with metaphors: they have their uses. But they are not proof; they are only metaphors.

Yet metaphors, as Freud would have been the first to assert, are rarely *mere* metaphors. They may be conventional locutions, the common property of many writers. And the mental image of the archeologist uncovering buried truths seems obvious enough to be consistent with the work of many psychologists. Yet employed as frequently and as pleasurably as they are in Freud, these analogies are likely to point to deeper meanings. Here, as elsewhere, dogmatism is thoroughly out of place. But there is at least some evidence that Freud envied Schliemann, who had uncovered ancient Troy layer by layer; envied him partly for the discovery itself, partly for his good fortune of realizing in adult life a boyish fantasy: "The man was happy as he found Priam's treasure," he told Fliess, "for happiness comes only from the fulfillment of a childhood wish"—a dictum significantly, and a little pathetically, followed by a renunciation: "That reminds me: I won't be going to Italy this year."[30] Fortunately, Freud did not need to rest content with envying Schliemann: he equaled him. At least once, Freud compared an analytical success with the discovery of Troy: buried underneath a patient's fantasies, he re-

28. *Studies on Hysteria*, S.E., II, 139; *Studien über Hysterie*, G.W., I, 201.
29. See S.E., XXI, 69–71; G.W., XIV, 426–27.
30. May 28, 1899. *Origins*, 282; *Anfänge*, 301.

ported to Fliess in 1899, he found "a scene from his primal period (before twenty-two months), which satisfies all requirements and into which all remaining riddles flow; a scene that is everything at the same time, sexual, innocuous, natural, etc. I still scarcely dare really to believe it all. It is as if Schliemann had once again dug up Troy, hitherto thought legendary."[31] Let others compare him to Copernicus, to Plato, to Moses; he enjoyed, and sometimes played with, such comparisons. But he also took pleasure in the less exalted if still distinguished identification with a great explorer of the human past.

Beyond indulging such private fantasies, Freud found the comparison of psychoanalysis to archeology apt in a literal sense: to his mind, the scientific excavation of prehistoric remains described psychoanalytic procedures more accurately than any other comparable discipline. Like the archeologist, the psychoanalyst confronts promising but deceptive surfaces, which hint at, but in no way guarantee, strange finds beneath. Like the archeologist, he must take care not to destroy his site with his probes; he must be patient, deft, delicate. Like the archeologist, too, he is a practical scientist guided by theoretical constructs open to revision.

All scientific disciplines are, of course, committed to the search for facts or laws not yet known, but the truths of psychoanalysis and of archeology are concealed in a particular way: to make the visible a dependable guide to the invisible requires the act of interpretation. For both sciences, the evidence is tantalizing and fragmentary, and both find it rewarding to work back from the present to the past and forward again from the past to the present: their materials appear in strata distinct from, yet historically and instructively related to, one another. And both, working as they do with fragments, make the disciplined leaps of a schooled imagination; as the archeologist reconstructs complete statues and whole temples from bits of busts and ravaged columns, so the psychoanalyst reconstructs the origins of a neurosis from distorted memories and involuntary slips. In the preface to his case history of "Dora," Freud makes this analogy explicit: "In face of the incompleteness of my analytic results," he wrote, "I have no

31. December 21, 1899. *Origins*, 305; *Anfänge*, 326–27.

choice but to follow the example of those explorers who are fortunate enough to bring to the light of day after long burial the priceless if mutilated remnants of antiquity. I have restored what was incomplete, following the best models known to me from other analyses; but, just like a conscientious archeologist, I have not failed to mention in each case where my reconstruction picks up and authentic parts end."[32]

Yet the neatest comparisons have their limits of application. The archeologist's material "resists" his inquiry in a metaphorical sense alone; the psychoanalyst faces the literal unconscious resistance of his patient. I have called psychoanalysis the science of candor; it is also the science of suspicion—suspicion systematized. For just as civilization is a web of deceptions, the mental life of the individual is a highly sophisticated system of falsity: of sublimations, displacements, reaction formations. Not even dreams are safe from the sly work of the censor who lives in us all, denying the undeniable, making palatable the unpalatable—especially to ourselves. And the more wicked the secret wish, the more elaborate the screen behind which it labors for its distorted fulfillment. Hence the psychoanalyst must be trained to distrust the most plausible explanations, reconcile the most palpable contradictions, seize the most evasive hints, and make sense of the most impenetrable nonsense. Digging down from layer to layer, he seeks the buried city. Incomplete as the archeological metaphor may be for Freud's life work, it is suggestive and elegant. What is obscure must be made clear, what is latent must be made manifest: that is probably the most important meaning that Freud's crowded shelves sustained.

3. STYLE OF A SCIENTIST

In September 1907, Sigmund Freud reported to his wife from Rome that he had just come upon "a dear familiar face" in the Vatican. "The recognition," he added, "was one-sided, for it was

32. *Fragment of an Analysis of a Case of Hysteria* ["Dora" Case], *S.E.*, VII, 12; *Bruchstück einer Hysterie-Analyse, G.W.*, V, 169–70.

'Gradiva,' high up on a wall."[33] One-sided as it was, the encounter gave Freud, as he said, great joy. This ancient bas-relief, showing a young woman stepping along gracefully, if a little emphatically, was a well-preserved and handsome object. Beyond this, it
reawakened cheerful, still vivid memories: just a year before,
Freud had written a psychoanalytic study of Wilhelm Jensen's
novella Gradiva, a story inspired, as it happened, by a cast of this
very relief. He had found the subject congenial and the writing
easy. In May 1907, shortly after he had published "Delusions and
Dreams in Jensen's Gradiva," he told Jung: "It was written during
sunny days, and I derived great pleasure from doing it."[34] Actually, it was Jung, a welcome recent addition to Freud's embattled
clan, who had first called Jensen's novella to Freud's attention,
and it was partly for Jung's sake that Freud had performed his
literary psychoanalysis.

His Roman encounter, resonant with unmixed positive memories so rare for Freud, pleased him so much that he bought a cast
of "Gradiva" for his consulting room and placed it at the foot of
his analytic couch. As if to leave no room for doubt that this piece
of art intersected, as it were, emotionally with his work, Freud hung
to its left a small reproduction of Ingres's Oedipus Interrogating
the Sphinx—of all artistic subjects the most pregnant anticipation
of the psychoanalyst's organized inquisitiveness. On this narrow
space of wall, archeology and psychoanalysis met and merged.

They do so even more emphatically in Jensen's novella, or
rather, in Freud's interpretation of it. The patient-protagonist of
Gradiva is an archeologist, Norbert Hanold, a withdrawn, un-
worldly Northerner who finds clarity and cure through love in
southern Italy, in sun-baked Pompeii. Hanold has managed to repress the memory of a girl with whom he had grown up and to
whom he had been much attached. Visiting a collection of antiquities in Rome, he stumbles upon a bas-relief depicting a
young and charming girl with a characteristic gait. He names her
"Gradiva," the girl who steps along, and hangs a plaster cast in a
"privileged place on the wall of his study, for the most part
crowded with book cases"—just as Freud, later, was to hang his

33. September 24, 1907. Freud, Briefe, 226.
34. May 26, 1907. Ibid., 251.

plaster cast of the same relief. Something, especially the stance of the figure, fascinates Hanold. It emerges that what makes the young woman irresistible to him is that she reminds him, though unconsciously, of the girl he had loved and "forgotten" for the sake of his profession. He has a nightmare in which he sees "Gradiva" on the day of Pompeii's destruction, and he begins to weave a network of delusions about her, mourning her passing as though she were a beloved contemporary, not someone who had died under the lava of Vesuvius in 79 A.D. He travels to Italy under the impulsion of nameless feelings and ends up in Pompeii, driven by the same inexplicable obsession. And there he sees "Gradiva" in the street and fancies himself back in ancient Pompeii on the day of its inundation. "His science," Freud comments, "has now placed itself completely in the service of his imagination."[35] The young woman turns out to be real, and German; "Gradiva" is, of course, the girl he once loved. And "Gradiva" is not only lovable but clever; she recognizes Hanold's archeological delusion for what it is: there was, she tells him, "a grandiose fantasy lodged in your head" of looking upon her here, in Pompeii, as before, as "something dug up and restored to life."[36] She knows that she can be restored to real life for Hanold only if she can help him to disentangle his fantasies. At the end of her "treatment," when Hanold suddenly asks her to walk ahead of him, the girl, understanding his appeal, steps forward in the gait he had first seen on the bas-relief. She has used his delusion in the service of his recovery.

Freud, a reader of demanding tastes, acknowledged that Jensen's novella was scarcely a distinguished work of literature, but he defended its psychological perceptions: sentimental though it may sound, "one must not despise the healing potency of love against delusion."[37] And he found it notable that in making the living "Gradiva" imitate the gait of the antique relief, Jensen had offered his reader the "key to the symbolism" which Hanold had employed to disguise "his repressed memory"—namely, archeol-

---

35. *Delusions and Dreams in Jensen's "Gradiva,"* S.E., IX, 18; *Der Wahn und die Träume in W. Jensens "Gradiva,"* G.W., VIII, 42.
36. Quoted by Freud in *Delusions and Dreams,* 32; *Der Wahn,* 58.
37. *Delusions and Dreams,* 22; *Der Wahn,* 47.

ogy. "There is actually no better analogy for repression, which both makes something in the mind inaccessible and preserves it, than the burial that was the fate of Pompeii and from which the city could reappear through the work of the spade."[38] Freud approved of Jensen endowing "Gradiva," no doubt unconsciously, with such psychoanalytical techniques as the fostering of associations and the interpreting of dreams. If in one way archeology was the agent of Hanold's neurosis, it is in another way instrumental in his cure.

While Freud's "Delusions and Dreams in Jensen's *Gradiva*" throws bridges from his profession to his passion for collecting, it also links psychoanalysis to another lifelong interest, literature, to weave an intricate intellectual pattern. *Gradiva* was his first published psychoanalysis of a literary work, an inquiry into "dreams that have never been dreamt at all."[39] He had tried his hand earlier, privately, at similar analyses of short stories by Conrad Ferdinand Meyer, one of his favorite modern writers; he had found Hamlet's hesitations immensely instructive; he had drawn his master metaphor, the Oedipus complex, from Sophocles, a metaphor (or, rather, a model) more commanding than any that archeology could supply. And he sometimes said that imaginative writers, in their own intuitive way, were doing his kind of work.

The interplay among Freud's work and his interests is even more active than this. The most instructive implication of Freud's collecting antiquities was, as I have said, "What is obscure must be made clear." That prescription propels us into the felicities of Freud's style, for leading his analysands to be clear about themselves was instrumental in making things clear to himself. And making things clear to himself was part of a wider enterprise: making things clear to his readers.

Freud the man of letters has been abundantly celebrated; the Goethe Prize was awarded to him in 1930 as writer and scientist "in equal measure."[40] Professional craftsmen like Thomas Mann or Stefan Zweig valued him not only as a savant, but as a col-

38. *Delusions and Dreams*, 40; *Der Wahn*, 65.
39. *Delusions and Dreams*, 7; *Der Wahn*, 31.
40. Dr. Alfons Paquet, Secretary of the Goethe Prize Committee in Frankfurt, to Freud, July 26, 1930. Quoted in G.W., XIV, 546n.

league. And all of Freud's biographers devote an obligatory page or two to the efficiency and beauty of his prose—not without reason. Freud's stylistic achievement is all the more remarkable considering the spectrum of his publications: introductory lectures before university audiences, technical communications to medical journals, ambitious speculations for a literate public. And Freud's published case histories—a genre that normally repels grace or wit —are classics in the literature of detection.

Freud was a born writer who never neglected the essentials of his craft. So far as I can determine, he had no program; he did not train himself to become a writer. He acted naturally and intuitively as a literary man from the beginning; his earliest surviving letters demonstrate that his energy, wit, and lucidity were not painfully acquired but were part of his character. In this sense, Freud was not a stylist at all; among the many tributes that other writers paid to Freud's prose, Alfred Döblin's is, in this connection, most interesting: "Note the simple, clear style," Döblin wrote on the occasion of Freud's seventieth birthday; "it is not really a style; he says, without artifice and without phrases, what he means; that is the way someone talks who knows something."[41] In short, Freud was most forceful, most amusing, most reasonable, most persuasive when he was most himself. And he was himself—which is to say, he could draw on his deepest inner resources, blocked by a minimum of conflicts—most of the time. That, after all, was what his self-analysis was about.

However informal and unacademic his growth as a writer, it is evident that he chose the right means and the right models. He disciplined his ear by reading French and English all his life, and his pen by translating books from both languages. He read continuously and intensely, though, of necessity, not all his reading

---

41. "Zum siebzigsten Geburtstag Sigmund Freuds," *Almanach für das Jahr 1927*, 33; quoted in Walter Schönau, *Sigmund Freuds Prosa: Literarische Elemente seines Stils* (1968), 258. I am indebted to Schönau's exploration of Freud's archeological analogies; for these, see also Suzanne Bernfeld Cassirer, "Freud and Archaelogy," *The American Imago*, VIII (1951), 107–28. Even greater is my debt to Walter Muschg's magnificently humane and intelligent essay, "Freud als Schriftsteller," conveniently accessible in Muschg, *Die Zerstörung der deutschen Literatur* (3rd ed., 1958), 303–47.

was for pleasure, or gave him pleasure. Working his way through the abundant technical literature for *The Interpretation of Dreams*, his first masterpiece, he comically complained to Fliess that this kind of reading was "a terrible punishment imposed upon all writing."[42] Freud could derive instruction even from the laborious syntax and rebarbative vocabulary of academic writers; he learned what to avoid. But his real teachers were stylists who were enemies of obscurity and strangers to jargon. While Freud explicitly acknowledges a debt only to Lessing, that spirited polemicist who created modern German practically singlehandedly, he highly valued, and rapidly absorbed, the qualities that distinguished other favorite authors: vigor, precision, clarity. It was for these qualities, after all, that he had made them his favorites. Freud's large corpus of writings, filled with casual allusions and apt citations from an impressive range of literature, show him, over and over again, for what he was: a cultivated German with an astonishing memory. He turns, on occasion, to such Austrian playwrights as Grillparzer, Nestroy—and Schnitzler, but he is equally at home, perhaps more so, with "North" Germans like Goethe and Heine, E. T. A. Hoffmann and Theodor Fontane, the lighthearted couplets of Wilhelm Busch and the profound aphorisms of Georg Christoph Lichtenberg. There is no literary character he quotes more frequently than Goethe's Mephistopheles, unless it be Shakespeare's Hamlet; and even in this choice of a figure from English literature he runs true to type, for since Goethe's famous analysis of Hamlet's character in *Wilhelm Meisters Lehrjahre*, debates over the meaning of Hamlet had been a preoccupation among educated Germans. Freud, of course, enlisted Shakespeare in his psychoanalytic investigations just as he enlisted Sophocles: both lent him the penetration that great poets possess, and magnificent metaphors. There was always something utilitarian about Freud's consumption of culture.[43] But the point remains that he had culture—German culture—at his command; he was neither a mindless technician nor a parochial Austrian. Late in life, Freud recalled that it was a public

42. December 5, 1898. *Origins*, 270; *Anfänge*, 288.
43. See below, 63–64.

reading of Goethe's "beautiful" essay on Nature that set him on the road to medicine—an instructive acknowledgment in that it seems to have been not simply Goethe, the rhapsodic naturalist, who moved Freud to his choice of career, but Goethe, the beautiful stylist.[44]

Among the most dependable proofs of Freud's professionalism is the size of his output. Freud practiced in the only way a writer can practice: by writing whenever he could find, or make, the time. In the early years, when he had few patients, he spent more time in his study writing than in his consulting room analyzing. But later, when he devoted ten or more demanding hours a day, five days a week, nine months a year to his psychoanalytic practice, and was compelled to write late at night, on Sundays, or in the midst of his summer vacation, he continued to publish extensively. However sincere his professions of indifference to the world, however serious his contention that one writes principally to satisfy an inner need, however pronounced his pessimism about winning recognition for his unsettling theories, his urge to communicate those theories to others agitated him from the beginning. It remained alive to the end: the last book he undertook, and did not live to finish, was a splendidly compact primer, an *Outline of Psychoanalysis*. In that fragment, as in his completed writings, his style was supremely right for his intentions.

While Freud was a natural writer, his cordial relations with literature were problematic to him. He conceded that poets and novelists were often right and profound about human motives and human conduct; they seemed to dredge up from their unconscious perceptions and insights that had often taken him, the scientist, years to discover and to demonstrate. The comparisons that the world found all too tempting to draw between the poet and the psychoanalyst were invidious: they made Freud's investigations look laborious, his discoveries imprecise and, in the derogatory sense, imaginative. When in 1896 the distinguished neurol-

44. *An Autobiographical Study*, S.E., XX, 8; *Selbstdarstellung*, G.W., XIV, 34. Scholars now agree that this essay is not by Goethe at all, but by his acquaintance Christoph Tobler. See the editorial note by Andreas Speiser in *Johann Wolfgang Goethe, Gedenkausgabe der Werke, Briefe und Gespräche*, ed. Ernst Beutler, 24 vols. (1949), XVI, 978.

ogist Krafft-Ebing dismissed Freud's theories about hysteria as "a scientific fairy tale," he chose, doubtless quite unconsciously, the very metaphor that would touch Freud at his most sensitive spot. Freud, the great man was insinuating, was guilty of perpetrating mere literature.

In the early 1890s, when he was starting his career as an innovating psychologist, Freud was still defensive about such charges. "I have not always been a psychotherapist," he wrote in his account of Fräulein Elisabeth von R., and he confessed that it still struck him as "odd that the case histories I write should read like novellas and that they lack, as it were, the serious stamp of science. I must console myself with the thought that the nature of the subject is evidently more responsible for this than my predilection." It so happens, he went on, that in hysteria traditional local diagnoses and electrical reactions lead nowhere, "while a thoroughgoing description of mental processes such as we are used to getting from imaginative writers permits me, in employing a few psychological formulas, to gather some kind of insight into the course of a hysteria."[45] Throughout his life, Freud was sensitive to being characterized as an artist; no matter how flattering the formulation, he disliked and distrusted it as just another form of resistance to the severe scientific propositions of psychoanalysis. But defensiveness was, for Freud, never enough, and he developed a position on the place of style in his discipline: he came to see psychoanalysis as a peculiar science which has, like other sciences, its appropriate mode of discourse but must, unlike other sciences, resort to literary devices which at once elucidate and endanger its theories. Since its materials are intimate, concealed, difficult to define, and impossible to quantify, psychoanalysis needs analogies, mental pictures. They may be inexact, but they are indispensable.

Psychoanalytic rhetoric, therefore, as founded by Freud, was by its nature rich in metaphor. The persistence of repressed memories "beneath" later experiences and the efforts of the psychoanalyst to "dig" below manifest dreams called, as we have seen, for metaphors from archeology. The organization of the mind—

45. *Studies on Hysteria*, S.E., II, 160; *Studien über Hysterie*, G.W., I, 227.

id, ego, and superego—could be clarified with borrowings from topography. The array of resistance to wounding truths, and of adaptation to the imperatives of culture, was so diversified that it invited Freud to draw analogies from the most varied of human occupations: warfare, politics, cookery, travel, family life, the arts. What could be more graphic than Freud's picture of a censor performing the unconscious work of repression and distortion? of mental defenses against sexual impulses as dams restraining raging floods? of the psychoanalyst conjuring up, and wrestling with, vicious and savage demons?

The services that such devices could perform for psychoanalysis were not confined to the vividness they lent to presentation. At least some of the metaphors, comparisons, and analogies that Freud so vigorously employed were, in his mind, almost literally descriptive: to assimilate mental life to warfare, like assimilating psychoanalysis to archeology, said something that was true rather than just picturesque. More than that, to draw the map of human experience as crisscrossed by the roads of analogy was to illustrate a conviction with which Freud, the nineteenth-century materialist, began his psychological inquiries, and which his accumulation of data and of theories would only strengthen: that human nature, however varied in its forms of expression, rests on essentially simple elements. Analogies disclosed substantial relationships: neurotics were like children or "savages," dreams like fantasies or psychoses, the public's resistance to psychoanalysis like the patient's resistance to his own analysis, not only apparently or suggestively but actually. Freud was aware that the scientist must not be dominated by the linguistic instruments that he himself has chosen; "psychology," he wrote in 1926, in *The Question of Lay Analysis*, "we can describe only with the aid of analogies. That is nothing unusual; the same is true elsewhere. But we must keep changing these analogies; none of them bears up long enough."[46] Whatever the limits of metaphor, Freud's ambition to discover far more than an explanation of hysteria and to solve far more than the mysteries of neuroses, to construct, in

46. S.E., XX, 195; *Die Frage der Laienanalyse*, G.W., XIV, 222.

short, a psychology of general validity, was supported and exemplified by the language he used.

Metaphors and analogies were only some of the literary devices
at his disposal; Freud resorted to many stratagems of persuasion.
While he was, as I have said, always himself, and his writing the
most direct and most expressive scientific prose we have, his art-
lessness was a high form of art. He was too alert to overlook himself as his greatest asset. But he was not self-conscious about his
unselfconsciousness; he did not cultivate informality in the calculated manner of the English gardener planting a wilderness. "A
clear and unambiguous manner of writing," he said in *The Psychopathology of Everyday Life*, "teaches us that here the author is
at one with himself," while, in contrast, "where we find a strained
and tortuous expression," we recognize the presence of an "inadequately settled and complicating idea or the stifled voice of
the author's self-criticism."[47] It was rare for Freud, the writer, not
to be at one with himself.

Awareness of self implied, for Freud, awareness of the others
whom he wanted to reach, to persuade, to enlist. He wanted to
make sure, he told a correspondent in 1932, not to fall into the
posture of "isolated lecturing," and to keep intact the mode of
discussion.[48] He kept it intact by deploying devices that have
been, in their freshness and variety, the envy of professional writers: informality, surprise, variations in pace, adroit admissions of
incomplete knowledge, patient handling of objections, and a
seemingly inexhaustible supply of telling metaphors.

Awareness is, of course, the psychoanalyst's professionally cultivated characteristic. He is trained, as I have suggested, to notice
what has gone unnoticed. Changing expressions, habitual gestures, unusual responses, casual slips, excessive emphases, slight
hints all, provide evidence for concealed truths. And the slighter
the hint, the more rewarding the work of interpretation. In fact,
the psychoanalyst becomes the detective of absences: of subjects
dropped, overtures rejected, silences prolonged. "He who has

47. S.E., VI, 101; *Zur Psychopathologie des Alltagslebens*, G.W., IV, 112.
48. Freud to Leon Steinig, June 1932. *Freud, Briefe*, 407.

eyes to see and ears to hear," Freud wrote with supreme self-confidence in his account of "Dora," "grows convinced that mortals can conceal no secrets. He whose lips are silent, chatters with his fingertips; betrayal oozes through every pore."[49] Freud's case histories are instructive on this point; they are studies in one psychoanalyst's sensitivity. Examining Fräulein Elisabeth von R. in 1892, Freud noticed that when he "pinched or pressed the hyperalgesic skin and muscles of her legs, her face assumed a peculiar expression, one of pleasure rather than of pain. She cried out—I could not help thinking: as though with a voluptuous tickling—her face flushed, she threw back her head, shut her eyes, and bent her body backwards." And he significantly adds: "All of this was not very obvious but still clearly noticeable"[50]—noticeable, that is, to Freud. Again, in 1902, "Dora" came to see him, fifteen months after she had broken off her treatment, "to finish her story and once again ask for help." Freud was not persuaded: one look at her expression was enough to "convince me that she was not serious with her request."[51] And in 1907, when Freud was listening to a patient known in the literature as the "Rat Man," he observed "a very odd composite expression" on the Rat Man's face as the patient recounted, with evident revulsion, some peculiarly sadistic punishments practiced in the East. Freud decided to read that expression as "one of *horror at a pleasure of his unknown to him.*"[52] It was a tenuous but sufficient clue to support a grave, and, it turned out, decisive interpretation.

An observer so finely attuned to moods and meanings could scarcely help being aware of his audiences. Freud's new science was unfamiliar and in many ways repellent; it offered no comfort to the prudish and no rewards to the prurient; it consorted, in the name of science, with the grossest of superstitions: dream inter-

49. *Fragment of an Analysis*, S.E., VII, 77–78; *Bruchstück einer Hysterie-Analyse*, G.W., V, 240.
50. *Studies on Hysteria*, S.E., II, 137; *Studien über Hysterie*, G.W., V, 240.
51. *Fragment of an Analysis*, S.E., VII, 120; *Bruchstück einer Hysterie-Analyse*, G.W., V, 284–85.
52. *Notes upon a Case of Obsessional Neurosis* [Case of the "Rat Man"], S.E., X, 166–67; *Bemerkungen über einen Fall von Zwangsneurose*, G.W., VII, 392.

pretation. Worst of all, it attacked mankind in its most vulnerable spot, its self-esteem. If Freud had not been a scientist of the utmost probity, resolutely refusing to dilute his message or to hunt for popularity, the acceptance of psychoanalysis would have come sooner. If Freud had not been, with all his probity, an advocate of genius, the acceptance of psychoanalysis would have been very much delayed.

Freud's strategies of persuasion all come back to Freud presenting himself as an explorer retracing his steps for the benefit of an intelligent and sympathetic, if inadequately informed, listener. His strenuous voyage, he implies, has more than repaid the strains it imposed with the unexpected and unexampled discoveries that have come along the way, and that have culminated in the historic solution of an ancient mystery, the riddle of the Sphinx. Freud acknowledged, without embarrassment at his failures or pride in his modesty, that he had taken wrong turnings at times; some seductive trails had led nowhere and some likely-looking terrain had yielded only dry wells. But he wondered out loud whether such frustrating detours were not the distinctive fate of the man who is first, of the pioneer who hacks a trail through uncharted jungle so that others may walk in safety—and patronize him. Freud recognized that the routes his landmarks had compelled him to follow seemed devious, and that the spoils he claimed were unpalatable. He knew that his critics were calling him doctrinaire and authoritarian and regretted the metaphors widely used to discredit him: to the best of his self-knowledge, he was neither jealous father nor manipulative politician, neither mad prophet nor infallible pope. Freud found himself insisting on the authenticity of his outrageous discoveries because they were, however outrageous, authentic; the court of experience, from which there is no rational appeal, continually confirmed his findings. It was true that no one had yet permitted himself more than a brief, shocked look at the fundamental realities he had been the first to lay bare; this timidity was only a vast collective piece of resistance, proof not that his disagreeable assertions were false, but that they were disagreeable. After all, in suitably disguised form—in myths, fairy tales, and tragedies, in the aphorisms of moralists and the folk wisdom of nursemaids—they had sometimes risen to the surface of man's consciousness, only to be rapidly repressed once more. Freud thought that he could understand the resistance, and explain it, along with the facts it resisted. He could be so generous and so understanding because he was a reasonable man speaking to reasonable men; he and his audiences, after all, shared the same literary culture and held the same moral values. If he quoted Goethe to them, or Shakespeare, they would recognize the allusion; if they regretted the beastliness of humanity he had uncovered, so did he. Freud, in short, could see without difficulty why his listeners might hesitate and object: had he not gone their way before them, experienced the same hesitations, offered the same objections?

It was his capacity for feeling the feelings of his audience, his gift for anticipating objections and thus disarming them, that made Freud into what I have called an advocate of genius. It was his empathy raised into a principle of style that led him to take his readers and listeners into his confidence, proceeding before their eyes to develop his argument, deploy his evidence, and build the proofs on which he would rest his conclusions. It was this style of empathy that made him cast some of his writings, and not his popularizations alone, in the form of dialogues, and to give his adversaries arguments sound enough to keep the debate interesting and compel him to stretch his powers of persuasion to its limits. This, too, is why he acknowledged patches of ignorance, incomplete cures, or even complete failures, and, in some matter-of-fact yet powerful postscripts, changes of mind; his science, Freud says over and over again, explicitly and implicitly, is after all still very young and will always be very difficult.

Freud had a picture in his consulting room, on the short wall, above a glass cabinet crowded with antiquities, that, suitably interpreted, documents his stylistic aspirations. It is a reproduction of Brouillet's painting of the great Charcot at work, *La leçon clinique du Dr. Charcot*, one of the most melodramatic renderings of an intellectual performance in the history of art. While an attendant holds a hysteric patient in the midst of a seizure, Charcot lectures to attentive listeners on her case. In the moving obituary that Freud wrote upon Charcot's death in August 1893, we see the reasons for Freud's choice, and for the attention that

Charcot's public performances demanded, deserved, and received. Freud had worked with the pioneering Parisian neurologist from October 1885 to February 1886, and the exposure proved to be of critical importance in his development as a psychopathologist. Freud had come to know Charcot well. With other students, he had accompanied him on his rounds in the Salpêtrière, identifying the ailments of the mental patients lodged there; an astonished Freud had played Adam to Charcot's God, receiving a splendid measure of "intellectual enjoyment" as Charcot named the diseases before him. One can read in Freud's obituary of this master his mounting dissatisfaction with the theories and practices, the ultimate hesitations, of Viennese medicine, and, quite as clearly, what kind of scientist and healer Freud hoped to make himself. This was not a passing identification; Freud would remember, and quote, Charcot all his life. Charcot, Freud wrote in 1893, was an unexcelled observer, a *visuel* who learned, and taught others, to override theory by experience. He took just pride in his discoveries, and "honest human pleasure in his own great successes." Like Freud he was not falsely modest, and enjoyed "talking about his beginnings and the road he had traveled." He was an indefatigable worker, a generous chief who put his discoveries at the disposal of his students, a discriminating scientist who could distinguish between solid knowledge and intelligent guesswork: "He would throw aside his authority to confess, occasionally, that one case admitted of no diagnosis, and that in another appearances had deceived him." And this candor linked Charcot's substance to his style, for, Freud goes on, "he never appeared greater to his listeners than when, with the most thoroughgoing account of his processes of thought and the greatest candor about his doubts and reservations, he strove to narrow the gulf between teacher and pupil." Later, Freud would employ the same tactics for the same purposes.

Charcot's candor in his informal weekly addresses, those famous *Leçons du mardi*, was matched by the elegance of his formal lectures, each of them, in Freud's admiring words, "a little work of art in construction and composition."[53] In translating

53. *Charcot*, S.E., III, 11–18; *Charcot*, G.W., I, 21–29.

two of Charcot's books, Freud was performing acts of piety and intellectual incorporation. But Freud was not born to be an epigone. Admiring Charcot, he became himself; what Charcot taught him, most of all, was that those artifices work best that are most natural—that, in short, honesty is the best strategy. He wrote his books as he practiced his psychoanalysis: responsibly. Freud knew that it might have had a beneficial effect on "Dora" to let her think that she was important to him. But he rejected this kind of operatic therapy. "I have always avoided playing a role, and contented myself with the less pretentious art of psychology."[54] The irony is transparent; he was not a humble man.

4. THE BOURGEOIS AS REVOLUTIONARY

While Freud's prose was superbly adapted to his purposes, his living quarters, to return to them for a moment, offered a suggestive contrast to the ideas he generated there. It is as if Freud had been making explosives in a drawing room. Freud was an irreproachable bourgeois who fashioned for himself an unmistakably bourgeois environment but who, at the same time, developed theories about human nature and human conduct as subversive as any set of ideas in history. The impression of stunning audacity has necessarily faded with the acceptance of his psychology, the entrance of his vocabulary into common speech, and the insistent attempts—attempts against which Freud warned more than once—to soften their angularities. It is only after one has reconstructed the mental atmosphere and scientific pieties of the late nineteenth century that the full measure of Freud's revolution emerges. Yet he made his revolution in the most unrevolutionary of surroundings. Its banners and slogans are all invisible. What was in evidence was photographs of friends, disciples, members of his family, and what I have called the profusion of things in his apartment, its orderly overcrowding: statues jammed

54. *Fragment of an Analysis*, S.E., VII, 109; *Bruchstück einer Hysterie-Analyse*, G.W., V, 272.

together, snapshots jostling one another on precariously small surfaces, pictures half-hidden by other pictures. A photograph of Michelangelo's *Moses*, on which Freud wrote a celebrated essay, peeked out, barely recognizable, above another picture and some Oriental figurines. There seemed to be no place for anything more. Indeed, the ornately framed mirror which hung, rather surprisingly, in the window of Freud's study, was a present put there precisely because there was no room for it anywhere else. Freud's famous analytic couch was only the most conspicuous instance of this domestic self-indulgence; it was covered with a heavy rug, with plush pillows and throws, and built up in the continental manner to let the patient not so much lie down as lean back. Berggasse 19 abounded in the kind of visual and tactile excess it has become almost obligatory to call "bourgeois comfort." The epithet is facile, complacent, inexact, and misleading; it begs, as we shall see, many questions. But it says something about Freud's tastes and choices: he lived like the very kind of respectable professional man whose style of thinking he was to undermine beyond repair.

While Freud's faultless respectability has been the subject of much remark, it deserves yet one more exploration. Freud's longings for domesticity took the conventional form of middle-class ease and modest plenitude—of comfortableness, *Behaglichkeit*. In August 1882, writing to his fiancée during their prolonged and self-denying engagement, Freud listed the things they would need for their "little world of happiness": a pair of rooms, some tables, beds, mirrors, easy chairs, rugs, glasses and china for ordinary and for festive use, decent linens, hats with artificial flowers, big bunches of keys, and lives filled with meaningful activity, kind hospitality, and mutual love. "Shall we hang our hearts on such small things? As long as a high destiny does not knock at our peaceable door—yes, and without misgivings."[55] Freud's were the fantasies that generations of lovers have spun out together, looking in shop windows and reading the advertisements—thoroughly and unashamedly bourgeois aspirations.

Once settled, Freud did all the things the good bourgeois is

55. August 18, 1882. *Freud, Briefe,* 29.

supposed to do. He worked hard, worried about money, loved his wife, fathered six children, played cards, attended lodge meetings, fixed a nameplate—"Prof. Dr. Freud"—to his door, smoked cigars, and went on vacations. He was a responsible paterfamilias; though inaccessible during his extensive, absorbing working hours and often absent even during his long summer holidays, he was emotionally available to his children. His son Martin retained, all his life, the touching memory of his father resolving a humiliating impasse into which the boy had fallen. Out on a skating expedition with a brother and sister, he had been slapped by a stranger for a remark he had not made, had his season ticket confiscated by the attendant, and (most humiliating for a boy whose head was stuffed with chivalric notions about revenge) had a lawyer volunteer to take the aggressive stranger to court. When the children returned home, full of the day's dramatic events, Freud listened to them attentively and then asked Martin to tell him, in private and in detail, about the whole affair. What the father said in the interview to soothe the boy's feelings and restore his pride the son did not retain for long. "I think," he wrote gratefully many years later, "this is typical of all similar treatment when a trauma is successfully dealt with: one forgets not only the injury but also the cure."[56] Freud was a very busy man, but when he was needed, he was there. This was hardly the style of the unshackled Bohemian or of the self-absorbed genius.

Freud's attitude toward sexuality, which is, after all, the key to his science, is congruent with this portrait. "You don't suppose," the distinguished psychoanalyst Heinz Hartmann once asked rhetorically, "that Freud, the eminently respectable Austrian bourgeois, was *pleased* with his discovery of infantile sexuality?"[57] Freud in fact presented himself in public as a reluctant Columbus, and we have no reason to question his self-appraisal. In April 1896, speaking in Vienna before the Verein für Psychiatrie und Neurologie, he insisted that in singling out "the sexual element" in the etiology of hysteria, he was following "no preconceived opinion of my own." Indeed, "the two investigators as whose dis-

56. Martin Freud, *Sigmund Freud: Man and Father* (1958), 43.
57. Private conversation with the author, June 21, 1967.

ciple I began my work on hysteria, Charcot and Breuer, were far from any such presupposition; indeed they confronted it with a personal aversion which I shared at the outset." It was "only the most laborious detailed investigations" that converted Freud to his view, "and that slowly enough."[58] The discovery of infantile sexuality was far more painful for him, and delayed by far stronger resistance, than his theory about the sexual origins of hysteria. There is an eloquent, if involuntary, bit of evidence about that resistance: in *The Interpretation of Dreams*, Freud remarks in passing that "we extol the happiness of childhood, because it does not yet know sexual appetite"—this from the very investigator who made infantile sexuality the subject of scientific study, and in the very book in which he adumbrates the Oedipus complex. It was not until the third edition, in 1911, that Freud added a cautionary footnote to this extraordinary passage, expressing reservations about childish happiness and innocence. But he never exorcised his original assertion, and there it remains, like a prehistoric monument to the tenacity of an older, less controversial attitude.[59]

If Freud's views on sexuality were unexpectedly complex and ambiguous, his attitude toward the arts was simply and unambiguously conventional. What differentiated him from the average Viennese bourgeois was less his taste than his sincerity: while many often went to the opera to be publicly seen and privately bored, Freud rarely went to the opera, lest he be bored. One may trust him to be fully awake to these feelings and to have explored their possible origins. In his essay on the *Moses* of Michelangelo, a gratifying source for those who like to denigrate him as a typical philistine, Freud frankly concedes that he derived far more pleasure from the subject matter of the arts than from "their formal and technical properties," though he knew that artists value them precisely for these qualities. His principal enjoyment in literature and sculpture and, to a far smaller extent, painting and music, was to explore their effects on him. "Where I cannot do this, as

58. *The Aetiology of Hysteria*, S.E., III, 199; *Zur Ätiologie der Hysterie*, G.W., I, 435.
59. See *The Interpretation of Dreams*, S.E., IV, 130; *Traumdeutung*, G.W., II–III, 136 and 136n. See also editor's note, S.E., VII, 128–29.

for instance with music, I am almost incapable of enjoyment."[60] Considering Freud's comprehensive cultivation and ease of literary allusion, it seems ungracious as well as unjust to brand him a philistine. But his appropriation of the goods that culture could provide suggests what I might call a higher philistinism, a consumption of culture less for its own sake than for the light it could shed on the scientific puzzles that interested him more than, and almost to the exclusion of, anything else. Hanns Sachs recalled that on one rare occasion when Freud was lured to the theater to see Max Reinhardt's production of *Oedipus Rex*, he greatly enjoyed the evening, but what gave him pleasure was a psychoanalytic train of thought that the tragedy had awakened rather than the performance. Freud made high culture pay.

Yet the presumed contradiction between Freud the bourgeois conformist and Freud the uncompromising scientist is almost wholly artificial. It follows from the plausible identification of the bourgeois with the conventional, which has itself become a convention. By the late 1860s and 1870s, when Freud was a young man, the term *bourgeois* had become a word of abuse among avant-garde artists, writers, and social critics. The bourgeois was, in a word, intolerable. But what made him intolerable remained a matter of dispute. Some damned him as a ruthless exploiter of his society, his workers, his family, and himself—as a materialist who, in his feverish pursuit of gain, stopped at nothing; he was a man with a hard face, a utilitarian philosophy, and an omnipotent checkbook. Others damned the bourgeois as the timid defender of the status quo, forever in search of safe investments, safe opinions, and safe emotional attachments—a man with conservative politics, comfortable slippers, and rolled-up umbrella. Ingenious theorists of the time, to be sure, found ways of reconciling these conflicting denunciations by seeing them as succeeding stages of historical development: the bourgeois, in this view, had begun as a buccaneer and ended as a *rentier*. But whether he was seen as the one or the other, or as both, the view was that the bourgeois loved money and hated art. And bold or timid, he was

60. *The Moses of Michelangelo*, S.E., XIII, 211; *Der Moses des Michelangelo*, G.W., X, 172.

an incorrigible hypocrite about his cultural tastes and his sexual behavior. The modern ideal of privacy, so typically bourgeois, was little more than a convenient mask behind which he could cheat his neighbor, indulge his vulgarity, and enjoy his mistresses.

However telling these assaults on the respectable, however perceptive the critics who made them, there was far more to bourgeois nineteenth-century culture than this. The word *hypocrite* is a tendentious epithet that has obstructed an objective investigation of the inevitable gap between professions and performance. In any event, by no means all bourgeois were hypocrites and by no means all hypocrites were bourgeois. Working men, peasants, and aristocrats normally loved money and many of them did not hate art only in the sense that they were wholly untouched by it. Moreover, no single code of conduct, no single type of hero, properly defined the middle classes as a whole; the self-confident merchants of Manchester or Hamburg had a sense of themselves wholly different from their more dependent fellow bourgeois in Munich—or Vienna. It is no accident that the radical ideas and avant-garde art which increasingly pervaded European culture from the middle of the nineteenth century onward were largely the work of bourgeois thinkers and writers: only a few of them were, like Marx and Engels, self-conscious renegades from their class. To be, as Freud was, a thoroughgoing revolutionary and a thoroughgoing bourgeois was by no means a paradox, an anomaly, or even a rarity.

One need not, then, step outside the boundaries of bourgeois culture to explain Freud. The struggle over respectability, over the place of the passions in conduct, was largely internal to the middle class. Freud's own views of the social stratum to which he belonged and in which he moved with ease clarify the nature and define the issues of this struggle. With a sensitivity to nuance hard to imagine today, nineteenth-century Europeans noted the manifestations and used the language of class. Movement within —or, for the most fortunate and unfortunate, movement between —classes was the staple of casual gossip and family politics, of plays and novels. Efforts at rising, or maneuvers calculated to enable one's children to rise, were the true business of most social strategies—of the schooling one sought, the marriage partner one found suitable, the taste one developed or demonstrated, the language one spoke or affected. The ladder of class was long and steep, and it had many rungs. There were many ways of being bourgeois, or, for that matter, anything else.

Underlying these refined distinctions, however, were the gross divisions with which everyone worked. And each class, as Freud saw it, stood in a particular relationship to culture, principally in the way it indulged or restrained the will. In his view—hardly untypical for the late nineteenth century—the middle class stood in the middle, between the "lower orders," who could not afford and had never learned self-control, and the aristocracy, who could afford and had not unlearned self-indulgence. The great debate over culture, in which critics as diverse at Nietzsche and Ruskin, Matthew Arnold and Max Weber participated, concentrated therefore on the bourgeoisie. While most humans were thought incapable of postponing gratifications, the bourgeois has presumably learned to do precisely this, to harness his libido for work. Self-control had been the historic achievement and became the heavy burden of the middle class. The frequent breakdown of that control in orgies of impermissible gratifications was only natural: the "illicit" passions can command elemental energies. "Hypocrisy,"—saying one thing and doing another—was, then, the tribute the bourgeois paid to his own rules, and the price of his inability to obey all of these rules all of the time. To claim a respectability one did not possess did more than help the individual to satisfy his desires in safety; it also helped to keep intact a social system that had produced splendid results—results that did not benefit the bourgeoisie alone.

Freud's thought made a double contribution to the debate. It was not ambiguous, for Freud articulated its two aspects with his customary lucidity; it was not ambivalent, for Freud was, as usual, wholly conscious of where he stood. It was only incomplete and, by design, unsystematic; Freud never published a treatise on ethics and repeatedly insisted that psychoanalysis was a set of scientific propositions rather than a *Weltanschauung*. Besides, as Heinz Hartmann once put it in an important lecture on *Psychoanalysis and Moral Values*, "it is not always easy to discern" in Freud's work on the history of civilization—precisely the late essays which are always quoted in discussion of Freud's thought on culture—"what derives from analytic research and what is the result of his use of psychoanalytic knowledge in developing the main themes of his personal approach to history."[61] The two sides of Freud's work, the psychoanalytic writings and the cultural-historical speculations, were not identical; but they were consistent with, in fact implied, one another. And, I must add, to deny that one has a *Weltanschauung* does not mean that one is, in fact, without one. Freud, in taking the part of science against authoritarianism or mysticism, at least implicitly supported some philosophies of life and opposed their opponents.

One side of Freud's thought has been emphasized at the expense of the other. Freud has often been hailed as a great liberator of men—and, despite that fatal phrase, "biology is destiny," of women, too. The accolade is fully deserved, and at least once Freud himself suggested that he thought so, too. In the summer of 1915, writing to the distinguished American neurologist James J. Putnam, he described himself as a highly moral man who accepted the ethical rules of modern civilization without question— all except those governing modern sexual conduct. "Sexual morality as society, in its most extreme form, the American one, defines it, seems to be very contemptible. I stand for an incomparably freer sexual life, although," he confessed, "I myself have made very little use of such freedom: only in so far as I myself judged it to be allowable."[62] It was a part of Freud's inner freedom that he did not need to impose his private preferences on culture as a whole. Whatever his own practices, he reiterated that modern man enjoyed himself too little and punished himself too much. In a much-quoted essay of 1908 on the effects of modern sexual restraint on mental health, he insisted that the pressures of civilization had become excessive. "Experience teaches that there is for most people a limit beyond which their constitution cannot comply with the demands of culture. All those who want to be nobler than their constitution permits lapse into neurosis." And he adds, with his characteristic reasonableness, "They would have

61. Heinz Hartmann, *Psychoanalysis and Moral Values* (1960), 17.
62. July 8, 1915. Quoted in Jones, *Freud*, II, 417–18.

been healthier if it had remained possible for them to be more wicked—*schlechter zu sein.*"[63] Freud's writings are pervaded with invitations to be more wicked: to accept eccentric behavior as normal, to give up punitive attitudes toward what were called the perversions—to accept, in short, instinctual life.

In a remarkable letter of 1935, written from Berggasse 19 to a woman, a stranger, who had confessed that her son was a homosexual, Freud chided her gently for not being able to bring herself to write the dreadful word. "May I question you why you avoid it? Homosexuality is assuredly no advantage, but it is nothing to be ashamed of, no vice, no degradation, it cannot be classified as an illness; we consider it to be a variation of the sexual function, produced by a certain arrest of sexual development." And he added, as consistent as he was being humane to the anguished mother, "Many highly respectable individuals of ancient and modern times have been homosexuals, several of the greatest men among them. (Plato, Michelangelo, Leonardo da Vinci, etc.) It is a great injustice to persecute homosexuality as a crime—and a cruelty, too."[64] When he addressed himself to more conventional sexual behavior, his liberalism was equally pronounced. At fourteen, "Dora" had responded with disgust to the sexual advances of an older man, a man she loved; Freud, in his report on the case, judged this rejection to be not praiseworthy moral conduct but a neurotic symptom: "I should certainly consider every person hysterical, in whom an occasion for sexual excitement elicits feelings preponderantly or exclusively unpleasurable."[65] Dicta such as these, delivered in Freud's most matter-of-fact voice, could only serve to enlarge the sphere of the permissible. His very theories pressed modern society to substitute clinical neutrality for high-minded condemnation. After all, if every human being is subject to the urges of infantile sexuality and the most murderous wishes against the most beloved persons, moral canons and cultural habits must be adjusted to take account of these over-

63. *"Civilized" Sexual Morality and Modern Nervous Illness*, S.E., IX, 191; *Die "kulturelle" Sexualmoral und die moderne Nervosität*, G.W., VII, 154.
64. April 9, 1935, in English. *Freud, Briefe*, 416.
65. *Fragment of an Analysis*, S.E., VII, 28; *Bruchstück einer Hysterie-Analyse*, G.W., V, 187.

whelming truths about human nature. And once again, style served substance. Freud was not Nietzsche; he was not, as Hartmann has said, " 'a transvaluer of values'—not in the sense, that is, that he wanted to impress on his fellow men a new scale of moral values."[66] But intentions and influence are two different things. Freud was no philosopher; he was just more effective than the philosophers. He was, partly without his active cooperation, a moral liberator.

But there is another side to Freud's social ideas that deserves equal prominence. Long before the trauma of World War I had assisted him in developing the postulate of the death instinct, long before he had portrayed human existence as a dramatic fight to the finish between the forces of life and the forces of death, he had been convinced that civilization must impose sacrifices on man's instinctual life by draining off energies from the libido and by restraining aggression in the service of social functioning. Although without such sacrifices civilization would be impossible, they had untoward, often tragic, consequences: unnecessary repression, excessive guilt—in short, neurosis. Freud saw no way out of this human predicament: mankind could not live without, and scarcely live with, exigent civilization. At best, the suffering could be alleviated, but to expect that it could be permanently cured was to indulge in the kind of magical wishful thinking appropriate to children, savages, and neurotics, but not worthy of grown men facing life, and death, with sober realism.

Freud presented this tragic vision of culture with his characteristic unwillingness to put pretty glosses on ugly truths; he had no wish to deceive himself and others. "I am far from offering an appraisal of human civilization," he wrote near the conclusion of *Civilization and its Discontents*. He had tried to keep free of "the enthusiastic prejudice" which claims our civilization as "the most precious thing we possess or could acquire, and that its path must necessarily lead us to heights of unimagined perfection." He thought he could "listen without indignation to the critic who, surveying cultural aspirations and the means they employ, suggests that one is bound to conclude: the whole effort is not worth

66. Hartmann, *Psychoanalysis and Moral Values*, 19.

the trouble." Freud could only hope that in this century when human beings could exterminate one another to the last man, "eternal Eros" would "make an effort to overcome his equally immortal adversary in the struggle." This sentence, the last in the essay he published at the end of 1929, was cast in the mold of heroic optimism. Two years later, Freud added another concluding sentence, a question further qualifying this already guarded hope: "But who can foresee the success and the result?"[67] Despite all this, Freud, the man without illusions, rejected the response to culture that his pessimistic way of thinking might seem to imply. He disliked the Socialist theories and Socialist states of his day, not because he disapproved of their attacks on exploitation and on private property—he had, in fact, a measure of sympathy for both these attacks—but because he thought they had fallen victim to a Utopian, wishful idealization of human nature. But while he had no faith in Socialism, he had no use whatever for the celebration of irrational forces, or for the primitivism that would evade the dialectic of civilization by abandoning civilization altogether. He had not labored in the sickroom of the human mind to join the party of disease; he had not descended to the sewer of human nature to wallow in what he had found there. He was no devotee of the id; he assigned no privileged position to that blind, imperious agent of the will, and valued the organizing rationalism of the ego or the nay-saying constraints of the superego as equally natural.

I want to linger over this point for a moment; Freud's particular brand of scientific rationalism has implications for Modernism as a whole. I have already noted that Modernism has usually been defined as a celebration of unreason, as a rejection, in anger, disgust, or despair, of the glib complacency, the shallow optimism, the self-satisfied evasions that marked bourgeois civilization.[68] Quite apart from its slanderous misreading of the nineteenth century, this interpretation of Modernism gratuitously impoverishes its definition by willfully slighting its rationalist component. Rationality need not be glib, shallow, or self-satisfied; science, sys-

67. S.E., XXI, 144–45; *Das Unbehagen in der Kultur*, G.W., XIV, 505–6.
68. See above, 26.

tematic objective inquiry, which is, in essence, reason organized, is not merely the assiduous servant of material interests and of a superficial philosophy of life, but also, indeed mainly, an exacting master imposing precise methods and holding out the promise of the most far-reaching intellectual consequences. Intelligence was as powerful a motor of Modernism as self-expression. With psychoanalysis Freud, probably the most influential master among the Modernists, demonstrated that it was more than possible, it was necessary, to be rational about irrationality. This demonstration was Freud's most Modern, most revolutionary act.

5. THE PLEASURES OF TRUTH

Freud's work gave him much pleasure, but it was not a pleasure he could do without. "I cannot imagine life without work as really comfortable—*recht behaglich*," he wrote to his good friend, the Swiss pastor Oskar Pfister, in 1910. "With me, fantasizing and working coincide; I find amusement in nothing else." He trembled at the thought, he added, of being disabled in advanced age, when ideas or words would no longer come freely. "With all the submission to fate proper to an honest man," he confessed to Pfister one very secret wish: "only no chronic infirmity, no paralysis of the capacity for work through bodily misery. Let us die in harness, as King Macbeth says."[69] The letter is as instructive as it is moving. There is that remnant, however small, of wishful thinking; there is the concentration on work as the single aim in life that brings us back to the pictures on his walls, the pillows on his couch, and the rugs on his floor—the overriding desire for comfort and coziness. Freud was, in this desire, as in so much else, like an ordinary bourgeois. He was just more honest.

Honest is an old-fashioned—I am tempted to say a bourgeois— word. Today, philosophers, and the literary critics who borrow their terminology, are far more likely to speak of authenticity, of

69. March 6, 1910. *Sigmund Freud–Oskar Pfister, Briefe, 1909–1939*, ed. Ernst L. Freud and Heinrich Meng ʹ(1963), 32–33.

good faith, of demystification. But *honesty*, a word frankly laden with approving emotions and redolent with pleasing images of truth-telling merchants, children, or physicians, fits Freud better than the chic vocabulary of our time. Freud was a supremely honest man.

Yet *honesty*, being an old-fashioned word, is also nonanalytical. It describes a quality of intentions and actions without digging into its psychic roots. And the roots of Freud's honesty are thoroughly buried. There is a familiar dictum in his essay on Dostoevsky that is peculiarly relevant here. In that essay, Freud shows himself perfectly prepared to discuss Dostoevsky the moralist and the neurotic, but, faced with his literary stature (since he rated him highly, not far below Shakespeare), he feels helpless: "Before the problem of the imaginative writer—*Dichter*," he writes, and one can almost hear the sigh of resignation, "analysis must unfortunately lay down its arms."[70]

With the problem of the imaginative scientist, analysis is in a scarcely better position. It is not surprising that Freud, the ruthless inquisitor into the minds and motives of others, should have proved an irresistible target for psychoanalysis—often a kind of retributive and reductionist psychoanalysis which tries to discredit Freud's discoveries by denigrating his character. Whatever the animus of Freud's self-appointed analysts, the impulses behind Freud's imaginative, audacious exploration of man's unconscious are far from transparent. We can uncover the necessary and still remain baffled by the sufficient causes of his work: it is far easier to understand the general conditions that made it possible than the specific conditions that turned his genius into an efficient instrument for research and translated the potentialities for scientific innovation into actuality.

The most conspicuous trait in Freud's character, indispensable to his capacity for generating insights and his patience in developing them into a general psychology, is his uncompromising commitment to truth. It was so powerful, he found it so natural, that he rarely troubled to justify, let alone analyze it. If it is im-

70. *Dostoevsky and Parricide*, S.E., XXI, 177; *Dostojewski und die Vatertötung*, G.W., XIV, 399.

possible to elucidate completely, its principal strands—curiosity, singlemindedness, and intellectual courage—are manifest. Freud, above all, wanted to know. That his passion for knowledge had its origins in his infancy is beyond doubt; we may apply to him the general observation he offered in the case history of Little Hans: "Thirst for knowledge and sexual curiosity seem to be inseparable."[71] Whatever its unconscious components, this desire was a prominent ingredient in that vitality that his most casual visitor could not help but notice and find attractive. In one respect, Freud was fortunate. He lived in an age when materialism was king, when researchers assumed—and in the "hard" sciences of physics or astronomy brilliantly demonstrated—that events follow strict causal laws. Freud fearlessly transferred this conviction, on which he never wavered, from the physical to the mental sphere. Now, to know was to subsume phenomena under general laws, rather than to call them names, and Freud found, if I may put it this way, that there was more to know and less to judge than most thinking people had imagined. When Freud, following Charcot, removed neurotics from the dismissive category of "degenerates" to place them on a continuous spectrum with "normal" people, he was reclaiming regions of the mind from moralizing for the exercising of scientific curiosity.

Freud himself thought scientific inquisitiveness central to his character. In his letters of the 1880s to his fiancée, in his letters of the 1890s to Fliess, and in his autobiographical essays of the 1920s, he returned, over and over again, to his driving desire to confront, and perhaps to solve, what he liked to call the "riddles of life." Looking back in his late years, he noted that he had never particularly wanted to be a physician. "I was moved, rather, by a sort of thirst for knowledge, which was, however, directed more toward human affairs than natural objects."[72] And he reflected that "after forty-one years of medical activity," his "self-knowledge" told him that he had never "really been, properly speaking, a doctor. I became a doctor through an imposed devia-

71. *Analysis of a Phobia in a Five-Year-Old Boy*, S.E., X, 19; *Analyse der Phobie eines fünfjährigen Knaben*, G.W., VII, 247.
72. *An Autobiographical Study*, S.E., XX, 8; *Selbstdarstellung*, G.W., XIV, 34.

tion from my original intentions; and the triumph of my life lies in finding once more, after a long detour, my original direction." That direction was, he explicitly adds, an overpowering "need to understand something of the riddles of this world and perhaps to contribute something to their solution."[73] In the heady days of 1896, when he was piling discovery on discovery, he triumphantly told Fliess in several letters that he was returning, by a circuitous route, to his first ambition, to do original work in philosophy. His life, as he saw it, had described several identical, fortunate circles, moving more than once from science to healing and back to science.

The almost compulsive reiteration of the same formulations across more than half a century suggests the depth of Freud's commitment to inquiry for its own sake. But his fundamental intentions were even more overdetermined than these lapidary confessions would suggest. Freud was no indiscriminate lover of humanity, no professional philanthropist—benevolent stances which, in any event, he was inclined to depreciate as derivatives of sadism, as self-protective reaction formations. But he was more humane than he readily allowed. His case histories and his private correspondence disclose his pleasure in a patient's progress, his delicacy in managing a patient's feelings. Since transference—the analysand endowing the analyst with the lovable (and, sometimes, the hateful) traits of others—is the single most effective weapon of psychoanalytic therapy, Freud could scarcely neglect the highly charged emotional situation of the analytic relationship; and his recommendations, like his practice, generally placed the patient's benefit above the psychoanalyst's convenience. Manifestly, he found the labor of healing always hard and often exhausting; but often he found it gratifying as well. He experienced in his own practice the clash between the imperatives governing the psychoanalyst-physician and those governing the psychoanalyst-scientist: the physician serves his vocation by keeping things private, the scientist serves his by making them public. Fortunately, it was rare for the conflict between his two roles to assume

73. *The Question of Lay Analysis, Postscript*, S.E., XX, 253; *Nachwort zur Diskussion über die "Frage der Laienanalyse,"* G.W., XIV, 289–90.

dramatic form. When it did, Freud unhesitatingly chose science over healing. "Analysis," he wrote wryly, wittily to Pfister in 1910, "suffers from the cardinal vice of—virtue; it is the work of an all-too-decent human being, who thinks himself obligated to be discreet." Psychoanalytic matters become comprehensible only if they are laid out with a certain completeness, with much detail. "Hence, discretion is incompatible with the sound description of a psychoanalysis; one must turn into a wicked fellow," throw out one's ideals, "behave like an artist who buys paints with his wife's household money, or provides heat for his model with the furniture. Without such a piece of criminality there is no good work."[74] Satisfying his disciplined curiosity and providing materials for the progress of his science were privileged matters.

Freud was the first to admit that the imperiousness of his need to know made him seem single-minded, even one-sided. He humorously denied being a monomaniac, and it is true that he was neither a fanatic nor a bore. But his concentration on his work was absolute. As he told Fliess in May 1895, "A man like me cannot live without a hobby horse, without a dominating passion, without—to speak with Schiller—a tyrant, and I have found him. And in his service I now know no moderation. He is psychology."[75] Hanns Sachs, who thought he saw a "red thread" of work in all that Freud did, said, and wrote, suggests that "utter devotion to one single aim in life" is "neither rare nor in itself precious. It may vary from collector's mania to the highest aims; it may make a person hidebound and sterile or it may become the source of a permanent flow of inspiration." Freud, whose family and friends all understood and accepted his master passion, belonged to the second class. "Many minds have been narrowed down to a pinpoint by an exclusive interest, but to the chosen few it has served as a means to expand over earth and heaven. To Freud it offered a new universe and he gave his all in return."[76] This impression seems to have been quite general among those who knew him well: there was something downright impersonal about his concentration on psychoanalytic matters. His attitude

74. June 5, 1910. Freud-Pfister, Briefe, 36.
75. May 25, 1895. Origins, 119; Anfänge, 129.
76. Sachs, Freud, 70.

recalls that of Frederick the Great, who took pride in calling himself the first servant of the state; Freud, with equal pride and less ideological distortion, could have called himself the first servant of his science: "Psychoanalysis," he wrote in 1935, in a late retrospective glance, "came to be the entire content of my life."[77] Five years earlier, he had begun his address of thanks for the Goethe Prize with a blunt declaration: "My life's work has been directed at a single aim."[78] This was the man who had told his friend Pfister many years before that he found life without work inconceivable, that to fantasize and to work were, at least for him, the same thing. This was the man who went to the theater to think about psychoanalysis—or, if this seems too harsh—who went to the theater and found himself stimulated to think about psychoanalysis.

To realize his overriding life's purpose, to occupy and map the terrain of the unconscious, the qualities of curiosity and concentration would have been, however valuable, insufficient. Freud's enterprise also demanded an uncommon supply of courage, the quality that translates honesty into action. One's first impulse—even Freud's—on sighting that terrain was to turn back. I have spoken of his unexampled audacity, his victory over inner resistances to his discoveries, his descent into the darkest reaches of human nature. I want to recall them here, for without them Freud's character, like his work, remains incomprehensible.

Facing up to things as they are characterizes Freud's life. It was not easy to be a Jew in Imperial Austria, especially a Jew with aspirations. In Vienna, especially at the end of the century, anti-Semitism was more than the confused broodings of psychopaths; it pervaded and poisoned student organizations, university politics, social relationships, medical opinions. To be the destroyer of human illusions, as Freud was by intention and by results, was to make oneself into a special target of the anti-Semite. "Be assured," Freud wrote in the summer of 1908 to his brilliant disciple Karl Abraham, "if my name were Oberhuber, my innovations

77. *An Autobiographical Study, Postscript, S.E.*, XX, 71; *Nachschrift* [Zur Selbstdarstellung], *G.W.*, XVI, 31
78. *Address Delivered at the Goethe House in Frankfurt, S.E.*, 208; *Ansprache im Frankfurter Goethe-Haus, G.W.*, XIV, 547.

would have encountered far less resistance, despite everything."[79]
Yet Freud persisted, both in doing psychoanalytic work and in
calling himself a Jew. There is, in this loyalty, a kind of defiance.
Freud was the opposite of religious; his view of religion as an illusion akin to neurosis applied to the faith of his fathers as much
as any other. He granted the existence of some mysterious bonds
that tied him to Judaism, and he attributed his objectivity and
his willingness to be in a minority at least partly to his Jewish
origins. But there was another element in this equation. "My
merit in the Jewish cause," he wrote to Marie Bonaparte in 1926,
after B'nai Brith had honored him on his seventieth birthday, "is
confined to one single point: that I have never denied my Jewishness."[80] To deny it would have been senseless and, as he also said,
undignified. The Jewish bond he felt was the recognition of a
common fate in a hostile world.

Individualistic and problematic as it was, Freud's Jewishness
made an intimate bond between him and Vienna. For Vienna,
never in reality the city of operettas and flirtations, was, even in
Freud's time, a city of ugly rehearsals; it made Freud the Jew
suffer even more because he was a Jew than because he was
Freud. A laboratory for every known species of anti-Semitism,
Vienna virtually compelled Freud to see himself as one among
a band of potential victims, as one among Vienna's Jews. It was a
role—I shall return to this point—that he took upon himself
with his accustomed courage. But the core of that courage was
neither sectarian nor local. It was intellectual. Freud was, first and
last, the scientist, bravely following the evidence wherever it led.

This is an expansive, and to many an unacceptable description.
Few will deny Freud the quality of bravery or an unusually developed capacity for listening. But was he a scientist—or, more

79. July 23, 1908. *Sigmund Freud–Karl Abraham, Briefe,* 1907–1926, ed.
Hilda C. Abraham and Ernst L. Freud (1965), 57.
80. May 10, 1926. *Freud, Briefe,* 365. Of the sizable literature on Freud's
ambivalent attitude toward Judaism, I want to single out Peter Loewenberg's
interesting "A Hidden Zionist Theme in Freud's 'My Son, the Myops . . .'
Dream," *Journal of the History of Ideas,* XXXI (1970), 129–32; and Ernst
Simon, "Sigmund Freud the Jew," Leo Baeck Institute *Year Book II* (1957),
270–305.

pointedly, did he found a science? Certainly, the claim of psycho-analysis to scientific status remains controversial. Experimental psychologists have denounced it as unscientific because it cannot be proved; critical philosophers, because it cannot be disproved. The psychologists have been irritated by the hermeticism of psychoanalytic inquiry, by the unduplicable history each psychoanalysis generates, by its resistance to experimental procedures. And the philosophers have been repelled by the commodiousness of psychoanalytic terms and the loose wording of psychoanalytic generalizations. The Freudian language, they have argued, can accommodate any psychological event whatever: any form of mental behavior can be compelled to serve psychoanalytic assertions. They see a concept like ambivalence as a vast, convenient cloak; it makes them uncomfortable that psychoanalytic mechanisms like repression, projection, or reaction formation invite the observer to believe the very opposite of what he is seeing: the show of affection covers deeply felt rage, the pacifist represses murderous wishes, the principled opponent of cruelty to man and beast has grown, as Freud wrote with bitter pertinence during the first World War, from a little sadist and tormentor of animals.[81] But a theory that must always be right, no matter what the evidence, can be right only in the most trivial way.

Freud was fully conscious of such objections from the beginning, and anticipated most of them. He knew that it would be as hard to establish the propositions of psychoanalysis as it had been to discover the materials on which they rested. But the obstacles to experimental verification did not trouble him. When he learned, in 1934, that an American psychoanalyst was conducting experiments to test psychoanalytic claims, he gave the enterprise his blessing—"It cannot hurt," he wrote—but insisted that it was unnecessary: "the wealth of reliable observations" on which his claims rested made them, he thought, "independent of experimental verification."[82] The stock of clinical confirmation, after

81. *Thoughts for the Times on War and Death*, S.E., XIV, 282; *Zeit-gemässes über Krieg und Tod*, G.W., X, 333.
82. Freud to S. Rosenzweig, February 28, 1934; quoted in the German original in David Shakow and David Rapaport, *The Influence of Freud on American Psychology* (1964), 129.

all, was vast and growing daily. Actually, by minimizing the value of experimental evidence, Freud was for once failing to exploit the full arsenal of argumentation in behalf of his science. For there has been, for years, impressive experimental evidence for such general concepts as the unconscious, and for mechanisms such as repression, dream work, projection. And these experiments have been more than exercises in the collecting of favorable instances which conveniently set unfavorable ones aside; the massiveness and variety of the experimental material suggests, however unsystematic and inconclusive it still is, the general applicability of psychoanalysis to the human experience.[83]

Despite all this, the objections to psychoanalysis, whether from philosophy or psychology, however malicious or obtuse, have had their uses. The early defensive strategy, when psychoanalysts would blandly reject all criticism as mere proof of the critic's own neurosis—an irritating, if understandable strategy—has now given way to responsible efforts at reformulating psychoanalytic claims,

83. The controversial literature on this subject is already large and steadily growing. Best known among the hostile appraisals are Robert R. Sears, *A Survey of Objective Studies of Psychoanalysis* (1943), which, though it fails to come to grips with case studies, is often cited; see also, among his other assaults on Freud, H. J. Eysenck, *The Uses and Abuses of Psychology* (1959). The symposium *Psychoanalysis, Scientific Method and Philosophy* (1959), ed. Sidney Hook, contains other attacks, most notably Ernest Nagel's essay "Methodological Issues in Psychoanalytic Theory" (38–56). The same symposium gave room to the magisterial, but not conclusive defense by Heinz Hartmann, "Psychoanalysis as a Scientific Method" (3–37). Richard Wollheim has edited a helpful anthology, *Freud: A Collection of Critical Essays* (1974), which addresses itself to the relation of psychoanalysis to philosophy; outstanding are Clark Glymour, "Freud, Kepler, and the Clinical Evidence" (285–304), and Peter Alexander, "Rational Behaviour and Psychoanalytic Explanation" (305–21). Apposite, though less technical, are two fine sympathetic studies of Freud, Lionel Trilling's splendid Freud Anniversary Lecture of 1955, *Freud and the Crisis of Our Culture* (1955), which stresses the toughness of Freud's mind; and Richard Wollheim, *Freud* (1971), the best brief analysis, in chronological order, of Freud's ideas. I have also learned from Philip Rieff, *Freud: The Mind of the Moralist* (rev. ed., 1961), especially from its ch. 9, "The Ethic of Honesty," and from David Rapaport, *The Structure of Psychoanalytic Theory: A Systematizing Attempt*, Monograph 6 of *Psychological Issues* (1960), which does not resolve the problems of method and foundations so much as clarify them.

disciplining psychoanalytic assertions, and clarifying psychoanalytic terminology. There is a new flexibility of attitude which constitutes, in effect, a return to Freud's own scientific style. For Freud steadily revised his insights as new information, and unexpected case histories, invalidated, and compelled modification of, earlier assertions. Some critics have accused him of rigidity because he was unwilling to abandon the fundamental theory of infantile sexuality; others have accused him of inconsequence because he changed his mind, for instance, on the etiology of anxiety. The critics cannot have it both ways, though, with Freud, they have tried. Actually, Freud was confident that his decisive discoveries were too solidly grounded to need revision, and, at the same time, quite consistently, that his science was so young, and so difficult, that it would have been a more than human achievement to state its propositions with utter finality. To him, what was most admirable in the scientific habit of mind, and yet most unusual even among scientists, was the willingness to live with uncertainty. "Mediocre spirits," he once wrote to Marie Bonaparte, "demand of science a kind of certainty which it cannot give, a sort of religious satisfaction. Only the real, rare, true scientific minds can endure doubt, which is attached to all our knowledge."[84] He did not add, though, it was implicit, that the capacity to tolerate this kind of doubt was the highest kind of courage.

It demanded, this courage, an unrelenting campaign against disguise and deception. In his letters to his fiancée, loving as they are, he reiterates the need for candor between them, the candor of friends. The obligatory tenderness that nineteenth-century middle-class men were supposed to pour out to their chosen women struck him as a form of condescension. "To live with one another," he told Martha Bernays in September 1882, "does not mean concealing from one another, or prettifying, everything disagreeable; helping means sharing everything that happens."[85] He

84. Quoted in Jones, *Freud*, II, 419. On the making of that scientific habit of mind, see, in addition to other titles, like Wollheim's *Freud*, Siegfried Bernfeld, "Freud's Earliest Theories and the School of Helmholtz," *Psychoanalytic Quarterly*, XIII (1944), 341–62.

85. September 25, 1882. *Freud, Briefe*, 30.

applied the same high standard of frankness in matters of greater gravity. "The art of deceiving a sick man," he wrote to Fliess in February 1899, "is really quite uncalled for. What has the individual come to, how slight must be the influence of the religion of science which is supposed to have succeeded the old religion, if one no longer dares to reveal that this or that person is now to die?" And he added with a Stoic's piety, "I hope that when my time comes, I will find somebody who will treat me with more respect and tell me when I must be ready."[86] This was early in 1899, when Freud was forty-two. He kept to this exacting ideal when his time did come: writing from London in April 1939, very old and very ill, he told Marie Bonaparte that there was a concerted attempt to envelop him "in an atmosphere of optimism." He was being told that his cancer was receding, and his poor condition only temporary: "I do not believe it, and do not like to be deceived—*Ich glaube nicht daran, und mag es nicht, betrogen zu werden.*"[87] The one thing he did not want, and did not like to give, was dishonest consolation.

That is why he treated religious and political dogmatism with contempt. The word is not too strong. He was quite unwilling to "stand up before my fellow-men as a prophet," he wrote on the concluding page of *Civilization and Its Discontents*, "and I bow to their reproach that I cannot offer them any consolation: for fundamentally that is what they all demand—the wildest revolutionaries no less passionately than the most virtuous pious believers."[88] On the rare occasions when he felt compelled to lie in the service of medical discretion, he regretted it. Describing the case of "Katharine—" in 1895, he had reported that her hysterical symptoms originated after sexual assaults by her uncle. Many years later, in a footnote he added in 1924, he disclosed that the assailant had actually been the girl's father; and he concluded that "A distortion like the one I introduced in this case should be altogether avoided in a case history,"[89] a candid effort to repair his

86. February 6, 1899. *Origins*, 276; *Anfänge*, 294–95.
87. April 28, 1939. *Freud, Briefe*, 451.
88. S.E., XXI, 145; G.W., XIV, 506.
89. *Studies on Hysteria*, S.E., II, 134n; *Studien über Hysterie*, G.W., I, 195n.

earlier lack of candor. Freud's whole science was, of course, a systematic assault on the lies by which men live, and which make them ill. But his urge toward honesty was something more than a professional rule; it was the principle of his existence.

The most remarkable, and scientifically the most rewarding, instance of Freud's honesty was, of course, his self-analysis. This long-drawn effort, tentatively begun perhaps as early as 1893 and never really concluded, has been well described and highly praised, but every new exposure to its inner drama must reawaken astonishment and admiration; it is a masterpiece of the scientific imagination, a masterpiece of the highest order. Freud had no precedents to follow when he undertook his self-analysis, no models to imitate. He had no one in Vienna to talk to, to test ideas with, and to gather courage from; he was, in that great center of cultivation and learning, wholly alone. He could count on only one friend and confidant, Wilhelm Fliess, whom he met on a few appointed occasions for scientific talk. Freud found these "congresses" refreshing and stimulating, but most of the time, Fliess was in Berlin, and Freud's sole resource was to write him long, immensely detailed letters, reporting his progress, his failures, his triumphs. Freud always learned much from his patients, but never more profitably than in these decisive years. He was a splendid listener, and he trained his sensitivity to the highest pitch of refinement, for he soon recognized that the hysterics who came to him for relief had, literally, much to tell him. They prepared him, at least in some degree, for what he was to find in himself; their dreams led him to his own dreams; their diversionary tactics, their fits of convenient amnesia, and their palpable misstatements alerted him to the resourcefulness of his own resistance.

But it was one thing to listen to his patients and quite another to listen to himself. This is what he implied when he thanked Fliess for "making me a present of an Other—*dass Du mir einen Anderen schenkst.*"[90] Yet Fliess, who in some respects and for some time functioned emotionally as Freud's psychoanalyst, was

90. May 18, 1898. From the German text in Schur, *Freud,* 544.

not an adequate substitute for the real thing, and Freud had to discover for himself even this rather mysterious role that his friend was unconsciously and intermittently playing for him.

The others being Other had two clear advantages for the tracing of subterranean connections and the imputation of concealed causes. They used overt signs—gestures as well as speech—which Freud found far easier to observe and absorb than the movements of his own mind, for which he had to rely solely on what Theodor Reik has called the third ear. Moreover, Freud could accept the disreputable fantasies of his patients with schooled professional detachment, with the physician's knowing gravity. But his fantasies, as unpleasant, as contrary to his bourgeois self-image as any his patients brought to him, were, after all, his own. There was no one to lift the burden of guilt from him for rejoicing in his infant brother's death, for having wanted his beloved father dead so that he might have erotic access to his mother— no one but himself. "A certain personal distance between analysand and analyst," writes Max Schur in illuminating pages on Freud's self-analysis, "is an important condition for the development of a typical transference in a regular analysis. In the latter, of course, the analyst provides the interpretations, including those of all transference manifestations, and thus influences in a subtle way the course of the analysis. Most of this was different in Freud's case."[91]

The flatness of this formulation, like that of most pages on Freud's self-analysis, exhibits the inadequacy of ordinary speech confronting the magnificence of a historic act. The risks of bathos or banality are exceeded only by the risks of prosy understatement. Freud's self-analysis was heroic beyond ordinary heroism: he performed it outside any known context; he had to make his own rules; he could not guess at its ultimate significance for his theories or consequences for his sanity. He did not know what he did not know. At the same time, he found his immense daring intellectually intoxicating: his explorations, rigorously and patiently pursued, might provide a master key to the whole range

91. Ibid., 76.

of human experience—to art, politics, and religion no less than to dreams, slips, jokes, and sexual life. But if he was proved right, nearly all other psychologists were fatally wrong. Hence the perils he faced were external no less than internal; Freud was undertaking his self-analysis in years when his professional colleagues were treating him as a charlatan, a maniac, and, worst of all for him, a mystic. He was rightly reluctant to publish the truths he had discovered about his inner self—even more reluctant than he had been to discover them.

It is impossible to date with any precision the time that Freud began his momentous self-scrutiny. By 1893 or, at the latest, 1894, the pressure for generalization always active within him had brought him to the recognition that the mental activities his patients reported to him strikingly resembled his own fantasies, thoughts, and wishes. Freud more than once expressed regret that the impetus to his greatest discoveries had come from the neurotics who consulted him; by 1894, he knew that his work would draw all humans, stable and unstable, within a single circle defined by the same sets of psychological laws. In the early summer of that year, he reported to Fliess his utter isolation in Vienna and his slow progress in his study of the neuroses. He was working on a project of general psychology, and, at the same time, on material he himself was generating. By May 25, 1895, in that important letter to Fliess in which he portrays himself as serving his tyrant, psychology, he reported ideas and procedures we are entitled to call, though Freud himself did not yet call them, self-analysis: "A satisfactory total conception of neuropsychotic disturbances is impossible if one cannot tie it to clear assumptions regarding normal mental processes. I have devoted every free minute to such work in the past few weeks, spending the night hours from eleven to two with such fantasying, translating and guessing—*Phantasieren, Übersetzen und Erraten*—and would stop only when I came upon some absurdity, or when I had truly and seriously overworked myself." As usual, analysis of self and analysis of patients reinforced one another: "Working with the neuroses in my practice gives me great pleasure. Practically everything is being confirmed daily, new things are being added, and the certainty of having the heart of the matter in my grasp does me good."[92] Then, on July 24, 1895, came the classic Irma dream which enabled him to understand what he was later to call "dream work." His materialist world view was beautifully confirmed: every scrap of manifest dream has its meaning, or set of meanings, and is related to the latent dream content that the analyst must excavate and interpret. Freud assigned the highest possible place to this dream in the making of his science; it was this very dream about which, in 1900, he wove the fantasy of the marble tablet that might single out his house one day. In August 1895, "after long mental labor—*nach langer Denkarbeit*"[93]—he confidently thought he had come to understand what he then called "pathological defense." With many setbacks, suffering many discouragements, he was making progress.

In 1896, after an agonizing terminal illness, Freud's aged father died. Freud had been prepared for that death, less than fully prepared for the emotions it was to release in him, and which his self-scrutiny permitted him to bring to the surface. Thirteen years later, in the preface to the second edition of his *Interpretation of Dreams*, he would note that his father's death had precipitated him into writing the book and inextricably entangled him in the most self-centered exploration in history: the book on dreams, he wrote, was "a piece of my self-analysis, my reaction to my father's death—that is, to the most significant event, the most decisive loss, of a man's life."[94] Dying was, as it were, the last service his father had done him; it aided Freud in understanding the operation of ambivalence.

The following year, 1897, was the year of decision. It was a time of intensified self-analysis, of ideas pouring out alternating with periods of paralysis, and of a setback that would have ended the inquiries of a lesser man. For some years, Freud had been increasingly impressed with the share of sexual conflicts in the making of the neuroses. He was not then, and never became, a pansexualist, and nothing irritated him more—and with justice—than to be accused of resorting to a single cause as the explanation of all human life. While he firmly held to the ubiquitousness of

92. May 25, 1895, *Origins*, 119–20; *Anfänge*, 129–30.
93. August 6, 1895. *Origins*, 122; *Anfänge*, 132.
94. *S.E.*, IV, xxvi; *G.W.*, II–III, x.

infantile sexuality and the importance of sexuality in all spheres of human existence, he was always ready to concede—or, rather, always insisted—that causes other than sexual ones helped to shape human motives, character, and conduct. To call Freud a reductionist is to distort his ideas and his teachings; while some of these distortions may feed on incautious, overly sweeping formulations of Freud's, the balance of his writings invalidates any such accusation. He knew, though he did not write about it at length, that life experiences give specific form to the working of elemental impulses. Even the Oedipus complex is far from uniform and depends in its working out on the impact of family constellations, of schooling, and of reading. But in the mid-1890s, when his psychoanalytic ideas were still in the formative stage, his patients were deluging him with tales of seduction in infancy, mainly by the father. These stories offered a convenient explanation for the onset of neurosis, which Freud was all the more inclined to accept as it fitted the theories he had been developing. In 1895, he and Breuer had jointly asserted that hysterics suffer mainly from reminiscences, and here were his patients, producing memories of traumatic events calculated to unsettle an unformed mind.

Common sense, analytic experience, and self-analysis conspired to make these stories ultimately incredible. His theory, remarkable alike for its range and its outrageousness, stood discredited. On September 21, 1897, Freud, just back from a summer's vacation, "refreshed, cheerful, impoverished," burst out to Fliess: "And now right off I want to confide to you the great secret that has been slowly dawning on me in the last few months. I no longer believe in my neurotica"—that is, in the seduction stories. He no longer knew, he added, where he stood.[95] One must visualize Freud's situation at this moment. He was forty years old, a psychopathologist with towering ambitions, impressive self-confidence, and small income. He had failed, sometimes barely, to secure the fame he wanted and thought he deserved. For several years he had been reconnoitering from an exposed outpost, with incredible tenacity, reaching for a general theory of mind. Now

95. *Origins*, 215; *Anfänge*, 229.

he no longer knew where he stood. He was like a brave officer venturing far into enemy territory only to sense abruptly that his troops have deserted him, and that, in any case, the war may not be worth fighting.

Freud recalled this critical moment more than once. In 1914 he thought that his erroneous seduction theory had been "almost fatal to the young science." When his theory "broke down under its own improbability" and its contradiction of ascertainable circumstances, "the first consequence was a stage of complete perplexity." The "ground of reality had been lost." At that time, he would gladly have given up the whole work; perhaps he had "persevered only because I no longer had the choice of starting on something else. At last came the reflection that, after all, one has no right to despond just because one has been deceived in one's expectations, but that one must revise those expectations"[96]—a typically Freudian appraisal of the situation: he knew that the world does not exist to gratify one's fantasies. In 1925, his memory was, if anything, more dramatic: "I was for some time completely perplexed. My confidence in my technique as in its results suffered a heavy blow." He needed to pull himself together.[97]

The letters he wrote in these decisive weeks tell a far more serene story. In the letter in which he announced the collapse of his theory, he observed that he felt neither in bad humor, nor confused, nor exhausted. And since he felt cheerful, he chose to interpret his doubts "as the result of honest and vigorous intellectual labor," and to take pride that, having got in so deep, he was still capable of criticism. Nor did he feel disgraced, but had "a sense more of victory than of defeat." Immediately criticizing his mood, in turn, he added that it was really not right. But was it wrong? If Freud had suffered a severe blow, and had to pull himself together, it took him little time to do so; if he felt ready to give up his work, he changed his mind practically overnight. By October, within a few weeks of giving his doubts a free hand, he had turned the recognition of his mistaken trust in his pa-

---

96. *On the History of the Psycho-Analytic Movement*, S.E., XIV, 17; *Zur Geschichte der psychoanalytischen Bewegung*, G.W., X, 55.
97. *An Autobiographical Study*, S.E., XX, 34; *Selbstdarstellung*, G.W., XIV, 60.

tients into a triumphant instrument for theoretical advance: it gave him insight into the prominent place of fantasy in mental life. By October 3, he could announce that "the last four days of my self-analysis, which I consider indispensable for clearing up the whole problem, have been progressing in dreams and yielding me most valuable disclosures and clues."[98] He was dredging up erotic feelings about his mother whom, before he was two and a half, he had seen "*nudam,*" using the Latin word in one of his rare accesses of gentility. By October 15, when he told Fliess that his self-analysis was the most important matter now in hand, he had grasped "the gripping power of king Oedipus."[99] Before the year was out, the structure of his theories needed only some final touches. As Freud told Fliess, in the paragraph in which he announced the universality of the Oedipus complex, the whole business was not easy. But "to be completely honest with oneself is a good exercise."[100] He had been just that, and psychoanalysis had been the result. The world—even Vienna, torpid, self-absorbed, resistant—was never the same again.

Where, on the cultural map, do these reflections leave Freud? He remains hard to place, which, with a genius, should not surprise us. As a genius, Freud broke molds, transcended categories. And yet, to leave matters here would be facile, evasive. Though a genius, Freud lived, as I have insisted throughout, in space, in time, in a definable culture. And that culture was larger than Vienna. It was not even centered there.

I said near the beginning that Vienna gave Freud rich materials for the exercise of mixed feelings. Indeed, nothing is easier than to compile a catalogue of Freud's comments and choices that document his incurable ambivalence. Writing to his fiancée in the mid-1880s, Freud wondered whether he would be able to stand living in Vienna;[101] nor did he want to die there: a grave in Vienna's Zentralfriedhof, he told Martha Bernays, was "the most

98. *Origins,* 218–19; *Anfänge,* 233.
99. *Origins,* 223; *Anfänge,* 238.
100. *Origins,* 233; *Anfänge,* 237–38.
101. To Martha Bernays, May 6, 1886. *Freud, Briefe,* 211.

distressing idea" he could imagine.[102] Life in Vienna, he wrote his sister-in-law, was really "too stupid";[103] and he punctuated his correspondence with disparaging epithets about the city: it was oppressive, disgusting, repulsive, depressing.[104] It was even, he told Ernest Jones late in life, astonishingly, a city in which he had lived for fifty years without encountering a single new idea.[105] At the same time, though his wife was from Hamburg, his teachers from all Europe, and his supporters scattered across Western civilization, Freud acted as though he could not possibly abandon the city which, he told the world all his life, he thoroughly detested. Certainly he had been free to leave; certainly he had had repeated incentives to move to such friendlier climates as England, where he had family, to start again. There was an element of defiant stubbornness in his residential conservatism: he found a certain exhilaration in what he once described, in a letter to his fiancée, as his "struggle with Vienna—*Kampf mit Wien*."[106] It is a measure of that stubbornness, I think, that he should choose November 1918, the very moment of disastrous defeat for the Central Powers and misery for Austria, to tell an interviewer about his "unbounded affection for Vienna and Austria," even though he knew their abysses.[107] He found undramatic gratifications in Vienna: his walks, his card games, his friends, and the peculiar reward attached to unbroken habit—the saving of energy. It was as if Freud, the intrepid explorer, needed a place on which to stand. There may even be a bit of truth in Ellenberger's aphorism, "Those Viennese who really disliked Vienna emigrated; those who loved it pretended to hate it, but stayed."[108] Complaining about Vienna, we know, was a widespread, affectionate Viennese sport.

Yet Freud's troubled loyalty to Vienna in no way defines his

102. See Jones, *Freud*, I, 179.
103. To Minna Bernays, July 13, 1891. *Freud, Briefe*, 223.
104. See, for a collection, Jones, *Freud*, I, 293–94.
105. Quoted by Martin Esslin, "Freud's Vienna," in Miller, ed., *Freud: The Man, His World, His Influence*, 43.
106. May 13, 1886. *Freud, Briefe*, 212.
107. Quoted by Johnson, *The Austrian Mind*, 444.
108. Ellenberger, *Discovery of the Unconscious*, 558.

cultural position; it did not preclude wider loyalties. In the decades of Freud's long education for psychoanalysis, Vienna was, as I have already noted, almost dominated by famous Germans from Germany. The university and leading hospitals filled some of their most prestigious posts with men who had been born and had reached distinction in the Reich. Their presence, and their prominence, made it easy to raise one's sights above the specifically Viennese, or Austrian, share in German culture. And it was in that larger German culture that Freud lived and worked. It is no accident that Freud, who disdained most praise, rejected most honors, and sabotaged most celebrations, should take enormous and undisguised pleasure in being awarded the Goethe Prize in 1930. The Prize, he wrote to Ferenczi, "has through its connection with Goethe something more worthy about it than many others. I am allowed to rejoice in it."[109] There was something in the Prize, he wrote, "that specially warms the imagination."[110] It was the imagination of a cultivated German that it warmed.

But Freud, if culturally a German, was a German with his discontents, though he liked to think that his unpopularity in Germany was not among them. "It seems to me," he wryly told a correspondent in 1931, "that I am *persona ingrata*, if not *ingratissima*, with the German people—and moreover with the learned and the unlearned alike."[111] But he emphatically denied that he found this in any way troubling: what others thought of him, he implied, did not affect what he thought of himself. This was largely, but not wholly true. Anti-Semitism was an exception; when he encountered that, his characteristic stubbornness and dignity came into play. "My language is German," he told an interviewer in 1926. "My culture, my attainments are German. I considered myself German intellectually, until I noticed the growth of anti-Semitic prejudice in Germany and German Austria. Since that time, I prefer to call myself a Jew."[112] His choice

109. August 1, 1930. *Freud, Briefe*, 395.
110. To Alfons Paquet, July 26, 1930. *Freud, Briefe*, 394.
111. "Letter to Georg Fuchs," S.E., XXII, 252; see 251n. Not in G.W.
112. The interviewer was George Sylvester Viereck, scarcely an attractive or dependable figure. Freud, in fact, came to find him unpalatable (see Freud

of one over the other only demonstrates how deeply anti-Semitism had penetrated his consciousness in his late years; earlier, he would have done what others did, call himself a German and a Jew at the same time.

Freud had another, more professional reservation about his cultural self-definition, though that, too, interestingly enough, emerged during his last years. In 1927, the year after he had chosen to call himself a Jew *rather* than a German, Freud once again placed himself in opposition to Germany. In a letter to Dr. Werner Achelis, a German psychologist, he confessed himself an unreconstructed devotee of the scientific outlook. That outlook was clearly much on his mind; in the very year he wrote to Achelis, he published his *Future of an Illusion*, a provocative essay on religion as neurosis which ends with the celebrated declaration of faith, "No, our science is no illusion. But it would be an illusion to believe that we can obtain anywhere else what it cannot give us."[113] Metaphysics, he wrote Achelis, was, to him, a "nuisance," an "abuse of thinking," a "survival" from earlier, more religious ages. He found it much simpler to orient himself in the Here-and-Now of facts—*im Diesseits der Tatsachen*—than in the Beyond of philosophy—*im Jenseits der Philosophie*. "I know precisely," he concluded, "how much this way of thinking makes me an alien in the German cultural world."[114]

The choice is as striking as it was unnecessary. True, for more than a century, many cultivated Germans had prized profound philosophizing and professed contempt for "shallow scientism." Germany, to the admiration and exasperation of other countries, had made itself into the homeland of system-makers, of deep metaphysicians. But, as usual, the imputation of a universal and exclusive national characteristic grossly ignores actual diversity.

---

to Viereck, April 16, 1933; *Freud, Briefe*, 409–10). But in 1926 he was welcome, and the interview, first published in 1927, and republished in 1930, in Viereck's *Glimpses of the Great*, esp. 34, called forth no protest, or even mild demurrer, from Freud. See *S.E.*, XXI, 169. We may accept therefore this quotation as substantially accurate.

113. *S.E.*, XXI, 56; *G.W.*, XIV, 380.

114. January 30, 1927. *Freud, Briefe*, 371.

The texture of German culture had woven into it a prominent strand of positivism, containing threads of French philosophy, English biology, and German science. And Freud normally knew this as well as anyone. He seems to have momentarily repressed Germany's share in this powerful way of scientific philosophizing, to have forgotten the dazzling array of theoreticians, experimenters, and clinicians—Germans mainly—who had collaborated to make him into the lifelong determinist, the tireless seeker after natural causes he was to become. There was more of personal animus in Freud when he wrote that letter—irritation, perhaps a moment of self-pity—than cultural analysis.

His momentary lapse cannot affect the results of that analysis. It is, in any event, trivial compared to the lapses of others in search of Freud. Victor von Weizsäcker, not an unreasonable man, may therefore stand for those others. When, four days after Freud's death, he sought to arrive at a verdict on Freud's contribution to science, he could find nothing better than a "racial" Jewish intelligence. "It has in truth, it seems to me," he wrote, "been Asian wisdom which has come to us with him."[115] Weizsäcker meant to pay Freud a compliment, but his judgment is no less absurd for that. It was not Asian wisdom that Freud offered the world but German wisdom. Now this, in the cosmopolitan scientific atmosphere of the nineteenth century, meant European wisdom. But that makes it no less German; after all, Germans had freely participated in shaping, and profiting from, that atmosphere. The very words that Freud had used in 1927 to denigrate metaphysics—"nuisance," "abuse," "survival" from religious ages—conjure up that atmosphere and his international pedigree, transmitted and mediated through Brücke, Nothnagel, and other distinguished men who taught Freud in the 1870s and 1880s; they are words calling up Comte, Darwin—and Helmholtz. That Freud came to feel rejected by Germany and that Germany in fact came to reject him changes nothing in this conclusion, and does not weaken his claim on German culture. Germany has often rejected the best that is in her.

115. "Reminiscences," in Nelson, *Freud and the 20th Century*, 62. Freud himself on occasion played with such "Oriental" derivations (see above, 43). But they are fleeting and unrepresentative.

II
ENCOUNTER WITH MODERNISM
German Jews in Wilhelminian Culture

1. THE STRUGGLE FOR CREDIBILITY

In the quarter century between the accession of Wilhelm II and the outbreak of the first World War, German Jews made distinct contributions to German culture, as Germans far more than as Jews. In many respects, to be sure, Germany's Jews remained outsiders. There were still social clubs that would not admit them, private industries that would not employ them, public bodies that would not appoint them. There were fanatics who would not leave them alone. Social theorists of all sorts, pseudo-scientists who flourished in the anxiety-provoking aftermath of the Darwinian debate, found it convincing, or useful, to hold Jews responsible for real or fancied modern ills: materialism, secularism, mobility.[1] For German Jews anxious to live and work in peace, as Germans, the persistence of exclusive organizations, outbursts of hostility, and anti-Semitic publicists appeared as depressing survivals. The centers of darkness and animosity still scattered across the social landscape seemed so unpleasant precisely because so much had happened in the way of liberalization and enlightenment.

But the main point was that much *had* happened. Thus, in these decades, when Germany's Jews read hostile propaganda, or

1. See above, 19–22.

suffered personal affronts, they did so as Germans. The prominent social psychologist Moritz Lazarus spoke for a whole generation when, some years before the accession of Wilhelm II, he called the "Jewish question" a *"German* question," a remnant of inhumanity that all Germans, Jews and gentiles together, must extirpate: "Everywhere and always, the question of humanity and justice is more important for the one who has to grant it than for the one who has to receive it. But we are Germans, we must speak as Germans."[2]

What was true before 1888 was even truer after; the accession of Wilhelm II brought to the German throne an adventurous monarch some of whose friends, as German Jews noted with relief, were Jews. Earlier, in 1880, under the impress of the "intellectual" anti-Semitism aroused by the demagogic court preacher Adolf Stöcker and the influential historian Heinrich von Treitschke, the assimilated Jewish writer Berthold Auerbach had exclaimed in despair that he had lived and worked in vain: *"Vergebens gelebt und gearbeitet!"* But in general, German Jews could read the auguries as highly favorable. Popular anti-Semitism, which linked the machinations of traders and bankers and the "corrosion" of traditional values to the Jewish presence in Germany, had not been dissipated. But it was less active than before. The political parties that had profiteered from the economic dislocations of the 1870s and 1880s and gathered votes with anti-Semitic platforms stood discredited in the 1890s. While racialists, who detested intermarriage and denied the very possibility of Jewish assimilation, introduced a new and more poisonous strain into anti-Semitism, they appeared to be eccentrics; many conservatives, let alone liberals, thought them unrespectable, even mad.

2. From Lazarus, *Treu und Frei* (1887), 57, quoted in *Moritz Lazarus und Heymann Steinthal: Die Begründer der Völkerpsychologie in ihren Briefen,* ed. Ingrid Belke (1971), lxxiin. I should note at the outset that I have concentrated my argument in this essay on those who were born, or chiefly lived, in the German Empire. As I said in my Introduction to this volume, I am aware of the utility (often, the indispensability) of comparative history. But here I have chosen to explore Jews living under relatively homogeneous circumstances. To have included Austrian and Czech and Hungarian Jews, important and interesting as they are, would have enriched but also diluted my inquiry.

Jewish assimilation into German society was not a theoretical matter.[3] It was practical. And, increasingly, in occupations in which Jews found a welcome, in disciplines into which they sent a few pioneering, lonely scouts, even in preoccupations, like that of self-defense or sectarian scholarship, in which they were almost wholly taken up with the advancement of Judaism, German Jews thought and acted like Germans. The defense organization they founded in 1893, the *Centralverein deutscher Staatsbürger jüdischen Glaubens*, proclaims, with its very name, a sturdy confidence in the prospects of assimilation: it was an organized body of *German citizens* of the *Jewish faith*, brought together by outside pressures, but made up of Jews proud of their citizenship and no longer afraid to profess their religious adherence in public. Some isolated exceptions apart, the self-conscious return to Judaism and the half-anxious, half-defiant affirmation of its essential separateness—the world of Buber and of Rosenzweig— were still very much in the future. If professional anti-Semites had not called attention to the presence of Jews in the arts, in literature, in journalism, there would have been no way of deducing their religious affiliation from the quality or the character of their work.[4]

The Germanness of Jewish high culture in these decades was not an effort at disguise. It was not craven self-denial, but a proprietary feeling for a civilization that had produced decent cosmopolitans like Schiller and Kant, ornaments to modern humanism like Goethe. By 1888, German Jews could look back to a century of emancipation; they had discarded, in large part, their narrow concentrations on "Jewish" professions, like peddling and money-lending. They had gone into the big, rapidly growing cities, and diversified their social and professional status. More and more, German Jews were rich, or prosperous, or poor, in the

3. Here and throughout this essay I shall deliberately use the difficult term "assimilation" in an inclusive way. German Jews used it quite indiscriminately to mean acculturation—comfortable integration into the larger social whole while retaining one's identity—or amalgamation—adoption of all the customs of the larger society through intermarriage, baptism, and change of name.
4. See below, 180–81.

way of other Germans; more and more, they were cultivated or philistine in the same way. The act of 1869 that had officially granted civic equality to the Jews of the North German Federation was extended to all of just-united Germany two years later. There were still severe limits on German Jews in politics, in the bureaucracy, in the army; anti-Semitism continued to mar student organizations. But the liberal professions were comparatively hospitable; where there had been no Jews in 1850, there were, anti-Semites complained, too many Jews half a century later. What the Germans call the "free" professions, notably medicine and law, fully justified their name as far as Jews were concerned. By 1907, about 6 percent of Germany's physicians and 14 percent of Germany's attorneys were Jewish.[5] These developments were so heady because they appeared to be part of a wider historical phenomenon, the seeming emancipation of the middle orders of society.[6] Jewish liberation seemed logical, and promised to be

5. See Ernest Hamburger, "One Hundred Years of Emancipation: Four Legal Texts," Leo Baeck Institute (henceforth LBI), *Year Book XIV* (1969), and Siegmund Kaznelson, ed., *Juden im deutschen Kulturbereich* (3rd ed., 1962), 720–97.

6. Among the general treatments, I have derived most instruction from Ernest Hamburger, *Die Juden im öffentlichen Leben Deutschlands. Regierungsmitglieder, Beamte und Parlamentarier in der monarchischen Zeit 1848–1918* (1968); Jacob Katz, *Out of the Ghetto: The Social Background of Jewish Emancipation, 1770–1870* (1973); Uriel Tal, *Christians and Jews in Germany: Religion, Politics, and Ideology in the 2nd Reich, 1870–1914* (tr. Noah Jonathan Jacobs, 1975), an important book from which I dissent in part; the essays, *Juden im Wilhelminischen Deutschland 1890–1914* (1976), edited for the LBI by Werner E. Mosse in cooperation with Arnold Paucker, of which the present essay, in a somewhat different version, is a part. *Bankiers, Künstler und Gelehrte. Unveröffentlichte Briefe der Familie Mendelssohn aus dem 19. Jahrhundert*, edited and introduced by Felix Gilbert (1975), throws a great deal of light on nineteenth-century German-Jewish history; I have learned much from the Introduction. Reinhard Rürup, "Jewish Emancipation and Bourgeois Society," LBI *Year Book XIV*, 67–91, is useful, though I must confess that I find this essay marred by what German historians have recently come to call, in justified self-criticism, the hunger for theory. Fritz Stern's *Gold and Iron: Bismarck, Bleichröder, and the Building of the German Empire* (1977), which considers the career of Bismarck's Jewish banker in detail, was published too late to be considered here.

lasting, because it came in the guise of general human liberation.

To proclaim, and indeed to feel, a principal allegiance to Germany did not necessarily involve a German Jew in repudiation of his Jewishness—not necessarily, though often it did. There were many Jews in nineteenth-century Germany who chose the perilous path of conversion, some from authentic religious motives, some to make a political point, many to shed the stigmata that compromised their opportunities. The exodus was not massive; while reliable figures are hard to come by, one authority has estimated that around 22,000 Jews converted to Christianity in the course of the nineteenth century. Most "Jewish" journalists and editors, and about half of the "Jewish" academics in Germany, were converts.[7] One thing is certain: waves of anti-Semitism made wavelets of conversion; times of calm reduced the urge to join the safety of the dominant denominations.

Yet there were those who left Judaism for real, rather than merely good, reasons: they fell in love with a Christian, and the children of their mixed marriage were normally lost to Judaism. Or they became Christians because they thought Christianity was true: Max Scheler, the sociologist and philosopher of culture, with a Protestant father and a Jewish mother, was baptized in 1888, at the age of fourteen, upon the persuasion of a teacher, and later, again from conviction, converted to Roman Catholicism.[8] Until the mid-1870s, the only and by no means certain way of laying down the burdens of Judaism was to practice self-effacement and convert to Christianity. By 1876, at least in Prussia, legislation allowed Jews to withdraw from their religious congregations without embracing another faith, and this liberal law, justly feared and fought by rabbis of all persuasions, increased the flight from Judaism.[9] It was the Marxists above all who took this route of escape from the opium of their fathers: Eduard Bern-

7. See Werner Becker, "Die Rolle der liberalen Presse," Werner E. Mosse, ed., *Deutsches Judentum in Krieg und Revolution, 1916–1923* (1971), 127–28. And see below, 174.

8. For conversion, and for Scheler, see Carl Cohen, "The Road to Conversion," LBI *Year Book* VI (1961), 259–79.

9. Ismar Schorsch, *Jewish Reactions to German Anti-Semitism, 1870–1914* (1972), 19–20.

stein was only one of many Jewish Socialists to renounce Judaism legally and officially.[10] But this need not have been taken as a distinctively Jewish act: in the same way, and for the same reason, that Bernstein repudiated his religion, his Protestant and Catholic fellow-Socialists repudiated theirs.

Still, it took two to make Germanness credible: the actor saying his loyal lines and the audience appraising his public performance. And the German audience was, even in the days of Wilhelm II, all too inclined to find these legal performances unconvincing. The family history of the sociologist Georg Simmel is characteristic: Simmel's father, a merchant, had converted from Judaism to Catholicism and married a girl of Jewish family who had been baptized a Lutheran. Simmel himself was baptized in his mother's confession, and, in 1890, married a girl of mixed Catholic and Protestant parentage.[11] Yet we shall see that, to judge from Simmel's career, this parental mimicry did him no service. Normally it took several generations, several intermarriages, possibly a change of name and of residence, before the past of the new Christian faded into invisibility.[12] Jews generally despised their baptized brethren as renegades, Christians despised them as opportunists. Converts, seeking to win by moving from one camp to another, lost in both.

A substantial number of Jewish intellectuals and artists keenly appreciated the distasteful aspects and limited effectiveness of

10. Peter Gay, *The Dilemma of Democratic Socialism: Eduard Bernstein's Challenge to Marx* (1952), 25n.
11. Michael Landmann, "Bausteine zur Biographie," in Kurt Gassen and Michael Landmann, eds., *Buch des Dankes an Georg Simmel: Briefe, Erinnerungen, Bibliographie* (1958), 11–12.
12. The practice of changing Jewish-sounding names to neutral or deceptively Gentile-sounding ones was widespread in this period. Thus—to mention only some of the figures that will later appear in this essay—the great theatrical director Otto Brahm was originally Abramsohn, his even greater disciple Max Reinhardt was Goldmann, the Expressionist poet Jakob van Hoddis constructed his name anagrammatically from Davidsohn, the distinguished editor Julius Rodenberg was really Julius Levi from the Hessian town of Rodenberg. Sometimes, Jews adopted names from reasons other than disguise: the novelist of Jewish Berlin, Georg Hermann, simply used his first and middle names, and dropped his last name, Borchardt, which was hardly Jewish. The practice deserves further exploration.

conversion, and, however irreligious they might become, refused to disclaim their Jewish origins. But this did not prevent them from regarding themselves as thoroughgoing, wholehearted Germans. They might go to synagogue on the high holidays, or confess their traditional allegiance by answering "Jewish" on the census questionnaire. But when they wrote monographs, painted portraits, or conducted orchestras, they did so in ways which, I must repeat, were indistinguishable from the ways of other Germans. Even Jewish historians concentrating on the Jewish past, extraordinarily sensitive to their surviving parochialism, did their utmost to imitate the documentary obsession of Mommsen and the Olympian detachment of Ranke.[13]

While most Jewish cultural activity was German in form and in substance, alike in manner and matter, the idea persisted that it was somehow distinctive, easily recognized. Anti-Semites, of course, thought it self-evident that Jews were irremediable aliens in the Teutonic world; many Jews, though they earnestly rejected the charge of being a "negative" or "destructive" element, accepted the general proposition that there was some "racial" quality in the Jewish character that emerged most distinctively in the products of high culture: in the exercise of cleverness, of restless intelligence, of a certain unmistakable inwardness. There is a historical and sociological study that desperately needs to be undertaken: that of stupid Jews. The material would be abundant, and the results would correct the widespread and untenable notion that Jews are by endowment more intelligent than other people.

The proposition that German Jews were wholly like Germans yet notably distinct seems illogical. For most German Jews of the Empire, though, the persistence of presumably unique qualities did not compromise their authentic Germanness. As they saw it, one could be a "typical" Jew and a true German just as easily as one could be, say, a "typical" Rhinelander and true German. In retrospect, nothing demonstrates more poignantly how solidly

13. Ranke, of course, as we now have good reason to know, concealed strong biases behind his massive scholarship, but the point is that this is not how his work appeared to his contemporaries. See Peter Gay, "Ranke: The Respectful Critic," *Style in History* (1974), 57–94.

Jews were anchored in Western culture than their acceptance of the dubious notion of "racial" characteristics; it was a notion they had learned from the general vocabulary of Western pseudo-science. They affirmed their distinctiveness like everybody else.

The question whether there was a recognizably Jewish way of thinking and feeling acquires particular urgency in the years of Wilhelm II, for they were years of cultural upheaval in which radical shifts in style were common occurrences. They were the years of Modernism, of rebellion and renewal in tastes and techniques. Foreign painters like Edvard Munch, foreign dramatists like Henrik Ibsen settled in Germany and became influential and famous there; cultural capitals like Munich were hospitable to new drama, and painting, and novels from abroad. The breezes of change did not blow in the arts alone: philosophy, psychology, economics, sociology were far different in 1914 from what they had been in 1888.[14] Germans often limped behind the developments in other countries which they studied gratefully and enviously. This shift of sensibility could hardly go unnoticed; there was as much excitement among its supporters as there was resistance among its adversaries. Emperor Wilhelm II, an opinionated and intrusive patron of the arts with views on every conceivable subject, had some fairly radical, though not consistent, notions about scholarship and education, but in the arts and literature he was a vocal supporter of the Academy. He commissioned monstrously large conventional battle scenes and even larger, even more monstrous sculptural groups, and took part in the noisy debate over Modernism by calling French art "filthy," and voicing his disdain for French culture by telling Chancellor Caprivi that Paris was "the great whore house of the world." Modern art was, for him, the art of the gutter.[15] It is not surprising that in the early 1890s the young Gerhart Hauptmann could cause a public scandal with his outspoken Naturalist plays.

It was in these exhilarating and threatening movements of

14. See below, 114–32 passim.
15. See below, 159. For the letter to Caprivi, dated July 20, 1892, see Hans Herzfeld, *Ausgewählte Aufsätze* (1962), 310–12; the expression "art in the *Rinnstein*" is in Wilhelm II's speech at the opening of the Siegesallee, on December 18, 1901.

thought and talent that observers thought to detect a peculiarly Jewish element. They would describe it as impressive or sinister, depending on their view of Modernism—and of Jews. And historians have by and large followed them. But I want on the contrary to argue that, like notions of Jewish rootlessness and cleverness, the charge—or boast—of presumed Jewish hunger for experiment in the arts and thirst for innovation in literature is largely myth, fostered in part by Jews themselves. There were German Jews in the avant-garde of high culture, but they were in the rear guard and in the center as well. Far fewer cultural revolutionaries and far more cultural reactionaries were Jews than historians have recognized. German Jews moved toward the mainstream of German culture as much as they were permitted to do so. There was nothing in the Jewish cultural heritage, and little in their particular social situation, that would make them into cultural rebels, into principled Modernists.

Max Liebermann, Germany's most famous painter in the Wilhelminian era, once explicitly and eloquently made this point late in his long life, near the end of the Weimar Republic. Attacked by a Nazi newspaper as unsuitable to do the portrait of President Hindenburg, Liebermann chose to take the slander lightly and professed confidence that Hindenburg would find the article as ridiculous as he did: "After all," he said, "I am only a painter, and what does painting have to do with Judaism?—*was hat die Malerei mit dem Judentum zu tun?*"[16] That puts the matter squarely and, I think, resolves it correctly, at least for the German Jews of Liebermann's generation. Liebermann painted Jewish subjects: his notorious *Der zwölfjährige Jesus im Tempel* (1879), portrays Christ as an adolescent Jewish boy; and he returned, often, to seek subjects in the Jewish quarter in Amsterdam. But he did not persist in treating religious themes, and the *Judengasse* of Amsterdam was a source of visual inspiration like any other—polo players, Dutch peasants at the harvest, fisherwomen repair-

16. Wolfgang Koeppen, "Max Liebermann—Juden in der deutschen Kunst," in Thilo Koch, ed., *Porträts zur deutsch-jüdischen Geistesgeschichte* (1961), 94.

ing nets, hunters out with their dogs. Liebermann was a little self-conscious and a little timid about the position of Jews in their beloved and precarious homeland, in a way that, before Hitler, German Jews would have called old-fashioned. But that was politics.[17] Painting had nothing to do with Judaism.

Liebermann was the only Jew among Germany's notable painters of his day, with the possible exception of Lesser Ury, a gifted but little-regarded Impressionist. Ury painted and etched bright, rapidly sketched landscapes and city scenes: much like Liebermann, he occasionally turned to explicit Jewish themes, doing ambitious canvases in which he depicted melodramatic Hebrew prophets or pathetic Russian refugees. Born in provincial Prussia in 1861, Ury lived mainly in Berlin, where he died, poor and relatively unknown, in 1931. His contemporary, Emil Orlik, who came to Berlin from Prague and died a year after Ury, had a more gratifying career: he became the portraitist of celebrities, doing popular drawings and etchings of actors or writers. He was an agreeable, lesser talent. Liebermann alone stood out.

His Jewish predecessors offered him little guidance, either in conduct or in style. They were, all of them, conventional and derivative, the kind of artist whose name appears in Jewish encyclopedias, but rarely in histories of art. Moritz Oppenheim, probably the best known among nineteenth-century German Jews to make painting his profession, successively adopted styles from his German and French contemporaries, ending up an unadventurous realist. When he died at an advanced age in 1882, he had experienced in his lifetime the whole history of Jewish emancipation in his native country. He chose Jewish themes like *David Playing Before Saul* or, more parochially, *Sabbath Blessing,* but he did not refuse secular subjects or commissions to paint portraits of gentiles. The career of Eduard Magnus, who was born in Berlin in 1799, described a similar curve: he was influenced, first, by that school of devoutly religious painters, the German Nazarenes, then by the neo-Classicism of Ingres, and finally by the academic Realism that seemed most palatable to the French

17. See Osborn, *Der Bunte Spiegel: Erinnerungen aus dem Kunst-, Kultur-, und Geistesleben der Jahre 1890 bis 1933* (1945), 70–77. And below, 182–83.

Salons and to German customers. Like Oppenheim, he portrayed Jews such as Felix Mendelssohn; like Oppenheim, he also did gentiles such as Jenny Lind.

Magnus had been baptized as a child; and in general, nineteenth-century painters of Jewish origin either were raised as Christians, or took care to become Christians on their own. Philipp Veit, who achieved a certain prominence as a Nazarene, was baptized, as was his brother Johannes, another Nazarene. Eduard Bendemann, who studied with the celebrated German artist Schadow, married Schadow's sister in 1835 and accepted Christianity at the same time. His new family coupled with his new religion gave him social acceptance and did him no harm in securing desirable commissions for portraits and murals. That such artists should be prominent in all accounts of "the Jewish contribution" to German art in the nineteenth century is a comment, not on the greatness of their work, but on the mediocrity of that contribution.

This general mediocrity partly reflected the ancient Jewish aversion to making images. Receptive as Jews have always shown themselves to the cultures in which they were embedded, much as they have always learned even from their persecutors, some of their cultural traits have been a response to internal impulses. The laconic prohibition of the Second Commandment was not absolute. In the third century, the builders of the Dura-Europos synagogue decorated its walls with frescoes depicting biblical scenes; in the eighteenth century, prosperous Jews in Western Europe, including orthodox rabbis, rather enjoyed having their faces immortalized on canvas. Even so, the weighty injunction against making graven images doubtless diverted artistically inclined adolescents to other, less potentially impious vocations. Yet if German Jewry failed to produce great painters, it did so not merely because they were Jews, but also because they were Germans. The German tradition—in contrast to the Jewish tradition—was, of course, extremely hospitable to art, as such familiar names as "Grünewald," Dürer, or Holbein amply attest. But in the centuries of German fragmentation ambitious young Germans took to music, or poetry, or business—pursuits for which Germans were widely thought to be peculiarly fit.

While for several hundred years German painters had been little more than footnotes in the history of art, this was to change around 1900, with the emergence of German Expressionism. But in this change, Jewish artists played only an insignificant part. As in other countries, in Germany the Modernists were rarely of Jewish origin. The whole sizable and brilliant catalogue of Impressionist, Post-Impressionist, Expressionist, and abstract artists between 1870 and 1914 contains only two Jewish names, Camille Pissarro and Amedeo Modigliani. And it is necessary to add that they both made very little of their origins.

The vagaries of fame compel the historian to distinguish between contemporary prominence and posthumous reputation. If, in 1900, the best-known German artist was Max Liebermann, painter and etcher, popular for his appealing landscapes, realistic genre scenes, and penetrating portraits, in 1957 the Museum of Modern Art in New York could mount a comprehensive retrospective on "German Art in the Twentieth Century"—a show that included the very medium, the etching, in which Liebermann particularly excelled—without including a single example of Liebermann's work. Its catalogue casually refers to Liebermann as the founder of the Berlin Sezession, as a "late realistic" Impressionist against whom Nolde and Pechstein found it necessary to rebel, and as an etcher who succeeded in capturing "the transitory effects he sought"—nothing more.[18]

This implicit verdict—condemnation by neglect—suggests, I think fairly enough, that Liebermann's brave rebellion of the 1880s and 1890s, though honorable and admirable, was local and relatively short-lived. Its historical importance is that it permitted other artists to go further. Liebermann began as an innovator and ended up as President of the Academy of Arts.[19] He found his

18. See Werner Haftmann, "Painting," in Andrew Carnduff Ritchie, ed., *German Art of the Twentieth Century* (1957), 34, 42, and William S. Lieberman, "Prints," ibid., 188. Significantly, Haftmann gets the date of Liebermann's founding of the Sezession wrong by six years ("Painting," ibid., 22).

19. The fullest account down to his later years is Erich Hancke, *Max Liebermann: Sein Leben und seine Werke* (1923); see, in addition, Max J. Friedländer, *Max Liebermann* (1924); and Karl Scheffler, *Max Liebermann* (ed. 1953).

mature style relatively early and held to it tenaciously; his paintings of the 1920s look much like his paintings of the 1880s. He
did not move to the right; he did not move at all. It was art that
moved past him, to the left. Liebermann's large body of work
supplies no support for the thesis that restlessness and rootless-
ness are inherent Jewish characteristics, for he was the most im-
mobile and respectable of artists. "In my life's habits," he said,
"I am the complete bourgeois. I eat, drink, sleep, take walks and
work with the regularity of a church clock. I live in the house of
my parents, where I spent my childhood, and it would be hard
to have to live anywhere else."[20] Fortunately for him, he could
still die where he was born, in Berlin, in 1935, at the age of
eighty-eight, before the Nazis could compel him to break off his
life-long love affair with his native city.[21]

Liebermann was German, Prussian, Jew, Berliner, all at the
same time, and with no obvious strain. His biographers have
moved easily from one of these characterizing epithets to another;
few have found it necessary to mention his religion at all. If there
is one name that perhaps fits him best, it is that of Berliner.
Liebermann spoke the unmistakable Berlin speech, enjoyed the
irreverent and unsentimental wit in which Berliners used to take
sentimental pride, and contributed *bon mots* to the lore of dry
Berlin humor. Liebermann's rather appealing loyalty to Berlin
was anything but parochial; it was an affection for a city that was
as cosmopolitan in its culture as it was individual in its tone.
Liebermann himself took the high cosmopolitan line: "All my
life," he said, "my first question always was: What kind of a human being are you? But never: Are you Jew, Christian, or
heathen?" To which he immediately added, without any sense of
transition: "I was born a Jew and will die a Jew."[22] This array of
convictions is characteristic for German Jews of the Wilhel-

---

20. Hans Ostwald, ed., *Das Liebermann-Buch* (1930), 34–36.
21. His widow was less fortunate: she committed suicide in 1943 to avoid
being transported to a death camp.
22. Ostwald, *Liebermann-Buch*, 19–20. Speaking of the reluctance of Dutch
Jews to pose, he wrote on August 27, 1905, to the graphic artist Hermann
Struck about his "dear co-religionists—*uns're lieben Glaubensgenossen*."
Anna Wagner, *Max Liebermann in Holland* (1972), 27.

minian generations. Few of them felt under the necessity to make choices; they were, as their defense organization reminded the world, German citizens of the Jewish faith.

Max Liebermann was undeniably born a Jew: into a prosperous, eminently respectable family that had moved to Berlin in the 1820s. That habit of self-discipline and obsessive labor which Max Weber has taught us to associate with the Protestant ethic was one quality he internalized from his authoritarian and demanding father, even though he would not follow the bourgeois career that his parents had envisioned for him. But a painter can be as work-driven as a merchant or a lawyer. In 1930, when an interviewer reverently exclaimed that the steady productivity of the aged artist was a sort of miracle, Liebermann felt compelled to puncture this pious mood: "No, no," he protested. "It's no miracle. It's been drilled into me—*das ist so eingeübt*. Over and over again that inner admonition: work!"[23] Liebermann thought that this iron discipline, originating in his father's insistence that he earn his own living, was a typically Prussian trait. He was a Prussian Jew and proud of being both Prussian and Jew at the same time.

He had some right to his self-esteem. His *œuvre* is something better than the labored product of a diligent hand. Liebermann had a good eye for character, an artistically profitable love of nature, and, despite his admiration for Millet, a healthy aversion to pathos. As a young apprentice painter he had traveled widely, learning and soon discarding the tricks of slick salon painters, visiting picturesque Dutch villages, undergoing, in France, the influence of the Barbizon school. When he returned to Berlin in 1884, to settle permanently, to get married and keep painting, his style was set: a realism touched with Impressionist light, a receptivity for tough-minded genre scenes, an openness to the commissions for portraits that inundated him. He had become a splendid and democratic social reporter. His first sensational painting, the *Gänserupferinnen*, dates back to 1872; what intervened between this rather self-consciously posed scene of peasant women plucking geese and the more natural, more luminous scenes he would

23. Ostwald, *Liebermann-Buch*, 15–16.

do later was his experience of the Dutch masters and his reception of the Impressionists: Millet corrected by Manet and Hals.

Though widely denounced in his younger years for his irreverence and "love of ugliness," Liebermann was far less an aesthetic revolutionary than an honest observer and a stubborn artist who liked doing what he did more than he needed success, though he craved success as well. Even his most courageous "political" act, his founding of the Berlin Sezession, seems radical only against the background of the stuffy Wilhelminian atmosphere. In the early 1890s, Berlin was rapidly growing; an influx of writers, publishers, and artists gave Germany's official capital its first opportunity to take up cultural competition with Munich. In 1895, the open-minded and sensitive Hugo von Tschudi was appointed director of the National Gallery—Wilhelm's reign was nothing if not inconsistent. And throughout this decade, Liebermann welcomed and fostered rebellion. He greeted the graphic work of Edvard Munch, who first exhibited his neurotic lithographs to general scandal in Berlin in late 1891, and joined a new group of painters, known as "The XI," in the same year. Then, in 1898, significantly the very year that he became a member of the Berlin Academy, Liebermann founded the Sezession, which, in defiance of official protocol, sponsored independent exhibitions of young painters. Impressionism, of the original French and the derivative German variety, was making its way in Berlin, and Liebermann had his share in this widening of taste.

But, having made his move to Manet and Degas, he would not move further. In some of his writings on art—and he wrote fluently and frequently—he would speculate on the travail of the new in the land of the old: each innovator took a step beyond the familiar, suffered derision and isolation until he became familiar and famous, when he, in turn, would become a target for the younger generation. "No one can jump over his shadow."[24] Having learned to understand and admire the Impressionists, and having sponsored his own little revolution in German art, Liebermann remained content with his vision of nature. For the styles of the twentieth century—Expressionism, Fauvism, Cubism, ab-

24. Liebermann, *Degas* (1899), 12, 20–23.

straction—he had no sympathy whatever. He refused to apply what he had learned about his past to his present; he would not jump over his shadow. In a late, revealing summing up of his artistic position, delivered in 1927 under the august auspices of the *Akademie der Künste*, Liebermann looked back at the artistic styles of the past quarter century, and summarily rejected them all for their hostility to nature. He thought that the call, "Away from nature—*Los von der Natur*," which had been resounding from France since the beginning of the twentieth century, had been a baneful influence on art. Fortunately, he noted, serenely and myopically, the threat was receding; with a certain *Schadenfreude*, he added that museum directors who had thought to anticipate a rise in the market by acquiring Expressionists by the carload now desperately wanted to dispose of their embarrassing accessions.[25] As we read these sentiments, as we visualize the aged and respected painter, erect in posture, still working hard, confident in his tone, we recognize the share of German Jews in German conservatism. We remember that none of Germany's true artistic rebels—Kirchner, Marc, Klee, Beckmann—was a Jew, and that the greatest of them all, Nolde, was a Nazi.

2. THE INVASION OF CULTURE

While Jews have not been traditionally associated with the arts, they have for many centuries been enjoined to pay devout attention to words. Clearly, this concern with language has critical psychological consequences. I bring no news when I say that language makes humanity human, or that the possession and management of words is as essential to the definition of the self as it is to the mastery of the world. For centuries, Jews maintained their identity by retaining distinct languages: Hebrew for the realm of the sacred; Yiddish, or Ladino, or other Jewish languages, for the realm of the everyday. By the nature of their work, whether as traveling traders or as sedentary intellectuals, Jews

25. Ostwald, *Liebermann-Buch*, 488.

often commanded other languages as well: that of the dominant culture in which they lived, or of the classical heritage which they were transmitting with their glosses and their translations. It meant no lessening of Jewish consciousness for a Jew to speak Arabic or Spanish—or German.

When, with Moses Mendelssohn in the eighteenth century, and in the nineteenth with emancipation, German became, not the second language of Germany's Jews, but their first, this shift of priorities engendered a psychological transformation, a transvaluation of identities, that was unprecedented in its scope. Its crucial importance has not been sufficiently recognized. What makes the modern Jew, everywhere outside Israel and largely even there, radically and permanently different from his ancestors is precisely that his first language is modern Hebrew or French or English or German. What preserves the Jew's separateness in this, our iron age, is far less his ancient religion or some distinct culture than his terrible memories; it is Hitler who has defined the modern Jew and continues to define him from the grave.

The conquest of German was a laborious process for the partially emancipated Jew. Looking back at his childhood in Anhalt in the early 1830s, the Jewish philologist and philosopher Heymann Steinthal recalled: "We children knew a fourfold German: our parents spoke the Jewish-German proper, sprinkling it with Hebrew words which, in living speech, they often gave a pronunciation that differed considerably from that of Hebrew prayers. The Christian boys spoke the central-German popular dialect. We Jewish boys talked neither like our fathers nor our mothers, nor even like the Christian children, who naturally talked exactly like their parents. Ours was a modified Yiddish—Judendeutsch. I must add that some of the older Jews and Jewesses, having a certain cultivation—for instance, my father, who had even learned French and wrote a fairly correct German—spoke in their intercourse with Christians precisely as the particular Christian did: dialect with the bourgeois; a pure, or approximately pure, German with persons of rank."[26]

But that was, after all, well before 1848. For Germany's Jews

26. "Aus den Jugenderinnerungen Steinthals," in *Lazarus und Steinthal*, 375.

of the Wilhelminian era, the German language no longer felt like a precious acquisition; it was a cultural endowment they had in common with other Germans. Hebrew remained a tongue for ritual. It meant as little to the converts, of course, as to the Social Democrats. But its emotional prominence also receded for those who studied it in their religious instruction. And Yiddish became a target of condescending fun for most German Jews, certainly for those who lived in cities and had aspirations to *Kultur*. Most Jews knew a few words of Yiddish, like *nebbich* or *mies*, which they pronounced as though they were German words. But then, most gentiles shared in the jokes that such vocables suggested— jokes, and a certain distancing derision, for Yiddish was, of course, the language of the *Ostjuden* who were migrating to Germany in increasing numbers. Linguistic incompetence came, for many German Jews, to be a mark of status and a support for identity: *not* to speak Yiddish was one thing a German Jew, as a good German, did. There were times when this pride in German reached monumental proportions. In the early 1940s, after the aged Expressionist poet Else Lasker-Schüler had found refuge in Palestine, it was suggested to her that her German poems—and her poems were all in German—be translated into Hebrew. She refused to grant permission: "But they are written in Hebrew— *aber sie sind doch hebräisch geschrieben,*" she said—an astonishing, almost mystical reply.[27]

Indeed, Germany's Jews made themselves into guardians of the German cultural tradition—or, to speak a little more cautiously and more precisely, they joined gentile guardians in keeping watch and crying alarm. Their assiduousness caused some bewilderment, but not always hostility. In December 1894, Theodor Fontane celebrated his seventy-fifth birthday, and saw a little ruefully that the Prussian aristocracy, his old chosen companions, the subjects of his histories and his novels, seemed to have forgotten his anniversary. He had received "a hundred letters" of congratulation, and he noted the names and addresses of the writers with surprise:

27. Reminiscence by Rachel Katinka, in Else Lasker-Schüler, *Dichtungen und Dokumente: Gedichte, Prosa, Schauspiele, Briefe,* ed. Ernst Ginsberg (1951), 597–98.

Aber die zum Jubeltag kamen,
Das waren doch sehr, sehr andre Namen,
Auch "sans peur et reproche," ohne Furcht
  und Tadel,
Aber fast schon von prähistorischem Adel:
Die auf "berg" und auf "heim" sind gar
  nicht zu fassen,
Sie stürmen ein in ganzen Massen,
Meyers kommen in Bataillonen,
Auch Pollacks und die noch östlicher
  wohnen;
Abram, Isack, Israel,
Alle Patriarchen sind zur Stell,
Stellen mich freundlich an ihre Spitze.

But, Fontane added, to be surprised did not mean to be disappointed; after all, these Jewish well-wishers too were of ancient nobility, like the Prussians, if from distant regions and with exotic titles. The main point after all was that they knew him and had read him:

Was sollen mir da noch die Itzenplitze!
Jedem bin ich was gewesen,
Alle haben sie mich gelesen,
Alle kannten mich lange schon
Und das ist die Hauptsache . . . "kommen Sie, Cohn."

I must add here, for the sake of the record and to underscore its complexity, that Germany's Jews found it so gratifying to be guardians of German culture in part because they did not know all the subterranean sources of ill-will against them. Even Theodor Fontane, whom they prized for his urbanity and his freedom from prejudice, had reserves of Jew-hatred in him that they would have been dismayed to discover. Not long after Fontane composed the affectionate apostrophe to his Jewish readers and well-wishers that I have just quoted, he struck a very different note in a letter to the distinguished pedagogue and philosopher Friedrich Paulsen. Thanking Paulsen for sending him an article in which he had adumbrated the "Jewish question," Fontane demurred from Paulsen's view that assimilation seemed to be failing because the *"Jews* do not want it." This, in Fontane's opinion, may have been true enough for the first two thirds of the nineteenth century, but now the *Christians* did not want Jewish assimilation. And Fontane thought he knew the reason why. "Down to 1848 or perhaps 1870, we were dominated by the ideas of the previous century; we had quite sincerely fallen in love with human rights and reveled in ideas of emancipation, which we had not yet had time and opportunity to test. This 'testing' is of recent date and has turned out most unfavorably for the Jews. They are irritants everywhere (much more than they used to be earlier), they mess up everything, obstruct the contemplation of every problem for its own sake. Even the most optimistic have had to convince themselves that baptismal water is not enough. Despite all its gifts, it is a horrible people, not a 'sour dough' yielding vitality and freshness but a leaven in which uglier forms of fermentation abound—a people afflicted from its very origins with a kind of conceited vulgarity, which the aryan world cannot get along with. What a difference between the Christian and the Jewish criminal world! And all of this, ineradicable." Fontane did not scruple to denigrate even his faithful correspondent, the eminent judge Georg Friedlaender, whose family, Jewish in origin, had been in public service for three generations, and whose father had been, as Fontane put it, an "orthodox, model Christian." And yet, Fontane noted, Friedlaender is a "typical Jew—*Stockjude*" who drives his "refined and amiable wife" to shed "tears of blood" because "he cannot get rid of his Jewish mentality." Nor could Fontane see any benign resolution of the "Jewish question" in the German future: "It would have been better if the attempt at assimilation had not been made." Physical assimilation, he thought, might be possible, spiritual assimilation—*eingeistigen*—was not.

This is an appalling document, and it was just as well for the peace of mind of Germany's Jews that it remained unpublished for decades. It discloses unsuspected *ressentiment* and bigotry in Fontane, a determined resistance to his life's experience that is particularly depressing to discover in a writer famous then, and celebrated since, for his penetrating observation, discriminating judgment, gentle humor, and Jewish friends. "I say all this," Fontane confessed to Paulsen, "(*must* say it), even though I have had, in my own person, nothing but good from Jews right down to this day."[28] This is more than the cranky outburst of an old man; it is just one more demonstration of the familiar assertion that the anti-Semite does not need Jews for his anti-Semitism, since the evidence has no influence on his views, but yields to the pressure of his private needs. And the letter is more even than that: it supports a more skeptical appraisal of the German Jew's situation than I am offering in this essay; it suggests that the pessimists among Germany's Jews may have been more realistic than the optimists.

And yet, the public Fontane was different from the private Fontane, and the private Fontane did not always think this way about Jews. And other evidence was equally mixed: favorable in large part, ominous in small details. One instance of good grounds for the optimistic readings was the esoteric *Kreis* which Stefan George gathered about himself in the years before the first World War. It did not escape observation at the time that this circle had numerous and important Jewish members. Prominent among this self-elected avant-garde busy rescuing high culture, the purity of language, and the elite from the threats of democracy were the polymath Karl Wolfskehl, the literary historian Friedrich Gundolf, the sociologist Georg Simmel, the cartoonist and designer Thomas Theodor Heine, and several others, all Jews at least in origin. Stefan George, in fact, broke with his early intimates, Alfred Schuler and Ludwig Klages, precisely over his

28. Fontane to Paulsen, May 12, 1898. Theodor Fontane, *Briefe an Friedrich Paulsen* (1949), 6. German Jews, it may be admitted, were at times a little credulous. Hermann Levi, writing to his father (for the correspondence, see below, 218), on July 14, 1886, praised the conductor Felix Mottl as his intimate friend: "Mottl and I are like brothers." (Bayreuther Festspiele, 1959, *"Parsifal" Program*, ed. Festspielleitung [1959], 18.) But shortly before Levi's death, trying to keep a singer named Bussart from leaving Karlsruhe for Vienna, Mottl showed his claws: "Vienna is beautiful, and you are right to want to go there. But I fancy that you would rather work with me than with the Jew Mahler!" (March 15, 1900. K2471,5. H.A., Badische Landesbibliothek, Karlsruhe.)

unwillingness to meet their demand for the expulsion of Jews from his circle.[29]

Quite as striking as the Jews' penchant for Stefan George was their passion for Goethe. As educated Germans, Jews remembered Fontane's birthday, acknowledged George's leadership, and celebrated Goethe's work. Kant, too, then in danger of suffering the kind of neglect into which cultural monuments often fall, was restored to his pedestal by Jewish hands. It was a young Jew, Otto Liebmann, who in 1865 published an eloquent polemic in Kant's behalf, and concluded it with a famous invitation: "Back to Kant—*es muss auf Kant zurückgegangen werden.*"[30] And it was a Jew, Hermann Cohen, who was to lead that return with his sympathetic, though by no means slavish, inquiries into the Kantian philosophy.

Cohen, of course, was a professor, and we may therefore profitably pause over his career, for the Jewish experience in the German university is an instructive chapter in the Jewish love affair with German culture. It was Treitschke, after all a famous professor in a great university—Berlin—who lent anti-Semitism his academic prestige. It was university students who embittered the life of the intelligent and academically ambitious young German Jew, whether on his way to the professions or (which was harder) aspiring to an academic post.

Germany's Jews, who made up about 1 percent of the total population, found access to the academic ladder far easier than ascent. While in 1909–10, roughly one *Privatdozent* out of eight was a professing Jew, the proportion among full professors dropped to one out of thirty-five.[31] Many professors, abetted by many public officials in charge of *Kultur*, continued to idealize "their" university as a Christian institution, or as the kind of

29. It was about Wolfskehl that the German classicist Ludwig Curtius was to say many years later, in a significant vignette, that what defined Wolfskehl was his "Jewishness," which was "one homeland of his religious-poetic being. The other was his passionate Germanness," and he claimed the two without inner conflict. "Karl Wolfskehl," in *Torso: Verstreute und Nachgelassene Schriften* (1957), 235–36.

30. *Kant und die Epigonen* (1865), 215.

31. Fritz K. Ringer, *The Decline of the German Mandarins: The German Academic Community, 1890–1933* (1969), 136.

"Germanic" bulwark in which Jews, no matter what their protestations, had little constructive part to play. To retrace the careers of German Jewish scholars in search of safe academic berths, and of the recognition to which their work entitled them, is to make a poignant voyage, marked by snubs, by frustrations, by manifest injustice. The pioneering *Völkerpsychologe* Moritz Lazarus advanced rapidly—in Switzerland. He was appointed *Honorarprofessor* at Berne in 1859, and received his professorship in psychology and *Völkerpsychologie* three years later, in 1862. He taught at Berne with great distinction, and received honors often reserved for older men: from 1862 to 1866, he was Dean of the Philosophical faculty, and in 1864, Rector of the university. Yet he tore himself away in 1866 to return to his beloved *"Vaterland"*; he felt, "as a *German*," that his duty lay back home.[32] His reward was some agreeable appointments, including one at the *Kriegsakademie* in Berlin, and, in 1873, at last, a post at the University of Berlin. But his title fell decisively short of the professorship he craved and deserved: famous and popular as he was, he was appointed only *ordentlicher Honorarprofessor*. It is not that Lazarus was despised and neglected; he held a good position in the academic world, had the opportunity to address large audiences, and even enjoyed public honors: on his seventieth birthday, Emperor Wilhelm I appointed him *Geheimer Regierungsrat*.[33] The point is that if Lazarus had been of Christian parentage, his titles would have come sooner and been more distinguished; his beloved fatherland was less grateful to him than Switzerland, where he felt only like a welcome visitor.

Heymann Steinthal, Lazarus' friend, fellow-psychologist and, later, brother-in-law, made it plain that he, too, had done less than he could in his chosen fields quite simply because he did not have the opportunities. He remained, for all his abilities, a lifelong *ausserordentlicher Professor* at the University of Berlin; in 1890, looking back at his long career, he wrote sadly: "As far as I am concerned, I am sure that I would have written other books, if they had only met me halfway—for example, if the

32. See Ingrid Belke, "Einleitung," *Lazarus und Steinthal*, xxii–xxx.
33. Belke, "Einleitung," xl.

Academy had invited me to become a member or if the Munich *Kommission* had entrusted me with writing the history of philology in Germany. And then I would have thought that I had lived my life to the full."[34] What Lord Melbourne is reported to have said about the Order of the Garter applies, in some measure, to advancement in German universities: there was no damned nonsense about merit in it.

The obstacles that academic Jews encountered under Wilhelm I persisted under Wilhelm II. As brilliant, productive, and versatile a philosopher as Ernst Cassirer—a prolific writer who breathed high German culture with his every breath—was called to a professorship only because the year was 1919, and the institution the new, self-consciously liberal University of Hamburg. There was one way to ease ascent on the academic ladder: conversion to Christianity. If we add the number of Jewish converts to professing Jews in German universities, the proportions rise from 12 to 19 percent among the *Privatdozenten*, and from 3 to 7 percent among the professors.[35] One day, when the *Privatdozent* Harry Bresslau, medievalist by profession and Jew by origin, complained to Ranke that his religious affiliation hindered his career, Ranke flatly and cordially advised him to be baptized.[36]

But there were exceptions, and Hermann Cohen was one of them. He grew up in a pious household and was destined for a rabbinical career. In late 1857 he entered the Breslau seminary that the moderate Reform rabbi Zacharias Frankel had founded three years before. It was a distinguished school, including among its teachers the historian Heinrich Graetz and the philologist Jakob Bernays. But Cohen, after more than three years of seminary training, decided to transfer from theology to philosophy; by 1861, he was inscribed as a student at the University of Breslau. It was a step, not a leap; Cohen never thought the right kind of theology to be in any way incompatible with the right kind of pihlosophy. Despite his consistent refusal to undergo baptism for the sake of promotion, Cohen's academic advancement was un-

---

34. Quoted in Belke, "Einleitung." ciiin.
35. Ringer, *Decline of German Mandarins*, 136.
36. See Friedrich Meinecke, *Strassburg, Freiburg, Berlin, 1901–1919* (1949), 27.

troubled, his life placid. The Neo-Kantian Friedrich Albert Lange was responsible for having Cohen called to Marburg in 1873 as a *Privatdozent*; three years later, after Lange's death, Cohen was appointed professor, and became the leading intellectual force in the Neo-Kantian Marburg School. And at Marburg he remained until his retirement in 1912.

Kant was Cohen's specialty, almost his obsession. He wrote his thesis on the relation of Kant's pre-Critical writings to his Critical system; he published notable studies on most aspects of Kant's teachings: his *Kants Theorie der Erfahrung* appeared in 1871, his *Kants Begründung der Ethik* in 1877, his *Kants Begründung der Aesthetik* in 1889. And he sought to introduce the thought of Kant to a larger public: in 1883, he offered the customary patriotic oration celebrating Emperor Wilhelm I's birthday on the subject of Kant's influence across German culture, an address later published as a pamphlet. Cohen's constructive writings, especially on ethics and on his rationalist system of religion, have Kant's categorical imperative and Kant's Critical method woven into their very texture.

The immense popularity of Kant among German Jews is easy to understand. Like Schiller, Kant supplied ringing, eminently quotable pronouncements on human freedom, a platform for brotherhood; and Kant's Critical philosophy provided a rationale for a religion of reason that permitted emancipated Jews to fit their own religious views into a universal—they hoped universally respected—scheme. And so Jewish scholars, Liebmann and Cohen, Jonas Cohn and Emil Lask, and, later, Hermann Cohen's most distinguished student, Ernst Cassirer, revived and renewed Kant's work, with its welcome mixture of humanism and criticism, and adapted it to construct a Neo-Kantian philosophy of culture appropriate to their own day with its new learning, its new sociology and anthropology.[37]

Admirers and detractors to the contrary, German Jews did not monopolize Kant. It has long been a favorite anti-Semitic strategy to criticize Jews for being unassimilable when Jews refuse to as-

---

37. See Jürgen Habermas, "Der deutsche Idealismus der jüdischen Philosophen," in Koch, *Porträts zur deutsch-jüdischen Geistesgeschichte*, 99–126.

similate, and to berate Jews for invading and debasing alien cultures when Jews try to assimilate. In fact, prominent as Jews were in the Kantian revival, they were not alone. One historian of the Marburg School has referred to the Neo-Kantian revival of the 1860s as the "third wave": "Back to Kant," he has argued, had been a persistent, if rather muted, call for some decades. Certainly Liebmann had been anticipated by Lange, at first Cohen's paternal protector and later Cohen's attentive reader, and by the historian of philosophy Eduard Zeller, who had spent his formative years at Marburg.[38] And this, of course, is precisely what made neo-Kantianism so exhilarating to its Jewish advocates: they were rediscovering a giant of German culture in the company of other Germans.

In the midst of his preoccupation with Kant and his other interests, Plato and *Völkerpsychologie*, Hermann Cohen continued to reflect about Judaism. He had, as he later recalled, left the seminary in disgust with the narrow ideas of a reviving, literal-minded neo-Orthodoxy. And in a youthful lecture on the Sabbath, written in 1869 and not published until 1881, he had further offended many among his co-religionists by urging Jews to move the Sabbath from its customary place on the calendar to Sunday. Jews, he said, should follow the Talmudic prescription and make themselves masters of the Sabbath, instead of its servants. Once masters, they would free themselves from the traditional Saturday-observance which "separates us from our people"—that is, the Germans. To identify the Sabbath with the national day of rest would be to take "a mighty step" in the "national fusion," a step greater perhaps than intermarriage.[39] Whatever one might think of these notions, they are not signs of indifference. This was the voice of a German Jew interested in Judaism, but interested even more in stirring the cultural melting pot in which German Jew and German gentile would become one. In the course of years, Cohen found the depth of his Jewish concern increasing. Looking back in 1914, during his retirement,

38. Henri Dussort, *L'École de Marbourg* (1963).
39. *Hermann Cohen's Jüdische Schriften*, II: *Zur jüdischen Zeitgeschichte*, ed. Bruno Strauss (1924), 71–72.

he dated his conscious return to Judaism to 1880, the year he had ventured to reply to Treitschke's assault on the Jews.[40] Cohen then spoke as a firm assimilationist but argued, against Treitschke, that Jews—as Germans—had every right, and in fact the duty, to profess the tenets of their faith. The persistent and sporadic outbursts of anti-Semitism left their mark on Cohen; the mass of his explicitly Jewish writings grew with the years, as did the earnestness of his Jewish commitment.

Yet he never abandoned the ideal of eventual fusion, and the outbreak of war in 1914 left him more hopeful than ever: he faced it as an aging patriotic German urging both Christian and Jewish Germans to recognize their present differences and the inevitability of their ultimate union. For Cohen's Jewishness was not merely, or mainly, apologetic. He took pride in being a Jew and in being a German, and, illuminated by the Kantian vision, he found the sources of both in a common root: the Greek heritage. Just as they had been in the remote past, so in the remote future *"Deutschtum"* and *"Judentum"* would be "most intimately intertwined—*innerlichst verbunden.*" With their ethical absolutism and their cultural ideal, to which Cohen himself owed the strongest allegiance, Germanness and Jewishness were more than compatible, consistent, or harmonious: they were simply the same.[41] The pamphlet makes painful reading today; it seems massively self-deluded, almost childish.[42] But in 1914, its views seemed reasonable to many educated German Jews—though not, I must add, to many German Christians, educated or not. Cohen was spared the bankruptcy of his cherished, lifelong cultural ecumenicism: he died in 1918. But as a Jewish type that flourished mightily in the Germany before the First World War,

---

40. See Cohen's polemic, "Ein Bekenntnis in der Judenfrage," *Jüdische Schriften*, II, 73–94. See also Hans Liebeschütz, *Das Judentum im deutschen Geschichtsbild von Hegel bis Max Weber* (1967), 214–19; and Liebeschütz, *Von Georg Simmel zu Franz Rosenzweig* (1970), ch. I, two books to which I am much indebted.

41. *Deutschtum und Judentum* (1915), passim.

42. See the critique by Emil L. Fackenheim, *Hermann Cohen—After Fifty Years*, Leo Baeck Memorial Lecture, 12 (1969).

Cohen remains representative. He was only one among many German Jews to become, in his mature years, more of a Jew without becoming less of a German.

Georg Simmel's life is as instructive as Hermann Cohen's, but far more pathetic. While Cohen was not harassed for what he was, Simmel was harassed for what he was not. He was rejected for being a Jew, though his religious consciousness was remote from any doctrine, any sect, including the Jewish; he was distrusted as a critical spirit, when he actually aimed his sociological and philosophical work at ambitious comprehensive generalizations. Some of his misfortunes, no doubt, followed his personality like a shadow—they were his "kismet," as he told Max and Marianne Weber in 1908, with some resignation.[43] Simmel was not merely brilliant, he seemed brilliant. Observers as different as Heinrich Rickert and Georg Lukács agreed that he was a wit— *"geistreich."* His wit was a quality prominent enough to be discussed both privately and publicly; a quality that Simmel thoroughly recognized in himself and manfully sought to control. And, worse, it was a quality which, many believed, characterized the modern Jew: Simmel was clever, abstract, mobile. Interestingly enough, while his hearers agreed that he was a magnetic lecturer who would invent the most dazzling constructions right before their eyes, they do not coincide in their physical description of him: they recall him as short, of medium height, and tall; as ugly or attractive; some remember his voice as high and penetrating, others as melodic and pleasing.[44] It is certain that Simmel's was a mind of stunning versatility and utmost refinement; his philosophy, Ernst Robert Curtius later said, "was the last word in intellectual subtlety. It was considered 'corrosive,' but its seductiveness was all the stronger as it dealt with matters that had not come up in philosophy till then: the financial system or Chinese art. Georg Simmel collected lace because it represented 'the highest spiritualization of material.' "[45] It was characteristic of

43. March 18, 1908, in *Buch des Dankes an Georg Simmel,* 128.
44. See Emil Ludwig, Paul Fechter, N. J. Spykman, Werner Weisbach, in *Buch des Dankes,* 155–56, 159, 186, 202.
45. "Charles Du Bos," in E. R. Curtius, *Essays on European Literature,* tr. Michael Kowal (1973), 248.

him to approach the "tragedy of culture" through the nexus that economic relations established in, and imposed upon, modern society: his *Philosophie des Geldes*, first published in 1900, pursued the meaning of money into the recesses of social bonds and of human nature. Such a choice spirit, moving at ease among a few other choice spirits, could hardly hope for favor from the establishment that determined appointments to professorships.

It will not do to stress the pathos of Georg Simmel's life. He enjoyed, after all, a devoted following among his hearers, a wide acquaintance among those he valued, sufficient means to travel and collect. But ultimate acceptance eluded him. Born in Berlin in 1858, he attended the University of Berlin, where he ranged widely among the offerings, studying history with Mommsen and *Völkerpsychologie* with Lazarus and Steinthal. Like Cohen, he did a thesis on Kant. In 1885, he began to lecture at Berlin as *Privatdozent*, and soon proved an enormously popular performer. It took him fifteen years to be named *ausserordentlicher Professor* at Berlin, a halfway house of semi-recognition he occupied until 1914, when he was fifty-six and was at last named to a professorship—not at Berlin, which he loved, or at Heidelberg, to which he aspired, but at Strasbourg, which seemed a mild form of exile. Like Cohen, he lived through the war as a firm, even enthusiastic German patriot; like Cohen, he died in 1918.

There the resemblance between Simmel and Cohen largely ends. The relation of the two scholars to their academic environment, to their religious tradition, and to the life of the mind, makes striking contrasts. Cohen's polemics aroused the admiration even of such adversaries as Treitschke; Simmel's conversational facility, aristocratic bearing, and enviable popularity induced his detractors to search for the most wounding epithets. In February 1908, after Max Weber and Eberhard Gothein had recommended Simmel for a post at Heidelberg, Treitschke's student, Dietrich Schaefer, gave the *Kultusminister* of Baden a savage appraisal of Simmel the man and the intellectual. He did not know, Schaefer began, whether Simmel was baptized. But it did not matter: "He is surely an Israelite through and through, in his outward appearance, in his bearing, and in his mental style—*Geistesart.*" His long, slow, rather insubstantial lectures are well attended; his manner, polished and assured, "is highly valued by certain circles of students which are very numerous here in Berlin." The ladies, and the "oriental world" which is invading Germany from the East in ever increasing numbers and settling in Berlin, are both well represented at Simmel's performances. Nothing much of "positive value" emerges from his lectures; they are filled, rather, with tantalizing suggestions that offer evanescent intellectual pleasure. But this is what his audience wants: "the wholly, half, or philo-Semitic lecturer" who performs at a university of this sort is bound to find a congenial public. But his teaching departs, in the most fundamental way, from "our German-Christian-classical" culture. For Schaefer, Simmel's most crippling defect and (by implication) most Jewish trait, was his commitment to sociology: to see society as the principal formative agent of human community in place of state and church is "a fatal error." Schaefer probably did not know Durkheim's proud boast that "sociology is essentially French." Had he known it, he might have adapted it to claim that sociology is essentially Jewish.[46]

It is easy to dismiss such vituperation as the outpouring of a virulent anti-Semite, a right-wing ideologue, a second-rate and envious epigone, who had the worst of Treitschke's opinions without Treitschke's larger gifts. But actually Schaefer's letter is symptomatic. It gives widely accepted notions about "Jewishness" their most impolite expression. Jewishness, on this view, is the quality of superficiality, of glitter, of intellectual tinsel sometimes disguised as false profundity, inherent in all Jews whether they profess their religion or deny it. Simmel, as I noted earlier, was born a Protestant, and had no religious allegiances of any kind. His loyalties were to German culture and to the science of society; his patriotism, as the war would prove, was fervent to the point of chauvinism. But to the likes of Schaefer, this was sheer masquerade whether conscious or unconscious; the quality of Simmel's work betrayed his ineradicable origins. Such non-Jewish sociologists as Gustav Schmoller and Max Weber would have re-

46. Quoted in Landmann, "Bausteine zur Biographie," in *Buch des Dankes*, 26–27. This letter has been explored, and printed in an English translation, by Herbert Menzel, in Lewis A. Coser, ed., *Georg Simmel* (1965), 37–39.

pudiated this doctrine, but there were many who, without sharing his viciousness, accepted Schaefer's diagnosis.

Schaefer was right about one thing: sociology was central to Simmel, despite all his other interests. "Simmel," Schaefer had written in his letter, "owes his reputation essentially to his 'sociological' activities." Simmel lectured and published on a dazzling variety of subjects: on the philosophy of history, the nature of culture, the structure of ethical theory; on artists like Michelangelo, Rembrandt, and Rodin; on German philosophers like Schopenhauer and Nietzsche; and, of course, on Kant and Goethe. His long essay on Goethe, published in 1913, is a tightly argued meditation on the central quality that, according to Simmel, makes Goethe immortal: his humanity. The book is the tribute of one German humanist to another. But Simmel's most significant work remains his sociology—notably his effort to establish the formal structure of social relations, and to distill the very essence of social conflict. Was this work Jewish in any way? Simmel was persistently interested in alienation. There is a famous little essay, "The Stranger," which is a brief excursus in his largest, most comprehensive work, *Soziologie*, first published in 1908. The stranger, for Simmel, is a dual being; he is part of a group, but in a curiously impermanent sense. He is not the wanderer who comes today and leaves tomorrow, but, rather, the one "who comes today and stays tomorrow"—the *"potential* wanderer." The stranger is the marginal man, at once near and remote, both at home and ill at ease in "his" community; hence he has that rare quality, objectivity, a quality that those who really belong in a group are too deeply engaged to develop. This gives the stranger freedom, but also exposes him to risks: he purchases the clarity of his vision at the price of being the first target of accusations if the community experiences any kind of trouble. This, in the light of subsequent history, is uncannily prescient; it becomes prophetic in view of Simmel's choice of the European Jew as the classic instance of the stranger.

Yet to perceive Simmel's sociological preoccupations as somehow Jewish provides information less about him than about us, not about his time but about ours. It is because in the decades after Simmel's death Jews have been targets of projection, compelled into alienation and self-awareness as strangers, that his work has been lent, posthumously, an intention it did not have, and did not display, in his lifetime. It is true enough that Simmel, in his anomalous position of the non-Jewish Jew, was a doubly marginal man; he was alienated from the community of his ancestors and from the society to which he laid claim, he was only partly at home in the German academy. And it is plausible enough to suggest that his situation may have given him a special sensitivity to the potential wanderer, the observant newcomer who comes today and, looking over his shoulder, stays tomorrow.[47] But the theme of the stranger, the dilemma of objectivity, was only one theme among many on which Simmel exercised his sociological imagination. The few pages on the stranger in Simmel's *Soziologie* enjoy no special status; they are among dozens of brief and brilliant forays into such hitherto despised topics as adornment, conversation, secret societies, or gratitude. It is our generation that has lifted the excursus on the stranger from its larger context and imposed on it a factitious centrality.

Simmel's intellectual ancestry was unimpeachably, almost aggressively German. He was enough of a cosmopolitan scholar to learn from Comte and, for a time, from Spencer, but he constructed his philosophical orientation by means of interminable debates with the classics of modern German thought. The last chapter of his last book, *Lebensanschauung*, completed in 1918, closes the circle of his German scholarly preoccupations in its *Auseinandersetzung* with Kant—the very thinker to whom he had devoted his thesis. It was from Kant that Simmel took his epistemological conviction that humans order the flux of their experience through inherent forms of thought. It was from Hegel that Simmel took his sense of life forever engaged in the struggle of creating and recreating the structures in, and through, which men live. It was from Marx that Simmel took the pervasiveness of alienation, the way in which individuals confront institutions that have escaped from the control of their makers. It was from Dilthey that Simmel took the idea of a special logic, different in kind

47. For Simmel, the marginal man, see Coser, in *Georg Simmel*, 1–2.

from the causal analysis of the natural sciences, appropriate to the sciences of society. It was from Lotze, finally, that Simmel took the centrality of the number three, the third force that underlies and reconciles the dualities and contradictions of life and death, spirit and matter.

I offer this catalogue as a tentative and schematic approximation to Simmel's intellectual debts. It would be absurd to be reductionist about Simmel, of all thinkers, and to dissect the totality of his system into the sum of its sources. Simmel was far too restless, far too ambitious, simply to adopt ideas from anyone, even from Kant. He could never be content with the role of the epigone. His favorite way of showing his appreciation was to debate with the thinker from whom he had learned. Indeed, Simmel molded the disparate elements of his mental world into a far-ranging, still controversial enterprise. He sought a sociology that would attain autonomy without being capable of generating causal laws. He sought the rules of association—*Vergesellschaftung,* which he called the "geometry" of human relations, but rejected both the view of society as an organism and the contrary view that it is a pure creation of mind.[48] Society is real enough, but it consists essentially of interactions and relations. Since these embody themselves in myriad instances, almost all human activities—the application of perfume, the spending of money, the conduct of debates, the formation of groups—lends itself to formal investigation. Several commentators have rightly noted that Simmel's description of his sociology as "formal" makes it seem more abstract than it really is: with all the abstractness of his ordering vision, Simmel presses for concreteness so persistently that many of his paragraphs are unduplicable gems of observation. To derive such a system, extreme alike in its abstractness as in its specificity, from any ethnic, racial, or religious origins is doomed to fail. Georg Simmel's sociology was no more Jewish, no less German, than Max Weber's.

Simmel died, as he had lived, beyond the bounds of classification. Late in life, he left the Lutheran church into which he had been baptized, not to return to Judaism, but to increase his own

48. See Coser, *Simmel,* 5.

inner freedom.[49] When he became aware that he was mortally ill with cancer of the liver, he sought the full truth from his physician, continued to work, and looked toward his own extinction with a philosophical calm that would later send commentators to hunt for metaphors from classical antiquity.

Hermann Cohen and Georg Simmel traversed two types of academic career open to German Jews in the Wilhelminian Empire: the first, rare, leading to complete success; the second, more common, leading to relative frustration. There was yet a third type, restricted to the rich: to pursue scholarship on one's own as a *Privatgelehrter*. Perhaps the most remarkable of these last was Aby Warburg, who sometimes flirted with a university post but could never bring himself to accept one. Warburg became a seminal art historian and creator of an unparalleled library whose influence was to spread, mainly after his death in 1929, beyond Germany, to Great Britain and the United States.[50]

While Aby Warburg's way into Germanness was largely prescribed by his family, his way into scholarship was wholly his own. The son of a pious Jewish banker in Hamburg, he belonged, as Felix Gilbert has pointed out, to a family of private bankers which retained its ties to Judaism.[51] When Aby Warburg wanted to marry Mary Hertz, of a local patrician family, it was not her parents alone who objected to the match; his parents, too, found it wholly unsuitable—the marriage was not concluded until 1897, after the couple had known one another for ten years. Yet, like his friend Albert Ballin, director of the Hamburg-America Line and one of Wilhelm II's Jewish friends, Aby Warburg was raised to be a patriotic German.[52] It is possible to speculate about the influence of Warburg's cultural situation on his art-historical interests, and Felix Gil-

49. Landmann, "Bausteine zur Biographie," 12.
50. Fritz Saxl, "The History of Warburg's Library, 1886–1944," a memoir printed in E. H. Gombrich, *Aby Warburg: An Intellectual Biography* (1970), 325–38.
51. Gilbert, "From Art History to the History of Civilization: Gombrich's Biography of Aby Warburg," *Journal of Modern History*, XCIV, 3 (September 1972), 390.
52. See Lamar Cecil, *Albert Ballin: Business and Politics in Imperial Germany, 1888–1918* (1967).

bert has cautiously done so: "The alienation from the Jewish world of his family," he notes, "and the identification with the social world of the Empire refined his feelings for the survival of residues from earlier times. It increased his perceptivity for the continuation of beliefs of an older culture in a later one." And, Gilbert adds, yet more cautiously, "His family background may also have directed his attention to the cultural role of a merchant class, and the part which the merchant bankers played in the Florentine civilization of the Quattrocento helped to strengthen his conviction that he had a right to belong to the ruling group of the Empire. . . . Consciously or unconsciously the conviction that he gave up something valuable for something still better must have helped him to rationalize his abandonment of a family tradition in favor of identification with the dominant political system. Consequently he was not inclined to probe deeply the weaknesses and defects of the German social structure."[53]

These subtle suppositions approach the core of the question to which this essay addresses itself. It may be that Warburg's tense, increasingly distant relation to Judaism in some way moved him to prefer art history over banking, and shaped his manner of doing art history once he had chosen it—or, rather, once it had chosen him. But the Jewish element in his life was by no means the only non-rational or unconscious ingredient in Aby Warburg's search for a vocation. He was a Jew, a German, a prosperous bourgeois, the citizen of a Free German City; he lived in worlds of mind, manners, and money. And he was profoundly neurotic; it was not simply external realities that pressed upon him. His perception of his world was intense and highly personal; it differed significantly from the perceptions of those who substantially shared it. When he was thirteen, already a passionate bookworm, he sold his birthright to his younger brother Max in return for all the books that he would ask Max to buy—a trade proving that the boys were no strangers to the Old Testament.[54] It is a bizarre and touching incident, but the point is that what

53. Gilbert, "From Art History to the History of Civilization," 390.
54. Gombrich, *Warburg*, 22.

Aby was ready to discard, Max was ready to accept. When the time came, the younger brother entered the parental banking business without hesitation.

Whatever the combination of ingredients in Warburg's tortured choice, his work was brilliant and, within his scholarly confines, epoch-making. The most obviously private elements in his art-historical inquiries are his preoccupations with the place of psychology in artistic activity, and with irrational elements in the general culture from which art springs. Almost from the beginning of his independent inquiries, Warburg insisted on placing the history of art squarely within the history of culture. Jacob Burckhardt, in many ways Warburg's model and in some ways his target, had made the leap from art history to cultural history three decades earlier, but implicitly, in his person, rather than explicitly, in his writings. For a variety of reasons, Burckhardt's most celebrated book, *Die Kultur der Renaissance in Italien*, published in 1860, omitted the arts; instead, Burckhardt wrote some separate essays on painting. And he did not integrate art into his comprehensive definition of "Renaissance," a period Burckhardt had had the unique merit to discover—or, as some disgruntled medievalists were beginning to complain in the 1880s, to invent. The years when Aby Warburg attended the universities of Bonn, Munich, and Strasbourg saw a mounting dissatisfaction with Burckhardt's conception of the Renaissance, its circumference, its nature, its very existence. Henry Thode, with whom Warburg studied in Bonn, had just made his name with the thesis that the "discovery of nature and of man," which Burckhardt had associated with the revival of pagan antiquity in the fourteenth and fifteenth centuries, was actually neither pagan nor antique. Thode saw the revival as a heritage from St. Francis and the Franciscans, who devoutly approached nature as a manifestation of the divine handiwork. The debate that Thode and his supporters had just initiated set Warburg his life's work: to study the survival and transformation of antiquity in the Renaissance. The world-famous library and institute that bear Warburg's name are rooted in this early interest.

If Thode set the theme for Warburg's vocation, other scholars, notably Hermann Usener, the celebrated psychologist of myths, and Karl Lamprecht, the controversial "scientific" historian of culture, directed Warburg to his method. He practiced it first in his dissertation on Botticelli's *Primavera* and *Birth of Venus* (completed in 1891) and perfected it later in substantial studies on art and culture in early modern Europe—in papers like "Francesco Sassettas letztwillige Verfügung" of 1907, and lectures like "Dürer und die italienische Antike" of the previous year. Warburg departed from the central concern of most art historians, the study of style, and pursued instead the transmission of whole ways of thinking; yet he sought to understand cultural traits not by means of facile guesses or private intuitions, but by cautious scholarship and patient inquiry. The point of his method was to secure the most general overview from the most minute particulars. He was interested in the relations of painters to patrons, but, quite as much, in the artist's way of rendering draperies. Warburg's favorite saying, *"Le bon Dieu est dans le détail,"* aptly sums up his need to get to the heart of individual experiences without losing, at the same time, the sense of the whole.

The saying, instructive as it is, says nothing about the other central quality of Aby Warburg's work: his concern with the irrational. Himself prey to inhibitions, depressions, and fears of insanity, Warburg was alert to the power of dark, unreasoning, often unconscious forces in culture; he was only too well equipped to recognize the prevalence, in the Renaissance and the Reformation, of astrological superstitions, magical hopes, apocalyptic panic. His penetration permitted him to support, and further refine, Burckhardt's complex dual vision of the Renaissance. More than other historians of his chosen period, Warburg could recognize that whenever enlightenment or reason seemed triumphant, the victory was precarious, temporary. In Warburg's nuanced portrait, the Renaissance appears as an unstable compromise, in which men had found an *Ausgleichsformel*, a formula that permitted them to live more or less comfortably with faith in man and in God, with energetic secularism and with devout religiosity. Even the recovery of antiquity that marked the Renaissance was a far from simple affair, for the antiquity that men recovered included the superstitions and magical practices that

ancient Hellenism had elaborated and spread over a world weary
of thought and rationality. Athens—as Warburg put it in one of
his famous formulations—had to be recovered from Alexandria.[55]

While the history of the Warburg Library reaches far beyond
the chronological scope of this essay, its beginnings fall into the
Wilhelminian Empire. From his earliest days Aby Warburg was
an avid collector. As a young man, he constantly begged his family for subsidies; writing home from Italy, he would describe some
invaluable and expensive work of reference, and ask for more
money. By 1904, when Warburg was thirty-eight, he had amassed
enough of a library to provide for it in his will. Ten years later,
just before the war broke out, Warburg formulated detailed
plans, in association with Fritz Saxl, for turning his library into a
research institute. But their realization was delayed by the war
and further postponed by Warburg's psychotic breakdown in late
1918. In 1911, when Fritz Saxl saw Warburg's library for the first
time, it already contained more than 15,000 volumes, mainly in
German and Italian, and embraced a baffling variety of materials
ranging from sober reference works to esoteric volumes on astrol-
ogy. It became Saxl's task to bring order to this chaotic wealth, to
make it accessible to the scholar. And his way of arranging the
books—of grouping them, cataloguing them, shelving them—
could only be one way, dictated by Warburg's perception of
man's mind at work in culture.

If it makes any sense to call Jews the people of the book, the
Warburg Library is, almost by definition, the most Jewish of
creations, a maze of volumes in which one title led to another
and the whole to a comprehensive vision of man defining himself
in words, pictures, beliefs—a mighty maze, but not without a plan.
Yet the particular definition that was Warburg's obsessive theme
was not explicitly, or even largely, Jewish. It was in fact not Jewish at all, for, while the Institute was rich in the writings of the
Jewish mystics (as it was rich in the writings of all mystics), its
central concern was the survival of antiquity into the modern

55. "Heidnisch-antike Weissagung in Wort and Bild zu Luthers Zeiten"
(1920), in *Gesammelte Schriften*, 2 vols. (1932), II, 491–92, 534.

Western world. Jews played their part in that world, but not as Alexandria battling Athens. The mind of Aby Warburg, German patriot and German scholar, is evidence that cultivated German Jews saw themselves as part of the Athenian forces—the forces of reason, of enlightenment, of *Bildung*. It was their mortal enemies and their eventual murderers who spoke for Alexandria, at its worst. But Warburg did not live to see that.

3. THE CONQUEST OF LITERATURE

To turn from the world of learning to the world of imagination— from philosophers, sociologists, and historians to poets, novelists, and playwrights—is to enter a denser atmosphere, enriched by occasional, if fervent, explorations of Jewish identity. The presence and importance of Jews in the decisive shift from the nineteenth- to the twentieth-century sensibility appear disproportionate to the number of Jews in Germany. And they *were* disproportionate; whatever hyperbole the skeptical historian detects and discounts, the Jewish share in German Modernism remains noteworthy. Still, the widely accepted picture of Jewish dominance in German literary culture is in large measure a mirage, produced by the false perspectives of proud, anxious, or hostile observers concentrating on the "Jewish element" at the expense of the rest. Upon closer examination, the Jewish contribution takes a far smaller place, distinguished but moderate, in the larger literary environment.

Not even the explorers of Jewish themes were in any way aliens in the German world. The interesting, though now largely forgotten, novelist Georg Hermann, for instance, was born in Berlin in 1871, a typical Berliner, and grew up, by his own confession, a German, with vague memories of Judaism and the almost compulsory disdain for the *Ostjuden*. He published, among other books, studies of Rembrandt and Liebermann, and a survey of Germany in the age of the Biedermeier. But his reputation in the late Wilhelminian Empire rested on his novels, which had Berlin

Jewry as their theme. His broadly conceived two-volume chronicle, *Jettchen Geberts Geschichte* (1906–9),[56] was an affectionate portrait of a Jewish family in the distant days before 1848; his very different short novel, *Die Nacht des Dr. Herzfeld* (1912) took an uprooted and unhappy Jewish intellectual contemplating suicide through a night of ruminations on the meaning, or rather lack of meaning, of life. Hermann commanded a certain depth as well as a certain range; he handled the leisurely epic and the psychological study with equal competence. Reviewers all across the country welcomed Hermann as a precise observer capable of distance, of humor, of penetration, of giving life to varied *milieux*. The writers to whom they most often compared him were Thomas Mann (*Jettchen Geberts Geschichte* became a "Jewish *Buddenbrooks*"), and, of course, Theodor Fontane. In short, Hermann's public saw him as he saw himself: as a German novelist writing with kindly yet satirical insight about a slice of German life. In his work, Jewish life is genre; he was a Wilhelminian counterpart to Terborch. Not surprisingly, Hermann, an unproblematic, middling German talent,[57] was at peace with his readers.

Unlike Hermann, the young Arnold Zweig would achieve a larger reputation after the war, but wrote, like Hermann, about Jews before it. His Jewish, and Zionist, sympathies were awake from his beginnings as a writer. In 1914, in his *Ritualmord in Ungarn*, he pilloried one of the most persistent lies to which Jews have been exposed through the centuries—the charge of rit-

56. Better known under separate titles, *Jettchen Gebert* and *Henriette Jacoby*.
57. That peace was destroyed by the first World War, which persuaded Hermann, as it did so many other German Jews, that the gap between himself and the other Germans could not be bridged. After Hitler's seizure of power he emigrated to Holland, where he was caught by the Nazis in 1943 and transported to one of the death camps. See Hans Scholz's essay appended to a shortened version of Hermann's novel *Rosenemil: Ein Roman aus dem Alten Berlin* (ed. 1962), 345–68; for Hermann's public outburst in 1919, see Eva G. Reichmann, "Der Bewusstseinswandel der deutschen Juden," in W. Mosse, ed., *Deutsches Judentum in Krieg und Revolution*, 523–24; Hans Kohn has an interesting examination of Hermann's novel *Die Nacht des Dr. Herzfeld*, "Der Roman des Entwurzelten (Georg Hermann)," in Gustav Krojanker, *Juden in der deutschen Literatur: Essays über zeitgenössische Schriftsteller* (1926), 27–40.

ual murder—by dramatizing an actual Hungarian case. But earlier, in his first novel, *Aufzeichnungen über eine Familie Klopfer* (1911), he chronicled the decay of a German Jewish family; its kinship to *Buddenbrooks*, a novel Zweig admits to reading several times, is closer than Hermann's two Jettchen Gebert novels. Zweig's individual brand of Socialist Zionism was a product of the war and the uneasy years of the Weimar Republic: he admired Nietzsche and Mann before he graduated to Buber and Marx.

Whatever our final verdict on its quality, Jewish participation in the cultural revolution of the Wilhelminian era is far from surprising. The term "free professions," normally applied to law and medicine, aptly describes that cluster of pursuits grouped under the compendious name of literature. In literature, public attention was freely bestowed and depended on the work itself; it was a world in which the exercise of talent or a gift for self-promotion counted most, and where personal experience provided most of the writer's materials. Naturally the experience of German-Jewish poets or playwrights was mainly of other Jews, or of encounters—sometimes reassuring, often traumatic—with German gentiles. Yet, these Jewish experiences differed markedly from region to region, class to class, and even individual to individual. Hence Jewish literary expression conformed quite closely to the general pattern of German culture. Jewish writers, much like Jewish professors, stationed themselves across the social, political, and stylistic map. Many of them were perfectly traditional, and rejected in their creative as in their critical work the experimental modes which Expressionists of all descriptions were beginning to employ around 1900. There were probably more Jews around Stefan George, "avant-garde" in self-consciously salvaging the dying Western tradition, than there were Jews among the Expressionist poets, who were in the same years proclaiming the need to destroy the old in behalf of the new. And the Jewish poets in the Expressionist avant-garde found that the non-Jewish poets in their camp wrote, on the whole, much better than they did.

Prominent among these minor, but very active, Jewish Expressionists were the young rebels whom Hans Tramer has called the "poets of the metropolis."[58] Habitués of literary cafes, founders of little cabarets, they confirmed their saturnine view of the modern world by listening to one another; in short, often unpretentious verse, they memorably recorded the glories and miseries of Berlin, the restless world city, and the malaise of industrial civilization. What many inchoately felt, they made palpable, and enjoyable. Some of these literary Cassandras secured brief notoriety with a single striking poem—the right verse at the right time. *Weltende*, which the eccentric Jakob van Hoddis wrote in 1911, today seems light-hearted, amusing, but to its first hearers it captured the sense of impending doom that haunted so many in the late Wilhelminian days, which were so prosperous and seemed so hollow. There is a wind abroad that blows the hats off the pointed heads of the bourgeois, there is a strange shouting in the air; roofers fall off the roofs and break, while it appears that the floods are rising:

Dem Bürger fliegt vom spitzen Kopf der
    Hut,
In allen Lüften hallt es wie Geschrei,
Dachdecker stürzen ab und gehn entzwei
Und an den Küsten—liest man—steigt die
    Flut.
Der Sturm is da, die wilden Meere hupfen
An Land, um dicke Dämme zu zerdrücken.
Die meisten Menschen haben einen Schnup-
    fen.
Die Eisenbahnen fallen von den Brücken.

Born in Berlin in 1887, the young van Hoddis drifted into the heady ambiance of experimental literary circles; he haunted the meeting places of poets and in 1910 founded his own, the "Neopathetische Cabaret," in which students and literati, Bohemians and actors, crowded together to attend public readings of the latest innovation. Hoddis' own innovation, as his most successful poem, *Weltende*, adequately demonstrates, was to endow visions of apocalypse with a strand of macabre wit. Things acquire a life

58. Hans Tramer, "Der Beitrag der Juden zu Geist und Kultur," in W. Mosse, ed., *Deutsches Judentum in Krieg und Revolution*, 334; I owe much to his perceptive comments.

of their own and move about the world in menacing but comical ways; the poet's mental associations, carefully disciplined in his published verse, reflect the disorder, the fatal instability, of urban existence. It is only appropriate that many years later, André Breton should celebrate van Hoddis as one of the first and finest practitioners of black humor.[59]

The perception of modern life as unhealthy, unstable, nerve-wracking, was not new. As early as the 1860s, social critics like Jacob Burckhardt and rather less pessimistic social observers like Walter Bagehot had noted a dizzying commitment to change abroad in the world. From the 1880s on, physicians, psychologists, and philosophers debated the causes and cures of modern "nervousness," and in the 1890s, Decadent and Symbolist poets often took anxiety as their theme: in 1897, in "Nerves," Arthur Symons anatomized what he called "the modern malady of love." To Symons, this malady was essentially an overcivilized self-consciousness, remote from any deep spontaneity. What the German Expressionist poets added to this popular notion was a sense of doom and a Surrealist play with realities. In 1912, a year after van Hoddis' *Weltende*, another Jewish Expressionist poet, Ernst Blass, published his first volume of poems, aptly entitled, *Die Strassen komme ich entlang geweht*. Like van Hoddis' work, to which it bears a family resemblance, Blass's verse uneasily eyes the modern world in motion, and wrings a measure of comedy from overwhelming anxiety. Another celebrant of the "new pathos" and admirer of van Hoddis' poetic vision was Alfred Lichtenstein, who addressed his native Berlin in verses that combine irreverent quotations from the German classics with the almost obligatory extravagant metaphors of the Expressionists, and tough-talking insults against his beloved city:

In fremden Städten treib ich ohne Ruder.
Hohl sind die fremden Tage und wie
   Kreide.
Du, mein Berlin, du Opiumrausch, du
   Luder.

59. See Breton's *Anthologie de l'humeur noir* (1969); and Victor Lange, "Jakob van Hoddis," in Wolfgang Rothe, ed., *Expressionismus als Literatur: Gesammelte Studien* (1969), 344–53.

Nur wer die Sehnsucht kennt, weiss, was
  ich leide.

Yet another Jewish Expressionist, Alfred Wolfenstein, began to
publish his ecstatic and despairing verse in the same days, just before the war. Prolific and emotional, Wolfenstein was haunted by
the anonymity of the great city; the street, its noisiness, its indifference, its unending flow of people and traffic, dominates many
of his poems as a kind of master metaphor.

These Jewish experimental writers were, like their non-Jewish
fellows, anything but systematic in their thought. They recorded
feelings, their senses rubbed raw by modern life. Their solutions
were as far-fetched as their descriptions. The contradictions that
subsist in all men were more obvious with them. Wolfenstein, it
has been said, "was a poet of the big city who hated the big city.
He was an activist who soon found activism dangerous. Again
and again he has been characterized as a Nihilist, but he persistently sought community, friendship, a Utopian world order.
His contemporaries saw in him a bold renewer of lyric language,
yet he incorporated many clichés and superficialities of his own
as well as of earlier . . . generations of poets."[60] All these poets,
confused on principle, were very young—young enough to die at
the Western front (like Lichtenstein), or to survive into the Nazi
period only to be murdered by their own government; van Hoddis,
who went mad shortly after his single and singular triumph, was
taken from an insane asylum in April 1942 to certain death. Alfred Wolfenstein became one of Hitler's later victims; he survived the war and the Gestapo, but committed suicide in Paris
in January 1945, after liberation.

Like all such enumerations, this listing of Jewish poets is likely
to create a misleading impression by overstating the importance
of those listed at the expense of those omitted. I must therefore
repeat that Jews were far from alone, or even dominant, in the
Modernist wing of literary Germany. In the dense and adventurous artistic milieu of Berlin, they often found one another con-

60. Russell E. Brown, "Alfred Wolfenstein," in Rothe, *Expressionismus als
Literatur*, 262.

genial: van Hoddis established his "Neopathetische Cabaret" in association with other poets who were all Jews like himself: Ernst Blass, Erwin Wassermann, W. S. Ghuttmann, Erwin Loewenson, Erich Unger, David Baumgardt.[61] Yet the principle of their association was not their shared religious origin but their common poetic rebelliousness. And with the exception of Else Lasker-Schüler, to whom I shall return, they were minor figures, overshadowed by three extraordinarily gifted poets, none of them Jewish: Georg Heym, Georg Trakl, and Gottfried Benn. All three were pursued by private furies which they translated, in their poems, into memorable pictures of the modern world. Heym was a visionary, as sensitive to the mystical meaning of color as van Gogh, as preoccupied with destruction and war and corpses as Benn, as unnerved by the demonic city as other poets in his time. Trakl, victimized by drink, by drugs, by intolerable nightmares of decay and corruption, alternately reported visions of paradise and visions of hell, both with a plastic power to which a van Hoddis could only aspire. And Benn, a trained physician, took the fearful sights of the morgue as horrifying and unforgettable metaphors for existence as such. These three poets make part of any history of modern literature; in contrast, most of their Jewish contemporaries (like most of the Jewish painters of the day) survive mainly in highly specialized treatments of the Expressionist movement in Germany.

There are some Jewish writers, however, who have earned a more substantial treatment: some because they are indisputably major writers, others because they are now after years of neglect receiving the celebration they have always deserved, still others because they appeared important in their day even though the sobriety of posthumous judgment has reduced their inflated reputations to their proper, smaller stature. The lyric poet Else Lasker-Schüler is an instance of the first group, the playwright Carl Sternheim of the second, and the novelist Jakob Wassermann of the third. Such revaluations are not a Jewish monopoly: only a handful—a very small handful—of once-famous German imaginative writers in the Empire has survived the scrutiny of later gen-

61. See Lange, "Jakob van Hoddis," 344.

erations. A novelist and playwright like Hermann Sudermann, then hailed as a great and bold artist, has, if anything, sunk lower in the critics' esteem than Wassermann.

Else Lasker-Schüler richly repays exploration here, for her long literary career touches both on the nature of the German avant-garde and on the meaning of Jewishness in Germany. In a well-known book, Helmuth Plessner has called Germany "the belated nation—*die verspätete Nation.*" Setting aside the thesis of the essay to which he gave this title in 1959, the name fits the German contribution to the Modernist sensibility. The Naturalist theater of Arno Holz and Gerhart Hauptmann, which shook theatergoers and alarmed censors in the early days of Wilhelm II's reign, burst onto the German cultural scene after the Naturalism of the French had run its course; some of Hauptmann's early plays and Holz's programmatic statements read like demonstrations of ideas that Zola had developed two decades before. The disciplined and hieratic Symbolist Stefan George, whose first significant book of poems, *Hymnen*, was published in 1890, is unthinkable without his experience of Mallarmé. In painting, the German Expressionists' experiments with technique, freedom of draftsmanship, and extravagance of color owed incalculable debts to Munch, Cézanne, and Degas, to van Gogh and Gauguin. Nolde, Kirchner, the *Brücke*, and the *Blaue Reiter* found their distinct styles before the War of 1914, but while they discovered congenial theoretical formulations in the writings of German academicians like Theodor Lipps and derived encouragement from one another, they took much of their inspiration from Paris, and from exhibitions of modern foreign painting in Munich and in Berlin. Gauguin's *Yellow Christ* is grandfather to Franz Marc's *Blue Horses*. Thomas Mann, a giant of German and world literature, who emerged into national fame in the middle of the Empire with *Buddenbrooks* (1901) and *Tonio Kröger* (1903), owed rather less to foreign sources; he wrote out of his personal history, his close and appreciative reading of the German literary tradition, and his study of Nietzsche and Schopenhauer. But Thomas Mann, though indisputably an important writer, was scarcely a radical in subject matter, in style, or even in perception. Mann severely subdued the urge for experimentation to traditional irony; in his work, as in his politics, the nineteenth century gave way to the twentieth with marked reluctance. He was, after all, almost fifty when he professed himself a convert to democracy after World War I; and his most famous novel, *Der Zauberberg* of 1924, in which he finally says farewell to his long, Teutonic love affair with death, induces the reader not only to marvel at his virtuosity but also to wonder what took him so long.[62] In an important sense, Thomas Mann was a characteristic expression of the belated nation.

Expressionist poetry in Germany exhibits the same pattern, unashamedly. Like the painters, the writers were delighted to follow the model of French cabarets and French little magazines, or, for that matter, Scandinavian playwrights like Strindberg or Russian novelists like Dostoevsky. Unlike a Nolde, whose Nordic "philosophy" emerged early, the poets were largely unpolitical or vaguely utopian; some were possessed, like the young Werfel, with messages of human brotherhood, and eager to throw themselves into the world with the greatest possible energy and the least possible restraint. They could, and did, learn from everywhere and everyone. As historians know, "Expressionism" is a term that defies definition; many of the artists and writers later grouped under this label had nothing to do with one another and often detested each other cordially. But there are some guiding impulses that, however tenuously, unite Hasenclever and Kirchner, Lasker-Schüler and Barlach. One useful strategy for sorting them out—it is one that John Willett follows in his short and lucid exposition, *Expressionism* (1970)—is to begin with the European setting and then focus on the German versions of Expressionism. For while this cluster of movements did not originate in Germany, it was in Germany that it achieved its most extravagant formulations. Expressionism was at once irrationalist and humanitarian; it was a shout of discontent—often, in the declamatory verse and plays of the Germans, a scream of despair—over fat philistines, shallow positivists, authoritarian fathers, exploiting capitalists. The formal preoccupations of the first modern avant-garde, the Impressionists, seemed to the Expressionists superficial

62. Peter Gay, *Weimar Culture: The Outsider as Insider* (1968), 127–28.

and tame; the scientific ideal of Neo-Impressionists like Seurat appeared little better than an artist's pact with the devil. What mattered was strident criticism and candid confession, liberation from the shackles of probability and respectability. To publish erotic wishes (the more bizarre the better), family confrontations (the more outrageous the better), horrible fantasies (the more repulsive the better)—in short, to convert private life into poetic material, was, in the German Expressionists' view, their first duty to themselves and to their art. Surprisingly enough, in this chaotic situation in which aesthetic control was at a discount and the invitation to dilettantism pressing, the level of performance was often high. This was so simply because for some years Germany's most gifted poets and painters worked, each in his own way, in the Expressionist idiom. Once the dutiful pupils of Europe, they became, briefly, Europe's influential teachers.[63] And Else Lasker-Schüler was among the most talented in this talented clan.

Commentator after commentator has exclaimed over Lasker-Schüler's poetry and failed to define its greatness. The critical literature about her is abundant now after years of politic silence;[64] sometimes it reaches for an ecstatic tone as Expressionistic as the poetry it praises. Few poets, perhaps, have been more lucid about their own impenetrability, more explicit about their secret sources of inspiration, more intelligent about their "stupidity," than Else Lasker-Schüler. Her early life, in her cherished Rhineland, was sheltered and, at least in retrospect, seemed rich and happy. But as an adult, she led an adventurous existence, moving from man to man and, later, from furnished room to furnished room. Her home was the literary café in Berlin. Yet her poetry is inwardness itself; it is rich in lush and elaborate images designed not to describe the world through which she wandered,

63. See Claude David, *Von Richard Wagner zu Bertolt Brecht: Eine Geschichte der neueren deutschen Literatur*, tr. Hermann Stiehl (1964), 205.

64. One can hardly read these paeans by German literary critics and historians without getting the uncomfortable feeling that one is watching an opportunistic expiation, as though to praise a Jewish poet is to relieve the burden of guilt for complicity in those years, 1933 to 1945.

but to embody the only landscape that mattered to her, her inner self. Just as Gottfried Benn translated his medical experiences into equivalents for his anguished private state, so Else Lasker-Schüler wrote about her sister, her mother, her lovers, her adopted Berlin (which she loved and hated as Sigmund Freud loved and hated Vienna) to lay bare, not universal truths, but herself. She was, in this, a German Baudelaire.

Born in 1869 in Wuppertal-Elberfeld into a pious Jewish family—her great-grandfather had been Chief Rabbi of the Rhineland and Westphalia—she made an early marriage with a physician in 1894; then, in 1900, shortly after her divorce, she moved to Berlin. There she met and married Georg Levin, who, though best known as a publisher, was a writer and a composer as well; as she transfigured all the persons she knew into fairy-tale popes and potentates, she gave her second husband the name under which he survives in German cultural history, Herwarth Walden. This marriage, too, did not last, but it proved vastly profitable to her as a poet; in 1910, the year before her second divorce, Walden founded what would become the principal avant-garde journal of the time, *Der Sturm*, in which Lasker-Schüler published some of her most famous lyrics. Her association with Walden threw her into all the currents of German Expressionism. She formed intimate and productive friendships with Peter Hille, with Karl Kraus, with Franz Marc, with others. Gottfried Benn, whom she briefly loved, and Georg Trakl, whom she strongly influenced, drifted into her ken shortly before the war; she knew those who counted and whose names, along with hers, would survive. She exploited all she saw and everyone she loved; while there are many who write in order to live, Else Lasker-Schüler lived in order to write. *Styx*, her first collection of verse, appeared in 1902; other volumes of poetry, drama, and experimental prose appeared in rapid succession. Most of her verse was short in compass, figurative in speech, erotic in feeling. Her most famous poem is doubtless "Ein alter Tibet-teppich," published in *Der Sturm* in 1910; Karl Kraus, overwhelmed by its pregnant brevity, republished it in his *Die Fackel* and praised especially the last three lines:

Süsser Lamasohn auf Moschuspflanzenthron
Wie lange küsst dein Mund den meinen
   wohl
Und Wang die Wange buntgeknüpfte
   Zeiten schon?

The poem, as Kraus did not fail to remind his readers, is only nine lines long; yet it elaborates a metaphysical conceit worthy of Donne: the poet visualizes her soul entwined with that of her lover as strands are worked together in a Tibetan carpet.

Then, in 1913, Lasker-Schüler published *Hebräische Balladen*, a typically spare volume of short poems in which she clothes her erotic life in themes drawn from the Old Testament, from Cain and Abel, from Joseph and the Pharaoh. It was a self-consciously Jewish book, but she had been parading her Jewishness for some years; her friend Peter Hille, a Roman Catholic poet, had, as early as 1902, called her "the Jewish poet—*die jüdische Dichterin*," and "the black swan of Israel, a Sappho whose world has broken into pieces."[65] But Jewish in precisely what way? There are three intertwined and overlapping ways for a poet to be Jewish—or, for that matter, anything else: by choice of audience, choice of language, or choice of subject matter.[66] The first of these does not apply to Lasker-Schüler at all. Her associates were pagans, Protestants, Catholics as much as Jews; she wrote for an elite uncrippled by the "mass culture" which she, in company with her fellow Expressionists, feared and despised, an elite that all who possessed sensitivity and good taste could join.

Her language presents a more difficult problem. She herself, in her myth-making Expressionist way, once said that she was really translating her verse from the Hebrew spoken in the days of King Saul into modern German. Jewish and gentile commentators alike have taken this mystification seriously. Kasimir Edschmid, the indefatigable propagandist for the Expressionist spirit, said that her work produces an "equation between verse and blood. She is one of the greatest poets, because she is more

65. In Lasker-Schüler, *Dichtungen und Dokumente*, 565.
66. See on this point, somewhat differently phrased, Hans Tramer, "Der Beitrag der Juden zu Geist und Kultur," in W. Mosse, ed., *Deutsches Judentum in Krieg und Revolution*, 324.

timeless than all others, she approaches the Song of Songs. One feels that in the strange vision of her verse, all Asia has become lyrical poetry."[67] It is strange, as I observed before in my appraisal of Freud, how the inappropriate thought of Asia suggested itself to German gentiles characterizing German Jews. But Jews fell into the same trap. In the mid-1920s, the Jewish critic Meir Wiener argued that what made Lasker-Schüler a peculiarly Jewish poet was her extravagant use of tropes, images, and metaphors that strike the reader as "Oriental"—not, he adds, without justice, for it is characteristic of Oriental literature like the Song of Songs and Persian lyrics to express ecstatic states in this manner.[68] More recently, Fritz Martini, most emphatically no Jew, has celebrated Lasker-Schüler's "Oriental-Hebraic" spirit, with which she infused her "lyrical form."[69]

I want to pursue this point further, for it gets to the heart of Jewish ethnicity. That Else Lasker-Schüler resorted to the Bible for some of her images and linguistic rhythms is undeniable: she affirmed it herself. But she knew nothing of Persian poetry when she wrote her own; her "Oriental" way of expressing herself could have come to her only through the collective unconscious—a notion as vague, and untenable, as any that have obstructed the inquiry into national or ethnic character. She did not even know much Hebrew, beyond the bits of prayer she remembered from the religious services she had attended as a young girl, a literary inspiration feeble compared to the powerful influences that came to her through all the young Expressionist poets with whom she lived on such close terms and in whose experiments she participated. And she read the Bible—the source of her lifelong favorite story, that of Joseph and his brothers—as did all Germans: in Martin Luther's vigorous translation. Moreover, the Bible was no more Oriental than the medieval Jewish poetry she might have known, but probably did not: Biblical tales, images, rhythms, had dominated Western art and literature for many centuries,

67. Quoted in Tramer, "Beitrag der Juden," 342.
68. "Else Lasker-Schüler," in Krojanker, ed., *Juden in der deutschen Literatur*, 179–92.
69. "Else Lasker-Schüler: Dichtung und Glaube," in Hans Steffen, ed., *Der deutsche Expressionismus: Formen und Gestalten* (1965), 125.

and the Bible is in fact central to any definition of Western culture. Milton's poems, Voltaire's polemics, Macaulay's speeches, the young Bertolt Brecht's satire depend on the Bible for their matter and manner alike, and their effectiveness, in turn, depends on their readers' intuitive possession of scriptural stories as part of the mental furniture they take for granted.

Indeed, the very division of "Western" and "Oriental" that underlies all these appraisals of Lasker-Schüler's work begs the question it purports to answer. It conjures up dark-eyed, sensual Jewesses and colorfully clad, mysterious Jews fresh from remote regions. An anti-Semite may accept this division because it is convenient; a Jew who adopted it had identified himself with the aggressor, and denied his long European history. The Jewish tradition, like the German tradition, was a long, complex mixture of mixtures, in which Greek, Near Eastern, Roman, Western medieval and modern influences were joined in incalculable proportions. And each of these strands was, in turn, a composite; as Aby Warburg well understood, even the antiquity that Renaissance scholars recaptured from the neglect of medieval monks was not the pure classical antiquity of Plato and Cicero, but a brew in which Alexandria and Athens were almost irretrievably mixed together. What Else Lasker-Schüler was doing when she leafed through her Old Testament was precisely what Gottfried Benn was doing when he recorded his visits to the morgue: revitalizing, in the company of other avant-garde poets, a German poetic diction that had been devalued through sentimentality, and diluted through false pathos. "To play," she wrote to her friend Karl Kraus in 1911, "is everything—*Spielen ist alles.*" When she wrote poetry, she was playing a serious German game.

Her playfulness included the rediscovery of German Romantic poets whose combination of candid self-revelation and expressive abundance found a welcome echo among the literary rebels of the Wilhelminian era. The Swiss literary historian Walter Muschg is close to the center of Lasker-Schüler's poetic enterprise when he notes that her "imagination is no 'gift of the Orient to the German language,'" but rather "a heritage of Romanticism. The Jewish tradition is only the special strain that rescues her from the sentimentality of the epigone, and recalls William Blake more than it does Isaiah." And then he perceptively adds, to the name of Blake, the names of Jean Paul, Bettina Brentano, and her brother Clemens Brentano.[70] In short, it is possible to call her inspiration "Oriental" only if one does not know the Jewish literary tradition, and to call her inspiration "purely Jewish" only if one does not know the German literary tradition. With Else Lasker-Schüler, as so often, ethnic characterizations are the fruit, not of insight, but of ignorance. One cannot accurately compare traits one does not know.

Still, Else Lasker-Schüler's subject-matter, and her sympathies, stamp her as a Jewish poet even before the first World War and long before the Hitler nightmare, which she lived through first in Switzerland and then in Palestine, where she died early in 1945. Yet even this criterion of identification is not unproblematic. Firmly, eloquently Jewish as she was, her Jewishness was drenched in poetry; it was wholly personal, profoundly unorthodox. In blatant contradiction to all Jewish teachings, she thought of Jesus as the Messiah who had come once and would come again; she played, in her poetic way, but in all earnestness, with the idea of Jesus as God's son. This idiosyncratic Jewishness was an essential aspect of Else Lasker-Schüler, the willful poet. But she had yet another side to her, her Germanness. Her last and, many think, her finest collection of poems, *Mein Blaues Klavier*, was published in Jerusalem in 1943, with an ecumenical dedication that has not gone unremarked: "To my unforgettable friends, men and women, in German cities—and to those who, like me, have been driven out and are now scattered in the world, in fidelity—*Meinen unvergesslichen Freunden und Freundinnen in den Städten Deutschlands—und denen, die wie ich vertrieben und nun zerstreut in der Welt, In Treue!*"[71] For Jews of her generation, Else Lasker-Schüler's early and emphatic religious affirmation was a notable exception; her forgiving, even affectionate

70. "Else Lasker-Schüler," in *Von Trakl zu Brecht: Dichter des Expressionismus* (1961), 125.
71. Lasker-Schüler, *Dichtungen und Dokumente*, 153. Claude David finds space in his rapid survey of German literature for reference to it. *Von Wagner zu Brecht*, 212.

dedication, in which she speaks as one German to other Germans, strikes a far more familiar note.

In contrast with Else Lasker-Schüler, whose style places her in the Expressionist camp, Carl Sternheim is nearly impossible to fit under any kind of rubric. He owed little to anyone or anything but his talents and his spleen—except perhaps to the temperamental and outspoken dramatist Frank Wedekind, who was the most appropriate ancestor that Sternheim could possibly have adopted: one outsider going to school to another outsider. Sternheim was representative in one respect; half-Jewish in origin, with a Jewish father and a Lutheran mother, he was wholly non-Jewish in feeling: "Not an atom of piety," Arnold Zweig observed, "in his whole work."[72] Indeed, when he mentions Jews at all, he does so with icy aversion, and the reason for his hostility is enormously revealing: in 1920, looking back at the Empire that had died just two years before, Sternheim accused Germany's Jews of being far too much at home with modern "mechanized spirituality." In the vulgar and profiteering world of the *"juste milieu,"* the Jew was, "for the first time in recent centuries, not in opposition to the life of the people," but in harmony with his fellow citizens.[73] In short, the trouble with the Jews was, to Sternheim's mind, that they were Germans. This rather rarely articulated but sincerely felt antagonism was not anti-Semitism so much as a special case of his social philosophy—or, more accurately, his social attitudes. Sternheim knew what he despised; he had an almost unlimited distaste for the *juste milieu* which nourished the genteel, safe, "cultured" hypocrite who prates of Goethe. Sternheim's animus was far from unique, or even unusual; the youth movement, George's guardians of culture, Expressionist poets and painters generally shared this Nietzschean contempt for the stupid Junker, the materialistic bourgeois, and the craven proletarian. But his style is wholly unmistakable; it is pure and simple Sternheim.

72. "Versuch über Sternheim," in Krojanker, ed., *Juden in der deutschen Literatur,* 312.
73. *Berlin oder Juste Milieu,* in *Gesamtwerk,* ed. Wilhelm Emrich, 9 vols., VI (1966), 132, 134. For some other anti-Jewish passages in his work, see Tramer, "Beitrag der Juden," 368. It will appear in the text that I do not accept Sternheim's appraisal.

Easy as it is to recognize his hand, his intentions remain hard to fathom. Sternheim was born in Leipzig, in 1878, and spent his early childhood in Hannover. His father was a banker and businessman (both occupations notoriously associated with Jews), who, beyond that, owned the local daily, the *Hannoversche Tageblatt*. Many years later, Carl Sternheim remembered how he would accompany his father to the theater to see the latest play, which the elder Sternheim regularly reviewed in his own newspaper. This glimpse of the two Sternheims is both charming and instructive: the grown man and the little boy, attending productions of the German classics and new dramas in choice orchestra seats, the father taking notes for his review and the son absorbing the atmosphere that was to become his life—two German Jews thoroughly at home in German culture. When the Sternheims moved to Berlin in 1884, the future playwright continued his explorations in the Belle-Alliance Theater owned by his uncle; there the boy saw brash comedies and musical extravaganzas.[74] By the turn of the century, Sternheim was trying his hand at poems and plays. But his famous style did not fully ripen until about 1910, with *Die Hose*, a "bourgeois comedy" first performed in 1911. That style is marked by bold inversions, the omission of definite articles, pungent declarative sentences, stunning *bon mots*, a "telegraphic style" which Sternheim, in defiance of realistic conventions, lent to all his characters with only minimal concessions to individuality. Sternheim did not think much of the Expressionists; hence, directors who continuously "fire his sentences into the orchestra like a machine gun barrage" do him an injustice.[75] At the same time, in the best of Sternheim's plays his characters convey a single impression: of breathtaking speed and a marked aversion to sentimentality. So disciplined a speech as this must be an instrument; its creator had made it to say something.

But what? Sternheim offers little assistance with his programmatic pronouncements, cast, like his characters' lines, in his inimitable manner. They can be, and have been, interpreted in con-

74. See Carl Sternheim, *Vorkriegseuropa im Gleichnis meines Lebens* (1936), in *Vermischte Schriften* (1965), 476, 486. See also Hellmuth Karasek, *Carl Sternheim* (1965), 7–8.
75. Karasek, *Sternheim*, 17.

tradictory ways. In one essay, Sternheim insists that art should not try to leave the world better than it is. The task of art is not to imagine a paradise, but to report things as they are, clearly, honestly, "crudely," omitting nothing essential. Yet elsewhere, Sternheim expressed vast admiration for Molière, "physician to the body of his age."[76]

The resolution of the conundrum must lie in Sternheim's position on the bourgeoisie, and that is anything but unambiguous. Sternheim characterized the series of loosely connected comedies he initiated with *Die Hose* as being "from the heroic life of the bourgeoisie—*aus dem bürgerlichen Heldenleben*."[77] But whether he wants to record admiration or detestation for the modern heroes he invents, or an impenetrable mixture of both, is open to debate. Surely it is obvious why Sternheim chose the name Maske for the family he follows from petty bourgeois to nobilitated industrialists: he is unmasking the Maskes, and through them, society and its conventions. The bald, curt exchanges among his characters reveal the lust behind sentiment, the petty greed behind high aspirations, the unremitting and invigorating struggle for profit and power that pervades family relations and social intercourse. It is not necessary to reconcile the divergent interpretations of Sternheim's intentions, nor is it possible. They represent the outer limits of his Nietzschean political universe: contempt for the safe middle of the road, adoration of vitality, and an urge to face realities. There is, in *1913*, written before the war, a famous speech that is a triumph of Sternheim's somber prescience, and chilling evidence of his conviction that the bourgeoisie was unable to control the forces it had unleashed: "After us, collapse! We are ripe."[78] After that collapse became reality,

76. For the first of these attitudes, see "Kampf der Metapher!" (1917); for the second, "Molière" (1917), both in Sternheim, *Gesamtwerk*, VI (1966), 28–38; see also Karasek, *Sternheim*, 22–27.

77. Students of Sternheim's work still debate which of the dozen or so comedies he wrote belong to this "cycle." Definitely the four plays involving four generations of the Maske family—*Die Hose, Der Snob* (1914), *1913* (1913), and *Das Fossil* (1923); to this quartet must be added *Die Kassette* (1912), *Bürger Schippel* (1913), *Der Kandidat* (1914), and *Tabula Rasa* (1916), a set of eight plays. Others are problematical.

78. Act III, scene 2; *Gesamtwerk*, I, 285.

Sternheim's inspiration faded; he died, miserable and ignored, in 1942. But the plays of this aristocratic anarchist, who loved what he hated, are being performed again, with increasing frequency. They bristle with energy. Unlike the plays of his master, Wede-kind—pioneering, brilliant, but sometimes inviting unwanted laughter—Sternheim's comedies remain very, and intentionally, funny.

The voluminous work of Jakob Wassermann—immense cycles of novels, a stream of novellas, polemics, confessions—is far less exhilarating. It is a cultural symptom; in no way avant-garde but in many ways deadly earnest literature. Wassermann was some-thing of a religious moralist, as intent on making myths as Stern-heim was to discredit them. His fiction explores the fates of the worldly converted to sanctity, the rich who give up their property to serve the poor, the innocent victimized by a society too indiffer-ent to muster generosity. Even before 1914, in his fictional treat-ment of the famous, mysterious foundling *Caspar Hauser* (1908), Wassermann was driven to portray what he called the "indolence of the heart." Yet he was also an eloquent, rather baroque story-teller; perceptively, his friend Thomas Mann paid tribute to his "magnificent mixture of virtuosity and holy seriousness."[79] By temperament Wassermann was a reconciler. For a number of years he had to battle against the insensitive demands of his family that he enter a commercial career which he hated and for which he had no vocation, yet he persisted in seeking their ap-proval. The same ecumenical impulse informs his unrelenting efforts to be a good German without denying his Jewishness.

Wassermann was not an observant Jew, but he acknowledged, and suffered with, his ethnic inheritance. His first ambitious novel, *Die Juden von Zirndorf* (1897), begins with an introduc-tory account of Sabbatai Sevi, the false Messiah of the seven-teenth century, and then moves to the nineteenth century to de-pict the Jews of the town of Zirndorf attempting to come to terms with their past and find their place in the present world. It is, as Wassermann senses it, a desperate enterprise: the Jewish tradi-

79. "Tischrede auf Wassermann" (1929), *Reden und Aufsätze*, 2 vols. (1965), I, 232.

tion is too enfeebled to give vitality to its belated descendants, but to reject it is to betray an inescapable heritage. The way out, if there is one, must be sought through Wassermann's protagonist, a Jew who rises above sectarianism to a higher humanity, to worldliness in the best sense of that word. We may read Agathon Geyer as a kind of idealized self-portrait; he is the kind of healer and reconciler that Wassermann hopelessly longed to be all his life, a secular saint, a Christian Jew and Jewish Christian.

Three years later, in 1900, Wassermann further developed his theme of purification through worldly religion; his *Geschichte der jungen Renate Fuchs* is the history of a young Jewish girl who, as her name plainly implies, is "reborn." She becomes, like Geyer, "agathos"—good: Wassermann's symbolism was never very subtle. And later, in tales like *Der Moloch* (1902) and in *Das Gänsemännchen*, his most successful novel, which he wrote before the war and published in 1915, Wassermann relives his own persistent confrontation: that of Jew and Christian, Jew and German, in perpetual conflict and perpetual search for harmony. Long before he cast up accounts in his famous short autobiography, *Mein Weg als Deutscher und Jude* (1921), he felt, and, I am tempted to add, wallowed in, the pathos of his situation. The rise of anti-Semitism during the World War only underscored what had been a depressing reality before. "Sacrifices," Wassermann wrote in *Mein Weg*, "are not enough. Wooing is misinterpreted. Mediation meets coldness, if not scorn. Apostasy is, for the self-respecting, out of the question on principle. Secret assimilation bears fruit only for those who are suited to assimilation, which is to say, the weakest individuals. Persisting in old ways means torpor. What remains? Self-destruction? A life in twilight, anxiety, and misery . . . ? It is better not to think about it." Yet while Wassermann probes with an almost voluptuous hopelessness into a love that is not returned, and avenues of escape which all alike are blocked, he cannot renounce his passion: "I am German, and I am a Jew, one as much and as completely as the other; one cannot be separated from the other."[80]

"It is better not to think about it," so Wassermann wrote in

80. *Mein Weg*, 125–26.

1921. But obviously he had been thinking about it in his early years and would continue to think about it until his death in 1934. In several of his novels he has gentile characters indulge in virulent outbursts against the Jews: Jew-hatred is a constant threat in Wassermann's life and work. Yet, he persisted in facing that threat from the standpoint of a German, and adopted that standpoint so completely that he parroted some of the very cultural clichés which he might have rejected—had he been less anxious. In an essay of 1919, Wassermann professed to see "profound reasons" for the "large numbers of literary men among the Jews." Jewish existence, he argued, displays the greatest possible contrasts: the Jew is "either the most Godless or the most God-saturated of all humans." He has faced the greatest obstacles, fought the hardest battles, made the hardest cultural adjustments, and all this "has predestined the Jews as a whole to a kind of literary role." The "Jew as European, as cosmopolitan, is a man of letters; the Jew as Oriental, not in the ethnographic, but in the mythic sense, with the transforming strength for the present day which he is bound to possess, can be a creator."[81] Challenged by Martin Buber in the early 1920s to clarify this dichotomy, Wassermann stood by it, called the "European" Jew sterile, formalistic, and solitary, and the "Oriental" Jew sure of himself, of his world, and of his humanity. "He is never sectarian, never particularistic, he has nothing of the fanatic, of one who feels slighted, he has within himself all that the others seek outside themselves. . . . He is free, and the others are servants. He is truthful, and the others lie." Vague and rhetorical as these assertions are, Wassermann further reduces what little specificity they have by insisting that the "Oriental" is "naturally" only a "symbolic figure; I could just as soon call him the fulfilled or the legitimate heir."[82] To call the Jew an Oriental, which was so often intended as an insult, and so often reflected a confused helplessness, here becomes a source of pride and self-confidence.

81. "Der Literat, Oder Mythos und Persönlichkeit," in Wassermann, *Lebensdienst: Gesammelte Studien, Erfahrungen, und Reden aus drei Jahrzehnten* (1928), 546–47.
82. See "Der Jude als Orientale: Brief an Martin Buber . . ." *Lebensdienst*, 176–77.

To be sure, as one of his adoring biographers put it in 1933, Wassermann did "not boast about his heritage of oriental blood."[83] On the contrary, Wassermann found it necessary to boast about his deep German roots; more than once he let his readers know that his ancestors had "demonstrably" lived in Franconia for over five centuries.[84] As with many other German Jews, his identification with Germany was both cause and consequence of what I have called selective anti-Semitism: an almost visceral contempt for Jews from Eastern Europe. The psychological strategy of this mechanism (mainly unconscious) is simple and pathetically obvious: it was to force all Jewish immigrants from the East—university students, horse traders, and itinerant peddlers, Russians and Ukrainians, Lithuanians and Galicians—into a single mold, and thus to fashion a convenient stereotype. This permitted German Jews to despise recent Jewish immigrants in company with other Germans; nothing, after all, unites one with others more than the possession of a common enemy. Moreover, Jewish anti-Semitism had a special function in the German-Jewish psychic economy: hatred of outsiders diverted self-hatred to other targets. Finally, and most important: to construct this target for Jew-hatred would, many German Jews fondly believed, disarm German anti-Semitism altogether. After all, much German anti-Semitism had been ethnic rather than racial; and many critics of the Jews advocated total integration as the best solution to the "Jewish question."[85]

Not surprisingly, many German Jews found such sentiments

83. Siegmund Bing, *Jakob Wassermann: Weg und Werk des Dichters* (2nd ed., 1933), 81. This biography, precisely since it is strongly partisan in Wassermann's behalf, is just one more instance of just how mischievous the notion of "Oriental blood-heritage" is: "The very origin of his passionate story-telling instinct—*Fabeltrieb*," Bing goes on, "may be a dowry from the Orient. It fits the picture of his often glowing work, and, by the way, his physical appearance." His "southern" and "dark countenance" suggests that "ancestors on his mother's side had settled in Spain before persecution drove them to the Rhine and Main."

84. See a letter to a "German philosopher," dated February 1923, in *Lebensdienst*, 161; and elsewhere.

85. See below, 182.

irresistible. Many of the eastern immigrants *were* palpably different from the old German-Jewish settlers, different in speech, in gestures, in habits, probably even in values. Selective anti-Semitism, then, seemed socially right and politically prudent—a deadly combination. History has shown this attitude to have been as futile as it was immoral. It was worse than a crime, it was a blunder, for it misread anti-Semitism as a distorted response to a real cause rather than a pure projection that has very little, if anything, to do with Jewish character or Jewish conduct at all. To be sure, Wassermann earnestly denounced those who would hold all Jews responsible for the objectionable behavior of some Jews, or hold these last responsible for their misconduct *as* Jews. But he was, at the same time, ready to take public distance from "Polish and Russian Jews unfortunately let loose upon Germany . . . in consequence of the war." He had no intention of denying, he wrote—using the very clichés he was deploring in the same paragraph—the "sins" that Jewish exploiters and usurers, "corrosive" Jewish literati and negative spirits of all sorts had committed "against the general life of our people." He confessed himself appalled at "Jewish traders, profiteers, and speculators," and then added his sonorous question: "What do I have to do with them? I, whose forebears, on my father's as on my mother's side, have lived and worked in the heart of Germany for six hundred years?"[86] Not merely in the substance of his patriotism, but in his very mode of affirming it, Wassermann strove to be a good German.

Like the experience of German Jews in German universities, that of German Jews in German literature thus exhibits a wide range of actual conflict and possible symbiosis: Wassermann, who was a good Jew, was not a Modernist; Sternheim, who was a Modernist, was not a good Jew; and Lasker-Schüler, who was both Modernist and Jew, made her mark in Expressionism in the company of Catholics, Protestants, and Teutonic atheists. German Jews of the Wilhelminian Empire, whether they wrote trea-

86. "Offener Brief, An den Herausgeber einer Monatsschrift für 'Kulturelle Erneuerung,'" Richard Drews (1925), *Lebensdienst*, 158.

tises or poems, had no way, and no wish, to escape from the larger cultural environment.

4. THE JEWISH PRESENCE

And yet: the historian of the Wilhelminian epoch cannot escape a sense of Jewish bustle, of incessant Jewish activity. That sense is not misplaced: Jewish apologists and anti-Semites were right to note that in these years Jews entered the cultural market in striking numbers. There was a kind of explosion of Jewish talent; Jews became drama critics and art critics, book dealers and art dealers, publishers and editors, managers of theaters and producers of plays. They were prominent in the pursuits that enjoyed high visibility. It was almost as though Jews, hitherto schooled to seek the protective coloring of inconspicuousness, now escaped into the most exposed possible positions. Jewish talent, as I have said, continued to flow in channels that others had made for them, but with legal emancipation and increasing social acceptance, the gifts cherished by Jews and the employments available to Jews were more happily matched than before. It is a commonplace to say that Jews prize verbal culture, but the commonplace was proved true in the Empire. For centuries, Jews had needed literacy for their prayers even more than for their business, and the road to prestige at home or in the community led through scholarship, or at least, verbal facility. In the Empire, this set of values was supplemented by the German Jews' sincere, even passionate affection for high German culture. To become a literary critic or the editor of a civilized periodical was, for a German Jew, to gratify both his traditional yearning for excellence in the world of words and his more recent, but no less exigent, love for the country of Goethe and Schiller.

The evidence for the massive Jewish presence in cultural service industries is all too familiar. Among the largest and most versatile publishing houses were two Jewish family firms, Mosse and Ullstein.[87] Both had begun rather modestly with newspapers, and

87. See below, 172.

both expanded their operations from dailies to weekly, monthly, and prestigious quarterly journals, and to the publishing of books ranging from best sellers to reasonably priced classics, from luxurious art books to serious fiction. Among Mosse's and Ullstein's most powerful editors, literary reviewers, and popular authors there were many Jews, or at least many of Jewish origin. Fritz Stahl led the revival of interest in Schinkel's architecture, almost a century old and in danger of being neglected in the riot of eclecticism that marked Wilhelm II's reign. Paul Bekker and Alfred Einstein brought their scholarship to bear on old and new music alike. Alfred Kerr, Arthur Eloesser, Monty Jacobs, Julius Bab vigorously seconded the innovative invasions of Shaw and Ibsen, and made themselves into guardians of taste and defenders of experimentation—within limits—in the confused but lively atmosphere of the German drama. There were literally dozens of others like them, Jews by birth though often not by profession, who wrote for the major dailies in Berlin and in the provincial cities: for Mosse's *Berliner Tageblatt*, for Ullstein's *Berliner Morgenpost*, for Sonnemann's *Frankfurter Zeitung*—this last probably the most prestigious among German newspapers. It was called "Jewish" only by the most bigoted of anti-Semites, for Jewish themes or Jewish interests were strictly marginal.[88] While newspapers that Jews owned, or for which they wrote, were far from unanimous in their political views, by and large they were inclined to be liberal in editorial policy, respectable in makeup, and moderate in tone. One can almost understand why anxious *völkische* elements felt encircled by Jews at home as they did by the Entente powers abroad: these and other "Jewish" newspapers, with commanding circulations and incalculable influence, seemed, with their liberalism, part of a chorus, probably a conspiracy.

While Jewish publicists were heavily concentrated in the liberal sector of German opinion, this clustering did not necessarily

88. "With its editors, Jews and non-Jews alike, the Jewish question did not occupy . . . the center of their interests. It was subsumed under the larger, more general problem of working for democratic, libertarian, progressive, tolerant policies." Werner Becker, "Die Rolle der liberalen Presse," in W. Mosse, ed., *Deutsches Judentum*, 78.

reflect their ethnic heritage. Others besides Jews were liberals, and many Jews held other political loyalties. Two extremely prominent editors of the Social Democratic Press, speaking for both the Marxists and the Revisionists, were Jews—or, rather, principled atheists of Jewish origin: Eduard Bernstein, who edited the *Sozialdemokrat* in its years of exile, until 1890; and Joseph Bloch, editor of the Revisionist *Sozialistische Monatshefte*. Even the *völkische* element did not lack its Jewish spokesmen. Its most notorious representative was Paul Nikolaus Cossmann, who converted in 1905, in his mid-thirties, to Catholicism; he had founded a literary-political journal, *Süddeutsche Monatshefte*, in Munich just a year before. Stridently conservative, virulently nationalistic, Cossmann and his chosen contributors gave wide circulation to the stock slanders about Jewish "corrosiveness," "materialism," "hatred of tradition"; the *Süddeutsche Monatshefte* is a vivid, if depressing, reminder of how far some German Jews could go in escaping from their past.[89]

Cossmann, it is fair to note, was an exception among German Jews, but the wide range of Jewish opinion remains a fact—in the fields of literary controversy and artistic production quite as much as in that of politics. If there was one area in which Jews made their mark in, and for, the German avant-garde, it was literary journalism. Fritz Schlawe, who has carefully reviewed the literary journals of the Wilhelminian Empire, has called attention to the "creative contribution of Jewish intelligence—*Geistigkeit*."[90] He is speaking in particular of the *Freie Bühne für modernes Leben*, best known under its later title, *Die Neue Rundschau*, but he might well have been speaking of other periodicals, like Siegfried Jacobsohn's *Schaubühne* or Herwarth Walden's *Sturm*. Founded in 1890 by the Jewish director Otto Brahm and published by the Jewish house of Fischer, *Die Neue Rundschau* had among its

89. The pathetic irony of Cossmann's end—he was forced in his last year to live in a ghetto and then transported to Theresienstadt in 1942, where he perished—has not escaped comment; see Werner Jochmann, "Die Ausbreitung des Antisemitismus," in W. Mosse, ed., *Deutsches Judentum*, 482–83; and Wolfram Selig, *Paul Nikolaus Cossmann und die Süddeutschen Monatshefte von 1914–1918* (1967).

90. *Literarische Zeitschriften*, part I, 1885–1910 (2nd ed., 1965), 28.

Jewish editors the distinguished music critic Oscar Bie. It was hospitable to new tendencies in German and European literature, fostered Naturalism, and later ventured into more radical movements. Its list of contributors is rich in famous names, many of them creators of a new sensibility: Wedekind, Shaw, d'Annunzio, Hesse, Rilke, Strindberg, Thomas Mann. At the same time, perhaps the most vigorous adversary of the *Neue Rundschau* was the *Deutsche Rundschau*, a highly respected cultural and literary journal founded in 1874, and subsequently edited, by the Jew Julius Rodenberg. While Rodenberg's critical standards were high, his literary-political bent was a measured dislike of new departures in the drama and the novel; to print Theodor Fontane was about as unconventional as he was willing to be.

Similar diversity reigned among Jews in the world of the theater. The most versatile and effective propagandist for the new Naturalism was Otto Brahm, who wrote dramatic criticism for the *Frankfurter Zeitung* and the *Vossische Zeitung*, and founded the periodical *Freie Bühne* to expand his audience for his cause. In 1889, he had opened a new theater, the Freie Bühne, in Berlin, with Ibsen's *Ghosts*, followed by Hauptmann's *Vor Sonnenaufgang*. Both playwrights were still rejected by the respectable theater-going public, but Brahm made them into the staple of the German stage, especially after 1894, when he became director of the Deutsche Theater, also in Berlin. Brahm's Naturalism was comprehensive and consistent. Not content with daring to put on stage what the salon dramas and historical spectacles of his time politely masked, he extended his Naturalism to his sets and his direction, both designed to exemplify the ruthless veracity which, he believed, his favorite dramatists exacted. "We open a free stage onto modern life," he proclaimed in the opening number of the *Freie Bühne*. "In the center of our enterprise stands art; the new art, which faces reality and contemporary existence."[91] What he wanted, as he put it simply, was the truth.

Since it was the famous Otto Brahm who imported to Berlin Max Reinhardt, who was to become even more famous, the contrast between the two is instructive. Reinhardt was one of the

91. Schlawe, *Literarische Zeitschriften*, 27.

first Austrian Jews to conquer Berlin; there were to be a handful of others before the war, and many more during the Weimar Republic. Reinhardt had begun his career as an actor, but soon displayed a marked gift for directing other actors and for seeing possibilities in new plays as well as undiscovered aspects to the classics. In 1905, after Brahm had moved to the Lessing Theater, Reinhardt succeeded him at the Deutsche Theater, where, for all his feverish activities elsewhere, he would stay for almost thirty years. Brahm had been an innovator in compelling the public to face realities they had not seen on stage before; Reinhardt was an innovator in offering the public fantasies it had not yet imagined. It is characteristic of Reinhardt that his favorite play should be Shakespeare's *Midsummer Night's Dream*; between 1904 and 1934, he staged it in thirteen versions and in several languages.

There was something daemonic about Reinhardt: he added house after house to his empire and restlessly experimented with the classics; seeing himself as a *Gesamtkünstler*, he redesigned theaters, superintended productions, coached his casts, developed controversial repertories. His thoughtful interest in his actors was famous. Any device that would serve to make things dramatic was welcome to his hand: a *Hamlet* in modern dress; a revolving stage for crowd scenes. Some of his magic has been described as opportunistic; Alfred Kerr, for one, thought Reinhardt too avid for commercial success. After all, Ibsen himself, and Hauptmann, had deserted the Naturalistic drama that Brahm had so memorably staged, so that Reinhardt's desertion was only following a trend. And Reinhardt's taste for the extravagant suggests a certain theatricality in the pejorative sense of that term. Actually, it is not true that Reinhardt restricted himself to ventures that were predictably successful; he staged experimental plays that were not in themselves commercially promising: Reinhardt's staging *made* ventures successful. But theatricality in a broad sense was central to his makeup; he was not avant-garde on principle any more than he was traditional on principle. His principle was spectacle.

One way of deflating exaggerated notions about the Jewish share in Germany's Modernist movement, then, is to recognize that many Jews were in fact anything but avant-garde. Another is to give proper weight to advocates of Modernism who were not

Jews.[92] True, Max Liebermann pleaded for French Impressionism at a time when Monet and Degas still seemed unpalatable daubers to most German art lovers. And one of Liebermann's most enthusiastic supporters, the Jewish art dealer Paul Cassirer, presented these painters to an astonished Berlin public around the turn of the century. In 1901, when Cassirer first exhibited Cézanne, then almost unknown in Germany, Wilhelm II led the pack against such subversions of the time-honored verities in art: "Paul Cassirer," he said, is "trying to bring the filthy art—*Dreckkunst*—of Paris to our country."[93] Far from being dismayed by such noisy opposition, Cassirer enjoyed his notoriety and fostered the graphic work of the more *outré* among the Expressionists—Kokoschka, Barlach, Pechstein.

There were other Jews on the cultural barricades with Max Liebermann and Paul Cassirer, but they were far from alone. The Jewish industrialist Emil Rathenau had the gentile designer and architect Peter Behrens appointed artistic counselor—*künstlerischer Beirat*—to his firm, the A.E.G.; the gentile publisher Albert Langen employed the Jewish cartoonist Th. Th. Heine on his satirical weekly *Simplicissimus*. If there were Jewish avant-garde publishers like Samuel Fischer and Kurt Wolff, raising the sights of the German reading public with their youthful authors, handsome designs, and venturesome tastes, they found themselves in cheerful competition with gentile avant-garde publishers like Reinhard Piper and Ernst Rowohlt. The promoters of German Modernism were an interdenominational troop. Count Harry Kessler, of unimpeachable German-British aristocratic stock, had a hand in the new painting, the new music, the new literature, the new architecture. He gave lucrative commissions to Henry van de Velde and Aristide Maillol, had himself painted by Ed-

92. "It is sometimes said," John Willett comments, reasonably enough, that German openmindedness to radical cultural influences from abroad "was due to the Jewish element in the big German cities, but there were after all influential Jews in other countries too, and of those most responsible for it a number were no more Jewish than [Roger] Fry." *Expressionism* (1970), 36.
93. See Tilla Durieux, specifically referring to Cézanne, whose "bold, exciting colors," she recalls, irritated viewers to "outbursts of fury." *Eine Tür Steht Offen: Erinnerungen* (1964), 53.

vard Munch, participated in the elegant, expensive, and advanced journal *Pan*, moved in experimental artistic circles that included Richard Strauss and Hugo von Hofmannsthal, and, after his move to Weimar, helped to make that city receptive to the radical aesthetic tendencies that he himself favored.

Less rich than Kessler but more strategically placed, Hugo von Tschudi tried to bring the Berlin National Gallery into the twentieth century. He was the first German museum director to buy a Cézanne. That was in 1899; nine years later, his tireless devotion to the modern brought his disgrace and "resignation." Julius Meier-Græfe, who directed the artistic section of *Pan* in its first year (1895), went on to bring French Impressionism to German readers in a series of influential books, including a study of Manet in 1902 and an ambitious three-volume *Entwicklungsgeschichte der modernen Kunst* in 1904. And the charter of modern art, Wilhelm Worringer's *Abstraktion und Einfühlung*, came out in 1908; a short but technical treatise on aesthetics, it was to enjoy a strikingly large following. (It is ironic in retrospect, but scarcely astonishing, to recall that the first truly enthusiastic reader of Worringer's bold work was Georg Simmel.) Worringer subsumed the history of all art under two contrasting postures in the world: the one, confident, serene, classical, imitates nature by means of empathy; the other, anxious, lost, fearful, defies nature to proclaim the autonomy of art. Neutral though he professed himself, Worringer clearly preferred the abstract to the concrete, the maker of unreadable works to the perfect copyist. This view, already foreshadowed in other treatises, mainly by Germans, provided a theoretical basis for shifting aesthetic sympathies to the kind of Asian and African art to which Gauguin and Picasso were already calling attention. Worringer mentions few contemporary artists, but in a footnote he refers the reader to the Magic Realist Ferdinand Hodler, before whose paintings, he writes, even a well-schooled gallery-goer is helpless, just because their ideal is not mimesis.[94] Worringer's dissertation gave Expression-

94. *Abstraktion und Einfühlung: Ein Beitrag zur Stilpsychologie* (1908; 5th unchanged ed., 1918), 13n.

ist and abstract art the most unimpeachable academic blessing; it was a decisive affront to the kind of art Wilhelm II thought it healthy for Germans to enjoy. Had Worringer been Jewish, he would have been denounced as corrosive of the Western Christian tradition in art. But Worringer was not Jewish.

The widespread perception, shared by German Jews and other Germans, that Jews were intimately involved in the making of the new culture had its elements of truth, but it was only half the truth, or less. In 1893, the historian Hans Delbück collected a bouquet of philistine objections to the art and literature then making their way against the outraged protests of the general public. One, by a Professor Dondorff, expresses what many felt: "Just thirty years ago," Dondorff wrote, "one would have been ashamed to profess oneself openly an Atheist: today one does it emphatically. Liberalism, Judaism, Mammonism, Socialism, Pessimism, Anarchism, Nihilism—that is the ladder down which we are climbing, rapidly and infallibly, into the abyss." Art has been granted "the monopoly of vulgarity"; the theater is turning into a "kitchen of filth"; schools dish out knowledge without conscience; the "sacredness of marriage" has been compromised; "discipline and virtue" have become laughing stocks. "The signature of our day is the brutish man of pronounced Semitic type."[95] The central animus of this view emerges more and more clearly as we climb down the ladder of Dondorff's lament: at the outset, Judaism is just one corrosive force among many; at the end, it is their essential cause.

This sense of the matter remains misleading and malicious even after we bracket Dondorff's accusation against the Jews. German Jews participated in Socialism, pessimism, liberalism, and the innovations in the theater and literature that so many feared as symptoms of decay. But it was a German "decay" which many non-Jews fostered, and more German Jews resisted than welcomed. Germany's Jews were woven into the very texture of German culture, and Germany dyed its Jews through and

95. Quoted in Georg Kotowski, Werner Pöls, Gerhard A. Ritter, eds., *Das Wilhelminische Deutschland: Stimmen der Zeitgenossen* (1965), 125.

through. They wore its colors—black, white, red—without apology, in fact with pride. It was not protective coloring, but their own. Or so they thought.

I end where I began, with German-Jewish self-perception during the Wilhelminian Empire. Unfortunately our appraisal cannot remain wholly untouched by our oppressive knowledge of what happened later. The vast and irrational tragedy of the 1930s and 1940s throws into glaring relief those unpleasant incidents of the 1880s and 1890s that their victims refused to take seriously, or from which, at least, they refused to draw serious inferences. Were not the slights handed out to Lazarus, Steinthal, and Simmel so many warning signals that the Jews' love for Germany was pathetically unrequited? After all, they were not exceptional: the virulent anti-Semitism of fraternities caused much anxiety among Jewish students and brought defensive measures; the contempt that outspoken *völkische* professors expressed for Jewish scholars could not go unnoticed; and the silence, half-approving and half-timid, of other, so-called liberal, professors drove some Jewish intellectuals to despair. Even those prominent Germans who consorted with Jews freely generalized about "*the* Jews," and permitted themselves an occasional anti-Semitic remark. This was true, as I have shown, even of Theodor Fontane. And Stefan George, though he valued his Jewish disciples and refused to sacrifice them to importunate anti-Semites, thought Jews to be somehow "a different kind of people." He "never allowed them," he told Ernst Robert Curtius in 1911, "to be in the majority," either in his company or in his *Jahrbuch*.[96] Was the German Jew's self-definition as a German, then, nothing more than a degrading infatuation?

Historians are always enjoined to discard present passions in understanding past events. We know how difficult the demand is on all occasions; the historian of modern German Jewry finds it almost impossible to obey. He must face his deepest feelings

96. Curtius, "Stefan George in Conversation," *Essays on European Literature*, 124.

before he can discipline them. The insistent questions that I have raised resound more loudly as we contemplate the fate of German-Jewish writers, of poets, playwrights, novelists. For the havoc that the Nazis made among them was far greater than that among other German Jews. I speak not about the toll at Bergen-Belsen or Auschwitz, for there, and in other death factories, murders were committed with dreadful impartiality; the list of those who died there was compiled by the hand of accident, of sheer bad luck. The Nazis swept up those who had not found a place of safety: Arno Nadel, the metaphysical poet, and Arthur Silbergleit, the lyrical poet, who both died in Auschwitz in 1943, and others—those I mentioned before and those that readers can supply. There was nothing uncommon about this way to death; physicians, lawyers, housewives, schoolboys went the same way. When the Nazis murdered Erich Mühsam, radical poet and journalist, in the concentration camp Oranienburg in 1934, they strangled him not as a poet but as a political figure. And when they took the hapless Jakob van Hoddis from his insane asylum, they were simply adding another statistic to the Final Solution. But German-Jewish writers, in company with their friends from Vienna and Prague, were decimated because they did the work of the butcher themselves. The list of suicides is long and commands attention: Kurt Tucholsky, in Sweden, in 1935; Ernst Toller, in a New York hotel room, in 1939; Ernst Weiss, in Paris, in June 1940; Walter Hasenclever, in a French internment camp, on the eve of rescue, in June 1940; Walter Benjamin, on the Spanish frontier, in September 1940; Carl Einstein, in Paris, in July 1941; Stefan Zweig, in Brazil, in 1942; Alfred Wolfenstein, in Paris, early in 1945. Were not the roots of the murderous disease that killed them well exposed half a century before?

Survivors should have the decency to refrain from supplying the easy answers with which they so often assuage their guilt for surviving. Much has become clear since 1945 that was by no means clear in 1935, and seemed inconceivable in 1895. The half-century from 1888 to 1938, from the accession of Wilhelm II to the staging of the *Kristallnacht,* was a very great distance; the road to hell was long, with many and unpredictable stages. The first World War itself made an enormous difference. At the front, familiarity brought suspicion and separation, not brotherhood; at home, failures in battle or fraud among suppliers were often put to the account of Jewish saboteurs and profiteers. The desperate years between 1914 and 1918 converted German Jews from an easy confidence as German citizens of the Jewish faith to a defiant Zionism, to self-imposed social isolation, and more often, to sheer confusion and disheartened aimlessness. Albert Einstein was only the most famous among Germany's Jews to discover his Jewishness after 1918. Jakob Wassermann's autobiography of 1921, *Mein Weg als Deutscher und Jude*, which I have quoted before, is more eloquent, more pathetic, than other self-searching revelations of these years, but it reflected a widespread mood, especially among those who had come to maturity in the Empire. Some of its younger readers found Wassermann's confession less tragic than depressing; it read to them like the desperate testament of "an older generation," hurt to the heart at not being fully accepted.[97] The response is significant: Wassermann was being criticized for wanting too passionately to be a German. But there is yet another point to be made about *Mein Weg als Deutscher und Jude*: if some of Germany's young Jews, inspirited by the rediscovery of Judaism, could not have written this book because they would have thought it undignified, Wassermann himself could not have written this cry of disappointment, of frustration and pain, only seven years before, because he would have thought it unnecessary.[98] After all, in August 1914, German Jews patriotically rushed to the colors, volunteering to fight and die in company with their gentile brethren in defense of German *Kultur* against English materialism, French decadence, and general encirclement. Among the signers of the notorious manifesto of ninety-three German intellectuals justifying the invasion of

97. See Krojanker, "Vorwort des Herausgebers," in his *Juden in der deutschen Literatur*, 12–13.

98. There is evidence in *Mein Weg* (see especially 45–55), that Wassermann pondered his problematic situation as German and Jew even before the war; but it was the events of that war, both in Germany and elsewhere, that brought his concern to the high point of public confession. For the shift of Jewish awareness during these years, see Eva G. Reichmann's splendid essay, "Der Bewusstseinswandel der deutschen Juden," in W. Mosse, *Deutsches Judentum*, 511–612, to which I can add very little here.

Belgium was Max Liebermann. In November 1918, Albert Ballin, the deposed Emperor's friend, committed suicide; Aby Warburg had his psychotic breakdown a month before, and while it is naive to attribute these events to a single and contemporaneous cause, Germany's humiliation and defeat played their part in the collapse of these two good Germans.

In fact, except among Zionists and truly cosmopolitan Socialists, the German Jew's sense of possessing German citizenship did not change, even into and through the 1940s. Else Lasker-Schüler was far from eccentric in fondly remembering her German friends in the midst of the second World War.[99] For most German Jews, wherever their exile, however much they had undergone, the Jewish-German symbiosis was not a mirage that had finally lifted but a reality that had been wantonly destroyed. They postulated two Germanies, one civilized and the other barbarian; Hitler's seizure of power had placed the latter in control, without therefore defining the former out of existence. Late in 1947, when Gustav Mayer, the aged German-Jewish historian of Socialism, sat down in London to write his autobiography, he professed that he could never return to the land of his fathers; he would never again feel at home in a country that had slaughtered six million coreligionists. But he added that he could not manage to think of himself as a pure Jew, or regard Palestine as his homeland. For that, he wrote, he carried "too much spiritual baggage." Uprooted as he felt from Germany, grateful as he felt to England, still, for his "emotional world, despite it all, home—die Heimat—was irreplaceable." The idea of the homeland was inextricably tied to "memories of one's family, abodes of one's youth, and one's mother tongue."[100] Most German Jews, even after the Holocaust, could adapt Goering's well-known comment about General Milch to their own situation: "It is up to me to decide who is a German."

These feelings, which even the Holocaust could not eradicate, had animated German Jews far more strongly in the decades before World War I. It is easy now to ridicule them for thinking

99. See above, 145.
100. Mayer, *Erinnerungen: Vom Journalisten zum Historiker der deutschen Arbeiterbewegung* (1949), 372, 374.

that if they behaved as Germans they would be treated as Germans—easy, but unhistorical in the extreme. However self-deluded it may now appear, in the 1890s this was a reasonable reading of their situation. I have already noted that the auguries in those years were favorable; political anti-Semitism was on the decline. In fact, when German Jews worried over truly vicious anti-Semitism in the Wilhelminian epoch, they looked to the Dreyfus case in France, and the pogroms in Eastern Europe. It is easy, also, to argue that the palpable decay of German liberalism should have been a warning to Germany's Jews, for it is where liberalism is strong that Jews are safe. But in fact the decline of German liberalism coincided with the prosperity of the Wilhelminian period and the expansion of Jewish possibilities. Nor were all German Jews necessarily liberals; while many of them lyrically celebrated the cosmopolitanism of Kant and identified themselves with philosophies preaching peace and brotherhood, there were many others among them who, in contrast, adopted the nationalism, even the chauvinism, of their non-Jewish neighbors. National liberalism, that cluster of ideas and policies which increasingly symbolized Germany for its neighbors—an active state, a powerful army, a militant foreign policy—did not appeal to German gentiles alone. For every Jewish Socialist, there was a Jewish conservative; the few Jews who secured leading posts in the new Empire were, by and large, enthusiastic—and not merely opportunistic—admirers of Bismarck. Some of them even found themselves to Bismarck's right.[101] When German Jews in responsible positions, as respected publicists or influential industrialists, spoke about Germany's place among nations, they said, "we," not "they." How else could they have spoken of their country?

Even the offensive treatment of Jews, familiar and frequent as it was, occurred in an atmosphere that made it seem a survival for Germans to overcome, not a portent for Jews to fear. The correspondence of Moritz Lazarus is punctuated with cordial letters to, and from, Protestant and Catholic acquaintances; in the midst of his travail over his academic career and in his controversies

101. Jacob Toury's excellent monograph, *Die politischen Orientierungen der Juden in Deutschland, von Jena bis Weimar* (1966), especially sections C to G, says the essential.

with anti-Semitic intellectuals he drew encouragement from his friendly exchanges with the theologian Ignaz von Döllinger, the painter Adolf von Menzel, and numerous other, less famous gentiles. Recalling her early life with Ernst Cassirer, his widow Toni Cassirer noted that around the turn of the century, when her husband first thought of applying for a university position, anti-Semitism was a known barrier. But he and other Jews like him thought this a fact of limited significance—it was not, Frau Cassirer adds, true in the arts—and a mere atavism that a great civilization like the German was likely to outgrow.[102] Anti-Semitism seemed, as I have said, a disease to which some Germans were susceptible, and others not—a disease, moreover, to which Germans seemed less susceptible than Russians or even Frenchmen.

The slights that many German Jews experienced, then, carried far less weight than the German culture in which most of them moved as their own element. Ernst Cassirer represents this Germanness, at once comfortable and passionate, to perfection. As his widow was later to recall, Mozart was his "true element"; he knew the chamber works, the symphonies, the operas by heart. They were, in her words, "the air he breathed." Precisely like Max Liebermann, Ernst Cassirer "counted among his friends as many non-Jews as Jews, and it never occurred to him to inquire into the origins of anyone." As a little boy, he had explored his grandfather's library and enjoyed his father's habit of quoting tags from the German classics. And in 1906, he had a memorable experience. He and his wife were making a pilgrimage to Goethe's house in Weimar and noticed that one of the guards was staring at him. Asked why, the guard confessed that seeing the handsome, tall, blond visitor before him, he had thought for a time that Goethe himself had come back to life. Nothing ever delighted Ernst Cassirer more than this—delighted, but scarcely surprised him. Whatever hindsight might detect, this was the world in which Germany's Jews, by and large, lived comfortably enough. It was the world in which the *Allgemeine Zeitung des Judenthums*, in its fifty-fourth year in 1890, could advertise itself

102. Toni Cassirer, *Aus meinem Leben mit Ernst Cassirer* (1950), 27–28, and see above, 15.

as a "spiritual gathering point for all cultivated Jews," a "*German* organ, standing faithfully by *Emperor* and *Reich*," with its italics most emphatically in the original.[103] And so when, at the outbreak of war, Emperor Wilhelm II made his famous remark disclaiming all further partisan and internecine conflict, and professing to see around him Germans only—"*Ich kenne nur noch Deutsche*"—German Jews naturally applied this bracing profession to themselves. They were wrong. But they had good reason to believe that they were right.

103. T. Cassirer, *Ernst Cassirer*, 21, 27–28, 68–69. The Jewish periodical, published by the Mosse Verlag, and costing 3 DM a quarter, thus advertised itself in the *Münchener Neueste Nachrichten*, March 18, 1890, No. 129, p. 4.

III

THE BERLIN-JEWISH SPIRIT
A Dogma in Search of Some Doubts

The Wilhelminian decades were, then, up to the outbreak of war, the high point in the arc of German-Jewish hope. Whatever the residual pockets of anti-Semitism, however persistent anti-Jewish prejudices in business and society, assimilation appeared to be proceeding. "The interweaving of Jewish existence with the German environment," judges Robert Weltsch, "reached, in those years, a culmination."[1] There were, even before 1914, some skeptics among Jews and gentiles alike, but most observers, as we have seen, thought the chances for Jewish integration into German culture to be highly favorable. Today, our eyes sharpened by the Holocaust, we see the symptoms of underlying Jew-hatred far more plainly; we have learned to attend less to gross caricatures in humor magazines than to the subterranean currents of potential disaster: to the smoldering, usually inarticulate resentment of many Germans against Jewish claims to speak for the German people, and the widespread readiness to project upon Jews whatever seemed most unpalatable in one's world, requiring only some catastrophe to translate itself into active anti-Semitism.[2] The first World War, with its anxie-

1. "Die schleichende Krise der jüdischen Identität—Ein Nachwort," in Werner E. Mosse, ed. in cooperation with Arnold Paucker, *Juden im Wilhelminischen Deutschland* (1976), 689.
2. I here closely follow the careful exposition by Werner Jochmann, "Struktur und Funktion des deutschen Antisemitismus," in W. Mosse, ed., *Juden im Wilhelminischen Deutschland*, 389–477.

ties, its deprivations and irreparable losses, was such a catastrophe; the Weimar Republic proved to be another. Yet the latent is, of course, by definition, the hidden, resistant to detection by its contemporaries. And during the Empire, really devastating Jew-hatred was, by and large, latent. To reproach Germany's Jews of that epoch with failing to see what was, after all, scarcely visible or wholly invisible is an exercise in the unhistorical.

That the German-Jewish symbiosis was tenuous at best received almost daily confirmation in the heady and troubling years of the Weimar Republic. Yet even then, the evidence remained ambiguous and the prognosis uncertain: German Jews continued to make contributions to German culture, to have non-Jewish friends and marry non-Jewish partners. Life for the German Jew was problematic but not hopeless; significantly enough, Zionism, the most radical way out of the German dilemma, found, right down to the accession of the Nazis and even beyond, only limited response. And there was one city, the great metropolis, Berlin, in which the symbiosis, though tense and imperiled, seemed to hold. Berlin was the great showplace and the supreme testing ground.

1. THE DOMAIN OF THE JEWS

In 1928, the Ullstein Verlag launched a new afternoon newspaper, called *Tempo*. It was a tabloid, racy in tone, visual in appeal, designed to please the Berliner who ran as he read. Instantly it acquired a nickname: "Die jüdische Hast"—Jewish haste or, better perhaps, Jewish nervousness. Unfortunately but understandably, we do not know the identity of the Berlin wit who baptized the newspaper thus. Was it a Jew, offering an open-eyed, half-derisive, half-affectionate self-appraisal that it would be humorless to call self-hatred? Possibly. Whoever it was, the nickname seems to say something apt about Berlin, about its Jews, and about the two together.

But what? Berlin and the Jews have long been linked, in the minds of the informed and the ignorant alike. Long before

Tempo was conceived, when Berlin was still an Imperial and not yet a republican capital, Theodor Fontane, local historian and loyal Berliner in addition to being a famous novelist and respected drama critic, saw the Jewish element as a distinctive, indelible, and important part of the characteristic Berlin style. That style, he wrote, was a felicitous blend of several ingredients, one of which was the "Berlin-Jewish spirit" that emerged among the educated middle strata of the city in the age of the *Aufklärung*. It was a spirit of "negation, criticism, practical jokes—*Schabernack*—and—once in a while, a witticism."[3] Since Fontane, the idea of a Berlin-Jewish symbiosis has become an article of faith, the only dogma that Jews, philo-Semites, and anti-Semites of all descriptions hold in common. Jews, it is said, making themselves at home in Berlin, transformed it, and imprinted upon it something of their rootlessness, their restlessness, their alienation from soil and tradition, their pervasive disrespect for authority, their mordant wit. The poet Gottfried Benn, hardly a sympathetic witness, said of the Jews in Berlin: "The overflowing plenty of stimuli, of artistic, scientific, commercial improvisations which placed the Berlin of 1918 to 1933 in the class of Paris, stemmed for the most part from the talents of this sector of the population, its international connections, its sensitive restlessness, and above all its dead-certain—*totsichere*—instinct for quality."[4] And in 1938, a Nazi writer named Tüdel Weller put it succinctly: "Berlin is the domain of the Jews."[5]

3. "Die Märker und das Berlinertum: Ein kulturhistorisches Problem," *Gesammelte Werke*, Second Series, IX (n.d., [1908]), 295–312. By now this is part of the Berlin mythology. Hans Ostwald, author of numerous affectionate anecdotal collections, puts the matter simply: "Ja, die Juden haben vielleicht einen grösseren Einfluss auf das Berlinertum ausgeübt als man ahnt." (*Der Urberliner in Witz, Humor and Anekdote* [n.d.], 14.) Amid the vast literature on Berlin, I want to single out Hans Herzfeld, ed., *Berlin und die Provinz Brandenburg im 19. und 20. Jahrhundert* (1968) and the splendid, already dated *Berlin-Bibliographie* (*bis* 1960), ed. Hans Zopf and Gerd Heinrich (1965).

4. "Doppelleben," *Gesammelte Werke*, IV (1961), 73.

5. Quoted in George L. Mosse, *The Crisis of German Ideology* (1964), 23. This was scarcely a new idea. On March 27, 1860, Hermann Orges, an editor of the *Allgemeine Zeitung*, wrote to the liberal politician Rudolf von Bennigsen: Berlin "is merely critical, negative . . . it will never generate a

The coupling of Jews with Berlin had at least some basis in reality. In Germany Jews clustered in cities, and the larger the city the denser the cluster. In the 1920s, while professing Jews made up less than 1 percent of the German population, more than 4 percent of all Berliners were professing Jews; and if we add those men and women of Jewish ancestry who had either converted to Christianity or left the Jewish community to become Dissidents, the share of Jews in the Berlin population would be even larger. For their own part, Germany's Jews saw Berlin as headquarters: after all one-third of them—nearly 200,000, and many of these prominent, even famous—lived there.

These bare numbers tell only part of the story. Berlin's Jews were more conspicuous than they were numerous. From 1880 on, a rising proportion of Berlin's Jews were foreign born; more and more of them were refugees from pogroms in Russia or misery in Austria-Hungary—*Ostjuden*, the target of hostility by gentiles and embarrassed derision by German-born Jews. In 1880, fewer than 3,000 of Berlin's 50,000 Jews—5.5 percent—were *Ostjuden*. By 1900, their number had risen to 11,000 out of 92,000—12.6 percent; by 1925, they were 43,000 out of 172,000, or 25.4 percent.[6] This change in the ethnic contours of the Berlin Jewish population aroused much comment; it was one element in its high visibility to which I shall return. But it was not the only element. In fact, Berlin-born or German-born Jews were just as conspicuous as the *Ostjuden*, for out of all proportion to their numbers they were concentrated in professions that brought them to public attention, and gave them a large clientele. Many of the publishing giants were located in Berlin and the biggest of these, Ullstein and Mosse, were owned by Jewish families. So were such distinguished publishing houses as Samuel Fischer's. Many of the journalists who wrote for their newspapers, many of the editors who edited their magazines, many of the authors who wrote their books, were Jews as well. A census of drama critics, editorial writers, even sports columnists, reveals a high percent-

---

great idea. . . . Add to this, that it is being Jewified—*verjüdelt*—more and more." Quoted in Adolf Rapp, *Grossdeutsch–Kleindeutsch* (1922), 178.
6. Compiled from tables in S. Adler-Rudel's valuable study *Ostjuden in Deutschland, 1880–1940* (1959), 164–65.

age of Jews in these journalistic subcultures. Only a few years ago the Berlin journalist Walther Kiaulehn, not himself a Jew, entitled an article on the Berlin drama critics of the 1920s quite simply, "Berlin Criticism was Jewish," and counted two non-Jews out of thirteen among the leading drama reviewers in the city.[7] In addition, the great Berlin department stores, Kaufhaus des Westens, Tietz, Wertheim, the targets of so much animosity, were owned by Jews. The Jews were strongly represented in the "public" professions—they were doctors, dentists, bankers, lawyers, commercial travelers. Even poor Jews were public figures, for many of them were peddlers. Other, literally, "style-setting" industries, were in the same situation: the share of Jews in the men's and ladies' garment industry—*Konfektion*—was notoriously large, almost overwhelming.

The Jews' prominence in Berlin has a long and respectable history, going back at least to Moses Mendelssohn. In the decades of the Berlin salons, early in the nineteenth century, Jews made their contributions to the life of Berlin in a distinctive way. Jewish salons, especially those over which women presided, became favorite centers of good talk, quotable wit, original thinking. But these contributions were not then, nor did they become later, in any special way Jewish. That Berlin, and certain professions, should be congenial to Jews is readily explicable, and has often been explained. Berlin was a world city, hospitable to the stranger; it was so welcoming not only because it gave its residents conspicuousness, but also because it allowed them to disappear. For both internal and external reasons, Jews had for centuries trained themselves for the commercial and intellectual life that found its proper soil in Berlin. Debarred from owning land, kept out of civil service positions, the army and the universities, reminded of their pariahhood by persistent discrimination and periodic persecutions, Jews lived where and how they could. The stream of Jewish intelligence ran within banks that others had made for it. Not nature, not race, not even religion, but history —and history made by non-Jews—determined the course of Jew-

7. "Die Berliner Kritik war jüdisch," in Thilo Koch, ed., *Porträts deutsch-jüdischer Geistesgeschichte* (1961), 205–27.

ish life. It was not an inborn love of money or of glittering things that brought the diamond trade to the attention of the Jews: diamonds were portable, and for marginal men like the Jews, at best tolerated guests, at worst hounded victims, mobility—quite literally—was at a premium. Berlin was the city where mobile men came to rest. Berliners, the familiar cliché had it, are from Breslau, and many Jews were from Breslau, and beyond. The heavy impact of Jews on Berlin, then, is undeniable. What remains in question is whether that impact was "Jewish."

My recital is still incomplete. Everyone understood—everyone, philo-Semite and anti-Semite alike—that even those former Jews who had repudiated Judaism by religious conversion to Christianity, or legal disaffiliation from the Jewish community, were still somehow Jews: it never occurred to anyone to treat radicals like Karl Marx or the conservative legal theoretician Friedrich Julius Stahl as non-Jews.[8] Berlin was full of Jewish agnostics, Jewish atheists, Jewish Catholics, and Jewish Lutherans. Indeed, these non-Jewish Jews were, if anything, more conspicuous than those who held, no matter how tepidly, to their ancient label, for they labored under the added reproach of cowardice, social climbing, secret service in a world-wide conspiracy—in a word: self-seeking mimicry. By the nature of things, these non-Jewish Jews were among the most prominent figures on the Berlin intellectual landscape: Maximilian Harden and Kurt Tucholsky were only among the best known of these converts.[9] Thus, the presence of

8. See Istvan Deak, *Weimar Germany's Left-Wing Intellectuals: A Political History of the Weltbühne and Its Circle* (1968), 24. And see Deak's survey, 24–29.

9. How problematic the question of Jewish converts is can be demonstrated from the career of Franz Werfel. His late writings invite the widespread impression that Werfel did indeed become a Christian. I confess that I shared in this impression, but a letter from Werfel's widow Alma Mahler-Werfel insists that it is false.

The late Mrs. Margaret T. Muehsam of the Leo Baeck Institute, New York, called my attention to such a letter in the Chaim Bloch Collection, archives of the LBI. Mrs. Mahler-Werfel writes that "Franz Werfel war weder Zionist noch Nationaljude—weder hat er den katholischen Glauben angenommen noch sich 'als Jude katholischen Glaubens' ausgegeben. Er hat

the Jew in Berlin was even more of an emotional than a physical reality.

Jews, God knows, can do without the anti-Semite, and in one respect it is also true that the anti-Semite can do without Jews: their actual conduct has little bearing on his opinions of them.[10] Jew-hatred, we know, is normally unrelated to actual experiences which do little, if anything, to dissolve an irrational conviction; prejudice is not accessible to evidence—that is what a prejudice is. The misconduct of individual Jews serves only as welcome confirmation of Jewish iniquity, while "good" Jews can be rationalized away as exceptions or as exceptionally clever. Of course the very conviction that Berlin was a Jewish city made a difference to the way the city was perceived and experienced: it is the nature of men's mental sets to see that which they seek. All in all, then, in imagination, in distortion, in reality, the Jew was woven into the very texture of Berlin, and made part—significant part— of its style.

These facts, figures, and fantasies are all thoroughly familiar. But familiarity is not always a good thing: often it impedes, with its very forcefulness, objective inquiry into what may be a myth. What I have outlined is dogma, but it is dogma in need of some doubts.

---

weder in Frankreich noch sonstwo die Taufe erhalten. Er hat als guter Jude gelebt und ist als guter Jude gestorben."

The letter is dated March 20, 1958, and Mrs. Mahler closes it with her statement that she would be thankful if the addressee, Rabbi Chaim Bloch, would contribute to the endeavor "dass diese immer wieder auftauchenden Gerüchte, die jeder Grundlage entbehren, endlich aufhören."

10. I say "in one respect," for in another respect—that the anti-Semite would be happy to eliminate all Jews from the world—the record is far from clear. It seems, indeed, that the anti-Semite needs the Jew; all Jews gone, on whom would he project his self-loathing, and practice his aggression? Freud makes this point in a famous sarcastic passage on aggression in his *Civilization and Its Discontents*: "The Jewish people, scattered everywhere, has in this way rendered most commendable services to their host cultures"—by acting as scapegoats (S.E., XXI, 114; G.W.. XIV, 474).

To begin with, what of the Berlin spirit itself? The essayist, the cartoonist, and the novelist drawing their quick character sketches may, indeed must, generalize with impunity. Their portrait of the "typical" Berliner is one that we all recognize: the Berliner is quick-witted—*schlagfertig*, sentimental about his lack of sentimentality, a born deflater of pomposity, self-importance, empty grandeur. He coins nicknames for everything, most tellingly for the bombastic—witness his pitiless characterizations of the *Siegesallee* and similar sculptural or architectural monstrosities that Emperor Wilhelm II inflicted on the Berlin landscape. He is serious about his humor and proud of it; no other city, I think, produces and sells so many collections of local humor as Berlin. Surrounded, especially during the Empire, by Prussian garrisons, deluged with colorful uniforms and solemn parades, the Berliner takes the tall, self-conscious, stupid, conceited Junker clotheshorse as an object for his entertainment and target for his wit. These tin-soldiers are not heroes for the Berliner: his hero is the anti-hero—a comic figure like Nante, that mythical but living *Eckensteher* who finds all effort, except that of making jokes, too much for him. Nante was the happy invention of the journalist Adolf Glassbrenner around 1840, but his spirit lingered; as late as 1890 he appeared to Theodor Fontane as the "panacea" with which Berliners could ward off any threats of a militarist regime. The Berliner's very language—so much imitated and so hard to imitate—with its peculiar grammar and its emphatic, unique pattern of pronunciation, seems designed for criticism, for good-natured but pointed irreverence. And in the making of this Berlin style, the Jew has played his part: Jewish humor, with its peculiar mixture of self-criticism and self-respect, was wholly incorporated into Berlin folklore, and Yiddish words, pronounced in impeccably German fashion, are wholly at home in the Berliner's vocabulary.[11]

We all recognize this portrait, I say, but what validity can it claim? Is it anything more than the stock Frenchman with his beret, his thin moustache, his frivolity, and his lecherousness?

11. For an amusing and dependable study of Berlin speech, including its Jewish component, see Walther Kiaulehn, editor and revisor of Hans Meyer, *Der Richtige Berliner in Wörtern and Redensarten* (1965).

The question of generalizations bedevils every responsible historian: he cannot live without them, but he cannot live with them in any comfort. How does one measure a spirit? Berlin had its myth-makers, its humorless men, its fastidious *Germanisten* who would never dream of uttering such Jewish-Berlin words as *shikse* or *risches*. Perhaps Berlin's resistance to the Nazis—unsuccessful in the end, but for years a source of disgust and despair to Goebbels—might be taken as the anti-authoritarian Berlin spirit in action. Or was that simply effective party discipline in Berlin's working-class districts, both Communist and Social Democratic, humor or no humor?[12]

Even if we accept something we call the Berlin spirit, a further question remains: what of its Jewish component? The penetration of Yiddish and Hebrew words, and Jewish jokes, into Berlin speech is easy to demonstrate but hard to evaluate. After all, does the presence of French words in that same speech—words like *genre* and *milieu*, pronounced, like other loan words, in the German way—tell us much about the place of French culture in Berlin life? Moreover, much of the Berlin spirit was a synthetic product: Berlin was sprinkled with cabarets, with their irreverent political chansons and their evocations of the Berliner *Schnodd-*

12. The serious historian is bound to become a little impatient with these generalizations. Thus—to cite only two—Hans Ostwald: "Det is dem Berliner sein Fall! Witz, Humor und Anekdote. Er ist nicht für Traurigkeit . . . Der Berliner hat eben nicht nur den berühmten hellen und offenen Kopf. Er kann nicht nur Witze machen, Witze, wie sie zwischen Pankow und Potsdam üblich sind. Er hat auch das, was ihm so oft bestritten wird, was scheinbar zu seinen grosschnäuzigen, schnoddrigen Redensarten und zu seiner angeblichen Krakehlsucht nicht stimmt—er hat auch Humor." Etc. etc. (*Der Urberliner*, 6). And more recently, Wolfgang Schadewaldt, praising this Berlin (but forgetting its Jews, and its resistance to Hitler), thinks he can generalize: "Die Helligkeit des Berliner Geistes, seine Weltoffenheit, Beweglichkeit, ist bekannt genug. Doch wäre mein Lob nicht vollständig, wenn ich nicht aus eigenster vielfacher Kenntnis auch dies hier anschlösse, dass der Berliner bei allem praktischen Sinn, allem auf das Konkrete gerichtetem Realismus auch das hochhält, was er Gemüt oder in berlinischer Lautierung 'Jemüt' nennt." "Berlin und die Berliner," in a cycle of five lectures, *Berliner Geist* (1963), 33. Surely all this is not purely imaginary, "there is something in it," and yet—the inclination that drives even serious scholars to offer such sweeping judgments is worth investigating.

rigkeit: Berlin was headquarters for the satirical press and of leading cartoonists like Heinrich Zille, the Rembrandt of the Berlin proletariat, and of Walter Trier, gentle satirist and illustrator of famous children's books. But was much of this not simply the outpouring of a commercial dream factory, manufacturing a myth that could be exploited, as remote from reality as the blue in the Blue Danube and the gaiety in Strauss's Vienna?

Yet, as Freud has taught us to recognize, fantasies too are realities of a sort; they mirror men's aspirations even if they distort their real situations. For novelists, playwrights, actors, film-makers, journalists, Berlin represented liberation, an escape from deadly provincialism. The Berlin climate, both intellectual and physical, was enormously bracing to them; it was demanding and exhilarating at the same time, the nemesis of stodginess, an invitation to freedom. Berlin of the 1920s, as Carl Zuckmayer remembered it, was "worth more than a mass." It ate up talents and rewarded them; it was like a highly desirable woman—arrogant yet everyone's dream. "Berlin tasted of the future and that is why we gladly took the crap and the coldness."[13] Indeed even those who hated Berlin testified to this spirit. In his *Rembrandt als Erzieher*, August Julius Langbehn mixed a doctrinaire's anti-Semitism with declarations of hatred for Berlin. Huge metropolitan centers, he wrote, consume but do not produce culture; it is against the "Berlin spirit—*Geist*" that the "pure German spirit" must protest and rise up.[14] Indeed, what is explicit in Langbehn—the conjunction of anti-urbanism and anti-Semitism—is implicit in later writers who, consciously or not, conflate Berlin and the Jew into a single emotion-laden image.

The Berlin-Jewish spirit thus emerges as a distinct political and intellectual force in the great debate between Modernism and tribal—*völkisch*—primitivism. And it made up part of the Berliner's self-definition, and may thus claim a certain reality.

But, once again, what of the share of Jewishness in that spirit? What is typically "Jewish" anyway? Is it the trading mentality—

---

13. *Als Wär's ein Stück von mir* (1966), 314. I have used this passage before, in my *Weimar Culture: The Outsider as Insider* (1968), 132.

14. See Klaus Müller-Dyes, "Das literarische Leben, 1850–1933," in Herzfeld, ed., *Berlin und die Provinz Brandenburg*, 703.

the death-grip on credit, the talent for cheating, the inclination to make usury into a fine art? The portrait of the Jew as trader was canonized in Werner Sombart's *Die Juden und der Kapitalismus*. But it is irrelevant here: after all, far too many other national and ethnic groups shared this concern for profit to make it a distinctively Jewish trait; one need only read Emperor Wilhelm II's disquisitions on Germany's need for a place in the sun to see the trading mentality displayed at its most rabid in the most *Ur-German* quarters.

I submit, then, that the obstacles in the path of determining "the characteristic Jewish mentality" are practically insurmountable. I have no intention of denying the existence or minimizing the significance of the Jewish presence in Berlin; denial is a childlike retreat to which all too many Berlin Jews resorted in dangerous times. I am questioning what we have too long taken for granted for the sake not of denial, but of precision. And precision is just what is lacking in these identifications. The persistent failure to identify Jews correctly—an abiding trait of anti-Semitic propaganda—is instructive in this context. The right-wing Hugenberg press, for example, celebrated Helene Mayer, the Olympic fencing champion of 1928, as a "typical Aryan girl," when, in fact, she was half Jewish. Again, the Heidelberg professor Friedrich Gundolf, Stefan George's closest disciple, a Jew whose family name had been Gundelfinger, was hailed by the same right-wing press as a "German genius."[15] Such anti-Semitic handbooks as Theodor Fritsch's *Handbuch der Judenfrage* of 1937 and Adolf Bartels' earlier *Jüdische Herkunft und Literaturwissenschaft* of 1926 listed as Jews the Communist Willi Münzenberg, the Social Democrat Karl Liebknecht, the novelists Thomas and Heinrich Mann, the playwright Bertolt Brecht, and many others who were not Jews at all, though some of them had Jewish wives.[16] Ambitious theoretical attempts to discover and define the Jewish spirit in literature suffered shipwreck as well, and in significant ways. In his widely read and highly regarded *Literaturgeschichte der deutschen Stämme und Landschaften* which just predates the

15. For both, see Arnold Paucker, "Der jüdische Abwehrkampf," in Werner E. Mosse, ed., *Entscheidungsjahr 1932* (1965), 434–35.
16. See Deak, *Weimar Germany's Left-Wing Intellectuals*, 28n.

Nazi dictatorship, Josef Nadler offers as the three most representative writers of the time Rudolf Borchardt, Hugo von Hofmannsthal, and Rainer Maria Rilke. Borchardt, from Königsberg, translator of Dante and celebrant of medieval German language, is, to
Nadler, the typical *Ostpreusse:* "Borchardt's inner structure is
spiritually East German." Hofmannsthal, Nadler tells us, is connected through his father's family with the "Sudeten-region" and
through his mother's side with Italian aristocracy. It is through
Hofmannsthal that "Vienna awakens to its own proper essence."
In contrast, Rilke is the essence of Prague art, which is "lovely
and deep, and dignified German-Jewish literature." Nadler de-
clares himself unable to believe in the "Corinthian nobility" of
which Rilke liked to boast; "we believe in the drops of Slavic
blood, even if they were few, and we believe in his Jewish mother,
of whom there are reports." Nothing could have been more unfortunate. Borchardt was Jewish; Hofmannsthal part-Jewish. Only
Rilke, that typical, quintessential representative of the Prague-
Jewish symbiosis, was wholly and purely "Aryan."[17]

Such intellectual disasters raise troublesome questions about
national or ethnic character. Would someone attending Leopold
Jessner's Expressionist production of Schiller's *Wilhelm Tell* or
Max Reinhardt's extravagant production of Shakespeare's *Midsummer Night's Dream*; watching Elisabeth Bergner do *Maria
Stuart* or Fritz Kortner do *Hamlet*; listening to Bruno Walter's
interpretation of Beethoven's Ninth Symphony or Paul Dessau's
interpretation of his own compositions, to Fritz Kreisler play the
violin or Artur Schnabel play the piano; reading Siegfried Treb-
itsch's translations of Shaw or Alfred Wolfenstein's translations
of Shelley suspect in any way that these artists and writers were
Jewish? Was that influential left-wing journal, *Die Weltbühne*,
more "Jewish" under its first editor, Siegfried Jacobsohn, than it
became under its second editor, Carl von Ossietzky? Was Brecht-
Weill's phenomenally successful *Dreigroschenoper* Jewish in its

17. Josef Nadler, *Literaturgeschichte der deutschen Stämme und Landschaften,* IV, *Der deutsche Staat (1814–1914)* (1928), 731, 923, 927, 891.
My attention was drawn to these passages by Eva G. Reichmann, "Dis-
kussionen über die Judenfrage, 1930–1932," in *Entscheidungsjahr 1932,*
521–22.

music but not in its libretto? Could one tell in any way, by read-ing his satirical sketches and his love-poems to Berlin, that Kurt Tucholsky was a Jew who had gone over to Lutheranism? Or, for that matter, would Tietz "in the hands" of gentiles have charged different prices, stocked different merchandise, offered wares in a different manner? The very questions—rhetorical questions I have asked before but find important enough to ask again—betray the absurdity of the inquiry. Does Jewishness lead to irresponsibility or tenacity, to vulgarity or refinement? If Max Liebermann, as we know, began as an aesthetic radical, he ended up as an aesthetic conservative.[18] If Max Reinhardt had a streak of cheapness in his magic which those in search of incriminating clues found "typi-cally Jewish," that streak was lacking in Otto Brahm, another Jew, who dominated the Berlin stage in the 1890s.[19] Just as there was no Jewish way to cut furs, there was no Jewish way to paint portraits, play Beethoven, produce Ibsen, or fence in the Olym-pics.[20]

2. AN INTERMITTENT CIVIL WAR

It is pathetic to see stereotyped thinking infecting many Jews as well. There were Jews in Berlin certain they could recognize a Jew—any Jew—by a certain appearance, a certain way of speak-

18. See above, 107–8.
19. See above, 157.
20. Nor, it seems, was there a recognizable Jewish way of selling crystal and china. In the Berlin of the mid-1930s, my father ran a sales agency with a gentile partner named Willy Pelz. My father was welcome every-where: with his handsome gray hair combed back in the traditional Goethean manner, his stocky but handsome appearance, his fine hands, his neutral name—Moritz Fröhlich—and his solid reputation for honest dealings, he had many loyal friends. In contrast, Pelz, obese, coarse, greasy, with unpre-possessing curly hair and curved nose, was far less popular. As the Nazis' grip tightened on all details of life, more than one customer told my father: "Why don't you get rid of that Jew Pelz?" But in late 1938, when the Nazi regime legalized and encouraged such illegality, the pure Aryan Pelz expelled my father from the profitable partnership without a penny's com-pensation. That much for racial characteristics.

ing, by all sorts of subtle, elusive signs. This conviction contributed to Jewish mistakes about their fellow-men, mistakes which were doubtless far less vicious in intention and unfortunate in consequences than the mistakes that anti-Semites made, though they were culturally quite as symptomatic. Just as Nazi manuals listed as "typical Jews" many who were in fact "pure Aryans," so Jewish manuals claimed as Jews many who had no right to that designation.[21] Late in the nineteenth century, Heinrich von Treitschke had called on his "Israelitic fellow-citizens" to "become Germans, to feel simply and plainly as Germans," without necessarily abandoning "their faith and their ancient sacred memories which are venerable to us all." This idea, that Jews must behave in a less "Jewish" way, was widely held in Berlin's Jewish circles in the 1920s. In addition to a fundamental split among Jews in Berlin it suggests a solemn search for total assimilation or, rather, the dissolution of "Jewishness" into a kind of "Germanness." This was not the self-hatred of Jews who changed their names and had their noses straightened; it was the almost desperate attempt to assert a German feeling that was genuine enough. Max Liebermann, a Berlin original if there ever was one, the subject of many delicious stories, worried over the bad reputation that the misconduct of one Jew might bring on all Jews. "Every wave of anti-Semitism," his friend, the art critic Max Osborn, reports, "only strengthened within him the obstinate pride in his ancestry. He was even a strict Jew, certainly not in a religious sense, but in this: that he watched jealously and suspiciously to see that no Jew sin against his race and religion by unworthy conduct and thus burden himself with heavy guilt for Jewry as a whole. Sometimes he would call to his atelier people of whom he had heard something unfavorable, to give them a piece of his mind. . . . He grew angry when a Jew became all too prominent because he expected, with good reason, some adverse reaction to follow." He recalled that he had warned his distant cousin Walther Rathenau not to accept a cabinet post—though, when Osborn reminded him that he, Liebermann, had accepted appointment as president of the Academy of Arts, Liebermann laughed and

21. See Deak, *Weimar Germany's Left-Wing Intellectuals*, 28n.

pleaded human nature.[22] With Liebermann, at least, this kind of caution was tempered by humor.

Others were more solemn than he. The Berlin attorney Adolf Asch recalled a saying that he had heard from Ludwig Holländer, executive director of that significantly named *Centralverein deutscher Staatsbürger jüdischen Glaubens*: "Step-children must be doubly good—*Stiefkinder müssen doppelt artig sein*."[23] Acting on this maxim, and incensed by slanders against Jewish "shirking" in the great World War, Asch joined other Jewish war veterans to found the *Reichsbund jüdischer Frontsoldaten* in the early 1920s. This organization collected and disseminated statistics which showed that the share of German Jews who had died in the war was 12,000 out of 1,200,000—1 percent of the total, exactly proportional to the population. He was worried by that "small number of Jews" who were ostentatious parvenus—*Protzer*, and who were profiteering from the early post-war inflation: this small minority, he recalled, "gave, as usual, a welcome opportunity to anti-Semites, to make Jewry as a whole responsible." And so, in 1922, he became chairman of a new *Selbstzuchtorganisation*—a "self-discipline organization"—which tried to keep Jews out of the limelight. Its activities included issuing warnings to "coreligionists to guard the dignity customary before and after the divine services on the High Holidays, and especially to ask Jewish women to avoid all showy luxury in clothing and jewelry."[24]

No Jew can read Asch's autobiographical fragment without a pang of guilt or, at least, of recognition. For like all minorities, Jews too incorporated at least some of the prejudices and stereotypes of the dominant majority around them. What Jew has not cringed at what he regards as ostentatious behavior—loud voices, sharp clothing, flashing jewelry, sported by those who "look Jewish" in a theatre lobby, a restaurant, a bus? Is it not significant

22. Max Osborn, *Der Bunte Spiegel: Erinnerungen aus dem Kunst-, Kultur-, und Geistesleben der Jahre 1890 bis 1933* (1945), 70–77.

23. Mr. Arnold Paucker tells me that this saying was not unknown to the Empire, but it seems to have gained wider currency in the Republic.

24. Dr. Adolf Asch, "Die Inflationsjahre 1919–1923," 5–8; typescript prepared by the author in London around 1957, Archives of the LBI, New York.

that Treitschke's call to German Jews to become wholly German formed part of a diatribe against Eastern European Jews? "The number of Jews in Western Europe," Treitschke wrote, "is so small that they cannot exercise a perceptible influence on the national spirit; but across our Eastern frontiers there pushes, year after year, from the inexhaustible Polish cradle, a troop of ambitious, trouser-selling youths, whose children and children's children will some day dominate Germany's stock exchanges and newspapers." What Treitschke wanted to avoid was an "age of German-Jewish bastardized culture—*Mischkultur*,"[25] a culture, he thought, that would have a damaging effect on German spiritual life. Were Liebermann and Asch and other Berlin Jews, with their anxiety to present a good front, and avoid untoward publicity, so different from Treitschke? There can be no doubt: many of Berlin's most influential Jews wanted Jews in Berlin culture, but not a Berlin-Jewish culture.

The rather startling convergence between the ideas of a hard-nosed cultural nationalist like Treitschke and a civilized Jewish artist like Liebermann suggests an approach to an answer to my question. The very idea of a Berlin-Jewish spirit was ambivalent at its heart. Some, like Fontane, saw the Berlin-Jewish spirit as a source of vitality—a good thing; others, like Langbehn, saw it as a source of contamination—a bad thing. Peculiar though it seems, the most widely accepted portrait of the Jew in Berlin life was drawn by the most unlikely collaborators: German Jews and German anti-Semites.[26] It was, in large part, a malicious generalization of an unfair caricature, and the caricature was drawn from what was perceived to be the Eastern European immigrant Jew. The drawings in the *Stürmer*, depicting a short, paunchy, swarthy lecher, with improbable black curls, weak eyes, fat lips, and a big hooked nose, was only the most vicious form of this caricature.

25. For this and earlier passages from Treitschke, see Hans Rosenberg, *Grosse Depression und Bismarckzeit* (1967), 108–9.

26. For perceptive observations on the problem that *Ostjuden* presented to their German co-religionists, see Eva G. Reichmann, "Der Bewusstseinswandel der deutschen Juden," in Werner E. Mosse, ed., *Deutsches Judentum in Krieg und Revolution*, 1916–1923 (1971), 511–612, esp. 523, 538–45, 562–63, 576–77.

It is no accident that the most self-hating among German Jews, like Rathenau, should take such pleasure in blond "Aryan" types to the exclusion of their own type; such homoeroticism as his played its part in the making of the caricature.

To be sure, materials for the caricature were abundant, and grew more abundant after World War I. The Eastern Jews in Berlin, like their native-born counterparts, lived together in distinct quarters of the city. But they were also set apart by their trades, their appearance, their speech. Thousands of Berlin Jews, well educated, impeccably German in their accent and their convictions, thought themselves superior to these invaders from the East, and conducted an intermittent civil war with their fellow-Jews. Indeed the Berlin Baedeker of 1923, with its customary mixture of snobbishness and gentility, suggests that the caricature was growing into a commonplace: "The loss of the Great War," we read there, "has effected vast changes in the social composition of Berlin. The brilliance of the imperial court has disappeared. New classes of society with new aspirations have risen to commercial power, while the former calm based on assured prosperity has given way to a restless self-indulgence. The large influx of foreigners, mainly from Eastern Europe, is readily noticed, whereas the activities of the intellectual and professional classes, who now live in comparative retirement, are not immediately apparent to the passing visitor."[27]

I am not accusing the Baedeker of using code language.[28] But the impression is inescapable that Baedeker, speaking of foreigners, means Eastern Jews. So, after all, did everybody else. So, certainly, did Berlin's Jews hoping that the *Ostjuden* might go away or, failing this, that Berlin Jews might maintain their distance, and that Germans would continue to differentiate between them and the newcomers. In minds like Treitschke's, this distinc-

27. Karl Baedeker, *Berlin and Its Environs* (6th ed., 1923), 50.
28. In 1922, Baedeker estimates, there were 121,000 foreign residents in Berlin, "many of whom had come from Eastern Europe." We know from other sources that in 1925, the number of foreign-born Jews in Berlin was 43,000, and that, when Baedeker wrote, the figure was actually somewhat smaller. Most of the foreigners in Berlin, then, Baedeker's insinuations to the contrary, were not *Ostjuden*. And what if they had been?

tion was an obvious one; with the rise of racial anti-Semitism, it began to dissolve, and the attempt to separate one's fate from that of the Eastern Jews proved a desperate miscalculation.

For this self-deluding attempt to escape their destiny as a people, the Jews of Germany have been given some hard words since the second World War. There are angry writings by East European Jews in which Hitler appears as a kind of divine scourge to punish those who would forget who they are. As historians we cannot follow in this path. Not all attempts at assimilation were as desperate or as foolish or as despicable as some publicists have maintained. If Jews influenced German culture, Germany influenced Jewish culture, and the striving for humanity that animated Schiller and the writings of some Romantics were of authentic universality. They expressed a longing that Germans and Jews alike could share. For many Jews the flight from tradition was not a cowardly evasion but a flight into humanity—a flight they undertook in the company of many non-Jews. The German Social Democratic movement asked not only Jews to leave their faith openly and ostentatiously: Protestants, too, were called upon to take the same step.

Even the irritable condescension of Berlin Jews toward their Eastern brethren, unlovely though it is, has its explanation. It was the product of ambivalence: uneasiness with Germanness on the one hand, identification with Germans on the other. The reasons for the uneasiness lay on the surface: Jewish emancipation had been recent, acculturation uncomfortably quick, intermarriage and baptism drastic but obviously insufficient ways of disappearing into German culture. The Berlin Jews knew they were Germans, but they sensed that other Germans did not always know it. The Jew was the only citizen of Germany, it seemed, for whom religious conversion was not the road to acceptance but a cause for suspicion. And he was dependent, more than others, on the unanimity of the powerful: a well-disposed academic potentate like Ranke might recommend his Jewish students for university posts, but anti-Semitic professors often would not employ them. And periods of sudden effervescence or of sudden depression brought outbursts of anti-Semitism to serve as reminders that the bridges Jews had built to their non-Jewish fellow-citizens could sometimes be blocked, sometimes be destroyed—even in cosmopolitan, hospitable Berlin. To distance themselves from the *Ostjuden*, then, was, for Berlin's German Jews, an appeal to fellow-Germans for full acceptance, on the time-honored principle that two who despise the same outsider will not despise each other.

But what I have called the intermittent civil war between Berlin's German and Eastern Jews was more than a matter of policy. It was also a matter of conviction. Berlin's German Jews made fun of their brothers from beyond the borders not merely because they wanted to demonstrate that they were Germans, but precisely because they *were* Germans. Like their gentile fellow citizens, they saw the new immigrants from the Ukraine and Galicia as uncouth, noisy, greedy, truly alien, and distinctly inferior. Thus, while the German Jew found *Ostjuden* embarrassing for fear that he might be identified with them, he found them so also because they were, to him, really embarrassing. The prejudice was just one more emblem of his Germanness.

Beneath the humorous use of the term "Berlin-Jewish spirit," then, beneath the habit of irreverence and quick repartee in which Berliners of all origins could rejoice, a harsher reality lay concealed. Yet it will not do to be solemn about it: of all qualities, solemnity is as uncharacteristic of Berlin as can be. If there was a civil war among Berlin's Jews, it was only intermittent, exacerbated in times of crisis, dormant in moments of calm. It rose and declined in intensity as the tensions between Jews and gentiles rose and declined. And even when times were desperate, as they became after 1930 and even more after 1933, anti-authoritarian humor did not wholly die out in Berlin. Nor did the Berlin-Jewish symbiosis totally collapse. It was the humor, indeed, that kept the symbiosis going in the Nazi years, pitifully reduced and driven underground, struggling against brutal pressures and overpowering odds. While it was far from proving the panacea for which Theodor Fontane had hoped, it provided a bit of skeptical armor against the Nazis' murderous propaganda and a saving remnant of affectionate care for Berlin's suffering Jews. With all the legitimate doubts I have raised, this much—this little—the dogma of the Berlin-Jewish spirit can rightfully claim.

IV
HERMANN LEVI
A Study in Service and Self-Hatred

1. AN ANATOMY OF SELF-HATRED

Hermann Levi was the most accomplished conductor in the German Empire who was also a Jew. A cultivated and versatile musician, he was born at Giessen in 1839, the son of a rabbi whom he greatly cherished and often astounded. Precocious, ridden by ambition, Levi displayed his talents early, at the Conservatory in Leipzig and later in private tuition with the composer and conductor Vincenz Lachner, once a well-known figure in German music. Lachner was not untypical of civilized Germans at mid-nineteenth century; he was free from all tinctures of anti-Semitism. In fact, he loved his favorite young pupil like a son and hoped to secure him for a son-in-law. Nothing came of it; but, shrewdly deploying his far-flung connections, Lachner could at least aid Levi's career.[1] Hermann Levi decided in his youth, and Lachner agreed, that he was destined to go far.

In the manner of the ambitious musician, Hermann Levi, too, tried his hand at composition: we hear, in 1859, of a piano sonata, and in the following year Levi performed his piano concerto at Mannheim. Posterity has condemned his compositions to ob-

---

1. See *Briefe Vincenz Lachners an Hermann Levi*, ed. Friedrich Walter (1931), 13.

livion, but Levi, alert and ambitious, anticipated that verdict.[2] Recognizing his own limitations he turned to the honored profession of conducting; he would rather be, as one friend put it later, a first-class interpreter than a second-class composer.

Conducting was a craft for which Levi's taste, his memory, his generosity, and his gift for empathy peculiarly fitted him. His first post was at Rotterdam; in 1864, he moved to the far more desirable conductor's post at Karlsruhe, working for a court where, as Lachner put it, "there was *no* difference between Christian and Jew."[3] By 1872, he was *Kapellmeister* in Munich, conducting both operas and symphonic concerts. Though not alone in the musical stable there, he soon made it plain to his fellows that he meant to be first among them. He proposed to put his stamp on the repertory, and he succeeded. The orchestras over which he presided already had a good reputation; Levi seems to have made them the equals of any orchestra in Europe. And so he stayed in Munich, appreciated and acclaimed, until his early retirement in 1896; and it was in Munich that he died in 1900, in his sixty-first year.

In Levi's day, Munich was in most respects Germany's cul-

2. Levi dedicated his piano concerto, labeled Opus No. 1, to Vincenz Lachner who (to judge from his letter to Levi, summer 1860), was delighted to accept the honor, but balked at Levi's expressed "veneration—*Verehrung*." This is an early instance of Levi's need to adore others (*Briefe Lachners an Levi*, 9.) Levi's compositions have almost literally disappeared; I could find none even in the extensive, carefully tended music division of the Bayerische Staatsbibliothek (henceforth Stabi) in Munich. Yet there is some evidence that Levi did not give up composition entirely. A *Lied* for *Singstimme* and piano acompaniment, "Der letzte Gruss," labeled Opus 2, No. 6, was published by Peters around 1895. (Br. A 438, Music Department, Badische Landesbibliothek, Karlsruhe.)

3. Lachner to Levi, April 29, 1863. *Briefe Lachners an Levi*, 14. In the same letter, a long, affectionately Machiavellian weighing of opportunities available to the aspiring conductor, Lachner argues that Levi, a Jew in a gentile world, *must* be "active in your own behalf." For Levi, Lachner wrote, picturesquely, "whose parish is *in partibus infidelium*, this is doubly necessary." (Ibid.) This piece of advice is precisely the opposite of the one that was to become current among German Jews later, to the effect that "step-children must be doubly good," that is, must retreat from public view. Step-children, Lachner was saying, must be as visible as possible in the world. (See above, xxx.)

tural capital; its vitality, though the source of reiterated laments, was beyond dispute.[4] Levi participated in it fully. He formed friendships with such prominent residents as Paul Heyse, later to win the Nobel Prize for Literature, and Franz von Lenbach, the best-known and highest-paid portrait painter in Germany. Emotional, sensitive, nervous, often prostrated by bouts of self-doubt, anxiety, and psychosomatic ailments, Levi was nevertheless a most welcome guest in Munich social circles. With his friends, Levi belonged to informal clubs, bought modern German paintings, and cultivated the kind of intimate, highly charged friendships that were so familiar a feature of the social landscape in Germany at that time. In contrast with many professional musicians, Hermann Levi was far from being an *idiot savant*. A discriminating reader, a competent, if amateur, translator from English, French, and Italian, a knowledgeable collector of books and paintings, an affectionate editor of Goethe's tales, he compelled even Cosima Wagner, who treated him with unbearable condescension, to respect his "elevated intellectual cultivation," and to pay him the highest compliment she was capable of paying a Jew: Levi, she wrote shortly after his death, would have been able to understand Richard Wagner's *Gesammelte Schriften*.[5]

4. The most instructive books on Levi's world are the reminiscences of the keen-eyed drama and music critic Alfred von Mensi-Klarbach, *Alt-Münchener Theater-Erinnerungen* (2nd ed., 1924); the sensitive autobiography of the cultivated art historian Hermann Uhde-Bernays, whose parents' house Levi frequented, *Im Lichte der Freiheit: Erinnerungen aus den Jahren 1880 bis 1914* (2nd ed., 1963); the informal reflections of the music critic for the Augsburg and Munich press, Theodor Goering, *Dreissig Jahre München* (1904). Important is the Intendant Ernst von Possart's long obituary on Levi, published in 1900 in the *Münchener Allgemeine Zeitung*, republished in 1901 as a pamphlet, *Hermann Levi. Erinnerungen* (from which I will be quoting), and taken over practically unaltered into Possart's interesting autobiography, *Erlebtes und Erstrebtes. Erinnerungen aus meiner Bühnentätigkeit* (1916), 290–320. Karl von Perfall's account of his quarter-century as Intendant, *Ein Beitrag zur Geschichte der königlichen Theater in München, 25. November 1867–25. November 1892* (1894) is pedantic, dry, often touching, and extremely informative.
5. To Houston Stewart Chamberlain, June 28, 1900. *Cosima Wagner und Houston Stewart Chamberlain im Briefwechsel, 1888–1908* (1934), 599. Levi translated libretti of operas from the French (Berlioz) and the Italian

Levi's need for appreciation and intimacy was unusually developed; his conduct was a lifelong exercise in assiduity. His longtime friend and associate, the actor and Bavarian Intendant Ernst von Possart, noted that Levi's uncommon modesty and helpfulness aroused some doubts about his sincerity, but insisted that Levi's honesty and goodness of heart were beyond reasonable question. Levi, he wrote, was a man of "overwhelming amiability—*hinreissender Liebenswürdigkeit.*"[6] Unlike its English translation, the German word explains the psychological mechanism at its root: one is *liebens-würdig*, worthy of love. Certainly for Levi, amiability was a kind of courtship, betraying an irresistible personal need. After he had known Paul Heyse for over two years Heyse invited him to say "Du" to him; Levi accepted this bid for intimacy, but warned his friend that he would have to practice the familiar address for a while, since he had "great, great respect" for Heyse: a striking bit of self-abasement for a man in his thirties, and in a responsible public position.[7] As late as 1882, in

---

(Mozart); his English was good enough to permit him to translate a lecture by T. H. Buckle, "Uber den Einfluss der Frauen auf den Fortschritt des Wissens," dated "Karlsruhe, 1. 10. 1867." (Leviana, I, 38; Handschriften Abteilung [henceforth H.A.], Stabi.) His preoccupation with Goethe was lifelong, but his scholarly interest in him, including his having a catalogue made of his extensive Goethe library and his collecting, for the Cotta publishing house, the tales and fairy-tales of Goethe, date from his last years. On December 30, 1899, when he was only sixty, he wrote pathetically to Cotta: "Now I have just one *great* wish! I am old, my health is frail, and I should like to live to see the appearance of the little book." (5a, Cotta Nachlass, Schiller National-Museum, Marbach a. N.) The year before, in 1898, he had the then-famous painter and graphic artist Hans Thoma, with whom he was well acquainted, design an *ex libris* for him and his wife Mary; it shows, poignantly enough, the Star of David. (See Leviana, I, 40; and Thoma to Levi, May 8, 1898, Leviana, I, 53 [Thoma, 7] H.A., Stabi.) There is an interesting description of Levi's apartment in Munich, complete with its good collection of recent, mainly German, art, in Walther Siegfried, *Aus dem Bilderbuch eines Lebens* (1926), 218–38.

6. Possart, *Hermann Levi*, 36–37.

7. December 14, 1874. Heyse-Archiv, VI (Levi, 5). H.A., Stabi. Half a year later he reiterated this: "I have," he wrote Heyse on July 22, 1875, "(in addition to my great love), a perfectly horrible—*ganz abscheulichen*—respect for you." (Heyse-Archiv, VI [Levi, 7]. H.A., Stabi.) It is evident from this letter that he considered his sense of embarrassment—*Befangenheit*

a New Year's letter to another friend, Wilhelm Busch, the famous satirist and illustrator, Levi justified his not having written for a while with a "kind of—timidity—toward you."[8] The hotel rooms, concert tickets, surprise presents that Levi threw at his acquaintances were like love letters sent into the world with reply prepaid—and written out.

Levi came by his *Liebenswürdigkeit* honestly. As Possart recalled, he always obeyed his father's instructions: "In his wisdom, the pious father, experienced in the ways of the world, early managed to imprint shrewd rules of conduct on the inquisitive boy, which made him welcome wherever he would present himself."[9] One can imagine what sort of advice the cultivated and cautious rabbi, who had witnessed the early stages of Jewish emancipation complete with setbacks, gave his precocious son about to enter the larger world. But Hermann Levi was neither a masochist nor a Jew by profession; he was a conductor. As such he made a high, and accurate, appraisal of his professional gifts, and of his need for what his teacher Lachner had called elbow-room. Even before he found himself in a position to assert his pre-eminence, as he did in the Munich of the 1870s, he recognized that he must be in command. In 1869, while he was pondering a call to Vienna, he told his good friend Johannes Brahms: "I cannot stand a subor coordinated position for long."[10] In Levi, self-confidence and

---

—almost ridiculous, but, after all, he did not have this "certain feeling" voluntarily.

8. The letter is reproduced in facsimile in *Wilhelm Busch, Sämtliche Briefe*, ed. Friedrich Bohne, 2 vols. (1968), I, between 232 and 233. Levi's wish to be ingratiating was insatiable; his correspondence is punctuated with offers to be helpful in any possible way. Writing to the critic Friedrich Pecht, New Year's day 1881–1882, he expressed pleasure at a favorable review and immediately added: "A thousand thanks, and if I can ever be of service to you in any way, dispose over me." (Handschriften-Sammlung der Stadtbibliothek München, Levi, Sammelstück 3.) Another effusion, catching his anxious tone to perfection, is a letter to Rudolf von Seitz, a well-known designer of interiors and facades in Munich: "Monday noon," Levi wrote him on April 8, 1881, "I am going to Bayreuth. Have you no commissions for me— . . . Please give me some commission to carry out!" (Seitziana, IV. H.A., Stabi.)

9. Possart, *Hermann Levi*, 19.

10. April 19, 1869. *Johannes Brahms im Briefwechsel mit Hermann Levi . . .* , ed. Leopold Schmidt (1910), 43.

self-abasement were not mutually contradictory; they were two aspects of the same temperament. He needed to be master in his chosen sphere because only then could he truly serve.

That service was, of course, to music, but not to music in general. As a young conductor, Levi had defiantly played the "radical" compositions of Schumann and Brahms;[11] throughout his career, he would give a sympathetic hearing to new works and unknown composers, and make notable efforts in the revival of old music. He was among the conductors who discovered Berlioz for Germany, one of the first to play Bizet and Chabrier outside France,[12] and, in the 1890s, a leader in the campaign to revive and purify such long-neglected and sadly disfigured Mozart operas as *Cosi fan tutte*. But the crucial musical experience of his life was Richard Wagner, the genius who, for Levi, made service worthwhile and indeed obligatory. Wagner became the agent of Hermann Levi's fame and his misery, his self-esteem and his self-hatred.

Levi's Jewish self-hatred antedates the currency of the term by nearly half a century. Like other generic words, *Selbsthass*, the frantic urge to escape the burden of one's Jewishness not merely

11. For Brahms's radicalism, see below, "Aimez-vous Brahms?"

12. He was conscious of what he owed his position in Munich. As he wrote to his father, the rabbi, on November 13, 1882: von Perfall, his Intendant and immediate superior, "naturally shuddered" at his passion for Wagner— *Wagnerei*. "But since I do my duty beyond that, he can't do anything to me." (Bayreuther Festspiele, 1959, *"Parsifal" Program*, ed. Festspielleitung, [1959], 11; from a collection of hitherto unpublished letters of Hermann Levi's to his father, 6–23. Actually, it was also a sense of adventure that helped to shape Levi's programming. On November 8, 1878, he reported to Heyse that he was going to perform, at his next concert, "a somewhat crazy, but yet interesting symphony by Berlioz," a sign of his slightly grudging, but still measurable respect for a composer for whom Levi, with his friend Felix Mottl, did much in Germany. (Heyse-Archiv, VI [Levi, 17]. H.A., Stabi.) Composers other than Wagner found reason to be grateful to Levi. Thus Emanuel Chabrier warmly thanked him, several times, most notably on February 1, 1890, for his efforts in behalf of his opera *Gwendoline*, in several languages, concluding: "Encore merci! merci! So! So! Danke schön!!" See also the charming letter of thanks by Alice Chabrier, of November 20, 1890, expressing her gratitude for Levi's *"confiance à ma Gwendoline chérie,"* and for raising the morale of its composer and freeing him from self-doubt. (Both in Leviana, I, 53 [Chabrier.] H.A., Stabi.)

by renouncing but by denouncing Judaism, collects a complex of feelings under a single rubric.[13] The term entered general circulation in 1930, through Theodor Lessing's book *Der jüdische Selbsthass*, part diagnosis and part display of a distasteful masochism which, it seemed, was more widespread among Jews than among other despised or persecuted groups—though not as widespread as Lessing claimed. But while the popularity of the term was new, the set of feelings it designates was far older: sensitive observers had noted the existence of a certain anti-Jewish animus among Jews as early as the 1870s and even before—one can find abundant and painful evidence of it in, among others, Heinrich Heine. It was before the first World War that Theodor Lessing, Jewish in origin, Lutheran by persuasion, and anti-Semitic in convictions, wrote Sigmund Freud an "ugly" letter denouncing psychoanalysis as a typical "abortion—*Ausgeburt*" of the Jewish spirit. In 1936, recalling the correspondence that ensued, Freud remembered how shocked he had been to learn that this Lessing was not a descendant of Germany's great philo-Semite Gotthold Ephraim Lessing, but himself a Jew: "I turned away from the man in disgust," he wrote. But then the analyst took over: "Don't you think," he asked, "that self-hatred like Th. L.'s is an exquisite Jewish phenomenon?"[14]

At the turn of the century, Freud had supplied materials for understanding this phenomenon through his discovery of the Oedipus complex and the mechanism of unconscious self-punishment. In the same years another Austrian, Otto Weininger, of-

13. "Speaking in terms of individuals rather than groups, the self-hatred of a Jew may be directed against the Jews as a group, against a particular fraction of the Jews, against his own family, or against himself. It may be directed against Jewish institutions, Jewish mannerisms, Jewish language, or Jewish ideals. There is an almost endless variety of forms which Jewish self-hatred may take." Kurt Lewin, "Self-Hatred among Jews" (1941), reprinted in Lewin, *Resolving Social Conflicts: Selected Papers on Group Dynamics* (1948), 186–200, one of the few attempts to deal scientifically (if briefly) with the question. The citation is at 186–87. There are interesting observations, from a psychoanalytic perspective, on Jewish self-appraisals in Rudolph M. Loewenstein, *Christians and Jews* (tr. Vera Damman, 1951).

14. Freud to Kurt Hiller, February 9, 1936. In Hiller, *Köpfe und Tröpfe: Profile aus einem Vierteljahrhundert* (1950), 308.

fered spectacular evidence for the terrifying power of *Selbsthass*. Weininger's short, sad life history is well known. He was born in 1880 into a Jewish family; in 1902, the day he took his university degree, he adopted Protestantism; in May 1903, he published the book, *Geschlecht und Charakter*, on which his problematic immortality rests; four months later he committed suicide in the house in which Beethoven had died—a melodramatic end to an (at least inwardly) melodramatic life. In his book, which an oddly assorted collection of misogynists and anti-Semites found congenial and quotable, Weininger postulated a sharp contrast between males and females, and between "Aryans" and Jews. It was a seductively simple system, with a false lucidity to which intellectuals, especially German intellectuals, have long responded: woman, representing sensuality, is ethically infinitely inferior to man; the Jew, embodying skepticism and the spirit of imitation, is equally inferior to the "Aryan." Certainly, by converting to Protestantism, Weininger had expected to make himself into an Aryan: his definition of Judaism was not a racial one. But evidently fearing the sinister influence of woman within him, and recognizing his indelible Jewishness, Weininger eradicated his two linked problems forever by shooting himself.[15]

True self-hatred could go no further. Other Jews fled their Jewishness in less sensational ways. Some confined their demonstrations to voting for anti-Semitic candidates on the ground that their candidate was more patriotic than his left-wing opponents. Others paraded their Germanness by parroting the ethnic and, later, even the racial slanders that were the staple of anti-Semitic literature. The Jewish writer and editor Moritz de Jonge, for one, wrote for the reactionary *Kreuzzeitung* and in the 1890s helped to edit an anti-Semitic newspaper. The over-compensation that tore him apart is palpable from his confession: "I wanted to be

---

15. Theodor Lessing devotes a score of pages to Weininger in *Der jüdische Selbsthass* (1930), 80–100. See also David Abrahamsen, *The Mind and Death of a Genius* (1946); the brief treatment by William M. Johnston, *The Austrian Mind: An Intellectual and Social History 1848–1938* (1972), 158–62 and passim, with bibliographical indications at 429; and Hans Kohn, *Karl Kraus, Arthur Schnitzler, Otto Weininger: Aus dem jüdischen Wien der Jahrhundertwende* (1962).

German, to think, to feel, to work German. My heart leaped
when I saw a German uniform, heard German military music."[16]
Such deserters were often psychologically unstable and politically
inconstant.[17] As Freud suggested in a brief analytical comment,
the inner conflict—*Zerrissenheit*—that bedevils the victim of self-
hatred reflects his inability to give up either an intense hostility
to his father or an indissoluble identification with that father.[18]

The parade of Jewish self-haters is depressing, their fate laden
with importunate ironies. Everyone knows what happened to
Walther Rathenau, the industrialist Emil Rathenau's brilliant
and tormented son. Banker, industrialist, man of the world, collector of art, publicist, social prophet, Walther Rathenau acknowledged his Jewishness and felt damned by it. His famous—
or, better, notorious—pseudonymous essay of 1897, "Höre, Israel," begins with the admission that its author is a Jew, and then
proceeds to accept many features of the anti-Semites' caricature
of the Jew. Rathenau's solution to the "Jewish question" was for
Jews to shed their objectionable qualities and become authentic
Germans. Rathenau adored Germanness not merely on political
or social, but also on physical grounds; his "romantic admiration
for the nordic race," for blond "Siegfried types," was a secret but
persistent leitmotiv of his life.[19] Yet once he was in the public
eye, in the early days of the Weimar Republic, these very Siegfried types vilified him as the "Jewish sow—*Judensau*"; and his
career as Germany's foreign minister was cut short in 1922,
when he was shot to death to the applause of *völkische* circles
whose tastes he had at least partly shared.

The end of Theodor Lessing was just as violent. The World
War had converted him from principled anti-Semitism to passionate Zionism, though he never wholly discarded his tendency

16. Quoted in Jacob Toury, *Die politischen Orientierungen der Juden in
Deutschland, von Jena bis Weimar* (1966), 268.
17. A number of them, including de Jonge, leaped from anti-Semitism to
Zionism.
18. In his letter to Hiller, February 9, 1936. In Hiller, *Köpfe und Tröpfe*,
308.
19. See above, 185. And Harry Graf Kessler, *Walther Rathenau: Sein Leben
und Werk* (1938; ed. 1963), 72.

to make sweeping collective judgments; he hated himself, his in-significant stature and dark appearance, too much ever to reach objectivity. Yet he could now at least say that whatever rootless-ness and decadence Jews might display, these defects were the fault of their oppressors. As a vocal pacifist and, however twisted, a public defender of the Jews, Lessing became a gadfly the Nazis were determined to silence; he fled to Czechoslovakia, but, in August 1933, like Rathenau before him, he was shot down by assassins.

The painful twists in Theodor Lessing's line on the Jews under-score the complexity of the term he helped to popularize. It was not solely self-hatred that induced the German-Jewish poet and translator Rudolf Borchardt to devote his life to the self-appointed mission of upholding the Graeco-German tradition against what he thought to be "Oriental" forces of debasement and decay.[20] It was perhaps not mainly, certainly not solely, self-hatred that made German-Jewish writers from Heinrich Heine to Kurt Tucholsky invent those comical, slightly repulsive figures representing a "certain type of Jew." That such a type existed does not justify the portrait or settle the question; the peculiar pleasure with which Jewish writers drew these telling and damag-ing character-sketches suggests that feelings other than the re-forming urge had guided their pen. Like other feelings, hatred is over-determined; it has more sources than the hater himself knows. A Jewish-born Socialist could attack Jewish capitalists from class-hatred rather than self-hatred—because they were capi-talists rather than because they were Jews. Or he might single out for special vituperation those whom he uncomfortably, perhaps unconsciously, identified as his own kind.

Interesting as dramatic figures like Rathenau or Tucholsky may be, they are special cases, embodying individual choices with

20. The debate over Borchardt, an ultra-conservative man of letters who is enjoying a measure of revival now, can be followed through Willy Haas's malicious, but not wholly undeserved attack, "Der Fall Rudolf Borchardt," significantly subtitled "(Zur Morphologie des dichterischen Selbsthasses)," in Gustav Krojanker, ed., Juden in der deutschen Literatur: Essays über zeit-genössische Schriftsteller (1926), 231–40, and Werner Kraft's defense, Rudolf Borchardt: Welt aus Poesie und Geschichte (1961), 34–73.

deep, private, psychological roots. In the long run, the diffuse, unspectacular sentiments of ordinary German Jews are more important for the historian's appraisal of the German Jew's place in his culture; they may not involve acts of anti-Semitism, or a flight into suicide, but remain on the level of embarrassment, a feeling of shame and rejection that would overcome them as they witnessed what they identified as "Jewish" display in public places, in business dealings, in political controversy, in the gutter press.[21] Typical for such flinching is Ludwig Jakobowski's novel of 1891, *Werther, der Jude*, whose protagonist is a Jewish student at the University of Berlin, deracinated and longing for assimilation. He is ashamed of his family ties to Eastern Europe and equally ashamed of his father, a banker, whose sharp business practices confirm in his mind the truth of anti-Semitic charges.[22] And in 1932, six months before Hitler came to power, the Jewish poet Ernst Lissauer, who had greeted the war of 1914 with a once-famous "Hassgesang Gegen England," noted in his diary that he could not take leadership in the cause of threatened German Jewry because he disapproved of "much that is Jewish." He thought that the "characteristic defects of Judaism" had shown themselves in "many Jews," in producers like Jessner and Reinhardt, polemicists like Tucholsky and Kraus.[23]

Whatever the proper moral response to such opinions, the term *Selbsthass* in no way encompasses their meaning. There is social snobbery in its disclaimers and generalizations; there is a measure of German chauvinism in them; there is even, however misguided, something of a didactic intention: to pillory the noisy, the vulgar, the sharp dealers might purify the behavior of other Jews and thus undermine the case for anti-Semitism. But the element that came to dominate, by the 1920s, this Jewish embarrassment at the spectacle of other Jews was a renewed fear. For centuries Jews had learned to be inconspicuous. Their synagogues

---

21. See above, 182.

22. See Ismar Schorsch, *Jewish Reactions to German Anti-Semitism 1870–1914* (1972), 47. A rather more complex later instance, from real life, is Adolf Asch's *Selbstzuchtorganisation*, which I have discussed above, 183.

23. Quoted *in extenso* in the thoughtful "Entscheidungsjahr 1932" by Robert Weltsch, in W. Mosse, ed., *Entscheidungsjahr 1932* (1965), 551.

had been placed for safety in the center of town near public buildings, with façades as plain as ingenuity could make them. And their communities everywhere had legislated against ostentation. The rings Jews could wear, the silk they could show, the public banquets they could attend, the songs they could sing in the streets at night—all this, and much else, came under the vigilant eye of those responsible for the government of the Jewish communities. And the reasons were, quite explicitly, that modesty in demeanor would please God and besides, it was prudent "not to show off in the presence of the gentiles."[24] Jews knew from experience and from the sacred books that display was not merely irreverent; it was dangerous. And then the world had opened up, to gentiles as to Jews. The liberal nineteenth century had permitted many Jews in many places to assert themselves, as it permitted others to assert themselves, to cross the boundaries of class and country with fewer impediments than ever before. What Jews and gentiles alike came to refer to as typical Jewish *chutzpah*[25] was essentially an invitation to freedom, a turning away from fear.

But this did not last. The decline of German liberalism and, even worse, the experience of the war and its tempestuous aftermath went far toward closing the avenues of Jewish approaches to host cultures. The old fear returned, but under new conditions and hence under incomprehensible guises. The long ascent of Jewish integration into German culture was, if not exactly over, certainly imperiled.

I have gone, in this account of Jewish self-hatred, far beyond the span of Hermann Levi's lifetime. There is good reason for this long chronological reach: impossible as it is to make dependable quantitative measurements of such matters, it seems most likely

24. From a regulation passed by Italian Jews meeting at Forli in 1418. Jacob R. Marcus, ed., *The Jew in the Medieval World: A Source Book, 315–1791* (ed. 1965), 194.
25. On this word, see Weltsch, "Entscheidungsjahr 1932," in Mosse, ed., *Entscheidungsjahr 1932*, 549.

A Jewish High Priest. Title page of *Levi-Kneipzeitung*, October 1, 1884.

to me that Jewish cringing at Jewish conduct, the most common and most banal expression of Jewish self-hatred, grew markedly during the Weimar Republic, far beyond what it had been before World War I.[26] But Hermann Levi's case of self-hatred, classic in its ravages and its persistence, proves that even during the

26. Kurt Lewin made a similar observation about Jews in the United States: "There are indications that the percentage of such people"—of Jews who adopt an "unmanly and unwise (because unrealistic) hush-hush policy" about their presence in society—"among leading members of the American Jewish community has increased since the First World War." "Self-Hatred Among Jews," in Lewin, *Resolving Social Conflicts*, 196–97.

heady days of the Empire German Jews found ample temptation to reject their heritage and deny their identity. And Levi's classic case also proves that Jewish self-hatred, precisely like other forms of anti-Semitism, required no objective evidence for nourishment; it fulfilled subjective needs. After all, Levi's master, King Ludwig II of Bavaria, who worked closely with his officials in charge of cultural matters, was no Jew-hater; not even his adored Richard Wagner, who influenced Ludwig in so many other ways, could induce him to give up his respect for Jews and his disdain for anti-Semitism.[27] And some of Levi's closest friends, like Paul Heyse and the aesthetician and critic Carl Fiedler, were half-Jewish yet wholly accepted in German society. None of this was enough to give Levi, the Jew, the inner peace that he craved and that forever eluded him. Over the years he tortured himself, and, we may surmise, bored his friends, with ruminations about conversion to Christianity.[28] And over the years he associated with men who were casual, occasional anti-Semites, like Wilhelm Busch,[29] or principled, furious anti-Semites, like Richard Wagner. He could not escape the truth: though only loosely tied to the religion that his father, the rabbi, professionally professed, Levi knew himself to be a Jew. In 1873, writing to a sick friend, he closed his letter of encouragement which typically noted that his own health was none too good, with the words, "Your suffering brother in Christo," a salutation he self-consciously transformed by substi-

27. Wagner's fruitless efforts, and Ludwig's resistance, are well discussed in Ernest Newman, *The Life of Wagner*, IV (1946), 636–38.

28. In 1874, Levi was admitted to membership in the musical fraternity Cäcilia in Munich. (The document, dated November 2, 1874, is in the Leviana, I, 14. H.A., Stabi.) While this fraternity explicitly admitted non-Christians, it was, just as explicitly, founded on Christian tenets, and mainly concerned with fostering church music. Levi's readiness to join this fraternity says something about his religious state of mind in the early 1870s. It did not change. As emerges from a letter that Wilhelm Busch wrote about Levi to a close mutual friend, Franz von Lenbach, as late as August 1891, Levi seems to have carried himself with thoughts of conversion to Roman Catholicism—and to have talked about it to his friends, at length. (See Busch, *Briefe*, I, 335.) Lenbach's letters to Levi, of which over a hundred have been preserved, are fraternal, amusing, solicitous. (See Leviana, I, 53. H.A., Stabi.)

29. See below, 205–6.

tuting, for the last word, the word "Israel."[30] In later years, in his notebooks and his correspondence, he broached his Jewishness as a recurrent refrain. Significantly, his most well-meaning friends would remind him of his origins, often in jokes. Doubtless the most startling of these reminders was a special little newspaper issued by his intimates in 1884 to grace a celebratory dinner on the occasion of his twenty-fifth anniversary as a conductor. It consisted of the usual feeble, largely inoffensive doggerel, but its title page bore the effigy of a caricatured Jew in the garb of a high priest whose face, with its kinky hair, heavy eyes, and huge nose, had nothing in common with Hermann Levi's finely cut features.[31] It looked precisely like the vicious drawings in which the Nazi propaganda sheet, the *Stürmer*, was to specialize half a century later.

Cordial invitations, thank-you poems, even letters of congratulation often bore anti-Jewish barbs that Levi obviously took with equanimity.[32] It is in fact doubtful whether he saw them as barbs at all, or for that matter whether they were intended as such. And the historian must note that gestures and remarks we would today brand as tasteless, tactless, or bigoted, did not in those years necessarily bear the burden that events in our century have

30. Levi to "Dear Friend," February 15, 1873. Leviana, I, 47, 2. H.A., Stabi.

31. Leviana, I, 18. H.A., Stabi.

32. Thus, when Levi was awarded the Bavarian Knight's Cross, the St. Michael's Decoration, the popular novelist Felix Dahn, who seems to have enjoyed sending rhymed postcards to his friends, congratulated Levi with a quatrain reminding him that he was, though a youth without reproach, of the tribe of Israel, and that many a Christian would look askance at him for wearing the St. Michael's Cross:

> Wer ist der Jüngling sonder Fehl?
> Er trägt den heilgen Michaël—
> Ist doch vom Stamme Israël!
> Und mancher Christ sicht darob scheel!

(October 9, 1878. Leviana, I, 53 [Dahn]. H.A., Stabi.) The document accompanying the cross, dated October 6, 1878, is preserved in the Leviana (I, 7), as are numerous other decorations and awards, including one bestowed on August 26, 1889, by Wilhelm II in his capacity of Prussian king (Leviana, I, 8. H. A., Stabi.)

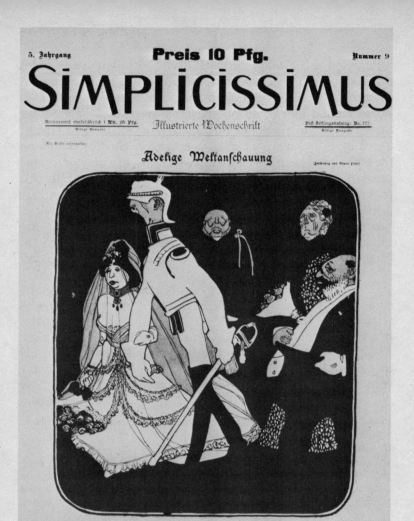

Bruno Paul, "Adelige Weltanschauung," *Simplicissimus*, 1900.

placed upon them. One need only glance at *Simplicissimus*, the famous humorous weekly that burst upon a waiting Germany in 1896, to see that what we would abhor today was accepted then. *Simplicissimus* did not present itself, and was not taken, as an anti-Semitic periodical. Its best-known and most prolific cartoonist, Thomas Theodor Heine, was a Jew. And its satire was ostensibly aimed at anyone else but Germany's Jewish citizens: at profiteers, exploiters, social degenerates, empty-headed Junkers, and corpulent priests. Yet the drawings of Jews that often appeared in its pages were satiric in temper and defamatory in line. They reiterate the familiar derisive stereotypes that had haunted Jews for so long: the vulgar Jewish plutocrat, the opportunistic Jewish convert, the fat pretentious Jewish dowager. A much-exploited theme for *Simplicissimus* was the effete and impoverished Prussian aristocrat rescuing the family fortune with a suitable marriage to a Jewish heiress. The savagery of Bruno Paul's cover cartoon on this subject, published in 1900, is anything but exceptional. Entitled "Aristocratic World View," it depicts a hideous, stunted, obviously Jewish girl accompanied by her no less hideous, no less obvious father, marching to the altar with an impecunious nobleman. "It is honor, love, and hunger," the caption informs the reader, "that make the world go round; for honor, we have the duel; for love, the corps de ballet; and for hunger, thank God, marriage for money."[33] It is impossible to decide who looks worse in such cartoons, the Jew or the Junker. But the Jew certainly looks very bad indeed, though I know of no Jewish protests against such malice; it must have seemed natural, perfectly innocuous.

Not surprisingly, then, there were many Germans who cherished their Jewish friends without ceasing to indulge in anti-Jewish remarks. One of these was Wilhelm Busch, Germany's best-known humorous poet and illustrator. Busch much preferred rustic solitude to urban conviviality; but on his occasional forays to Munich or Frankfurt from his native village near Hannover, he had made friends with such Jewish literary men as Paul Lindau, editor, journalist, playwright, and such Jewish musicians

33. *Simplicissimus*, V (1900), No. 9, p. 69.

"Christian and Jew under one roof. . . ." Studio photograph of Wilhelm Busch (left) and Hermann Levi, 1881.

as Hermann Levi. Busch was, indeed, one of Levi's most loyal and most patient listeners.[34] In 1881, he had joined Levi for a comical photograph which immortalized the two friends under a studio umbrella in a stance of affectionate cordiality; here they are, Busch noted in his gently sardonic caption, "Christian and Jew under one roof, no better than they should be—

Christ und Jud unter einem Dach—
Sie sind aber auch danach."

34. See below, 223.

"The Three Graces." Studio photograph of, left to right, Franz von Lenbach, Paul Lindau, and Wilhelm Busch, ca. 1880.

An earlier photograph, still more comical, had posed the Jew Lindau with Busch and with their mutual friend, Franz Lenbach, entwined in the posture of the three Graces.[35]

Yet these intimate associations did not keep Busch from inventing Jewish characters for his humorous tales matching, indeed accentuating, current hostile caricatures. In several poems, Busch speaks of "the" Jew, with his hooked nose and devious ways, physically ugly, morally corrupt, and financially unscrupu-

35. For the first photograph, see Joseph Kraus, *Wilhelm Busch in Selbstzeugnissen und Bilddokumenten* (1970), 91; for the second, ibid., 81.

Wilhelm Busch, "Schmulchen Schiefelbeiner," from *Plisch und Plum*, 1882.

lous.[36] And he illustrates rhymes like these with savage drawings. His most obvious and most distasteful Jew, "Schmulchen Schiefelbeiner," appears in *Plisch und Plum*, a tale he published in 1882, a year after he had had himself photographed with Hermann Levi, fraternally under one umbrella. This photograph and such drawings seem to have nothing whatever to do with one another. Levi certainly did not think that they did, nor did Busch's other readers, whether Jew or gentile.

36. For instances see "Die fromme Helene" (1872), in Wilhelm Busch, *Gesamtausgabe*, ed. Friedrich Bohne, 4 vols. (1959), II, 204; and "Plisch und Plum" (1882), ibid., III, 479–85.

And yet, when we have paid this tribute to the relativity of human perception, it remains true that Hermann Levi had a special weakness for such humor, perhaps provoked it and certainly indulged in it himself. What permitted him to adopt so undignified a posture was the psychological mechanism technically called identification with the aggressor. Victims of kidnappers and inmates in concentration camps have succumbed to it, and it is an essential ingredient in all Jewish self-hatred. Its symptoms were certainly marked in Hermann Levi. But at this point, once again, the historian must intervene to amplify, to place, the conjectures of the psychologist. There were many Jews in Germany in Levi's day who chuckled at jokes directed against Jews and who, indeed, made many such jokes of their own. Thus the Jewish publishing house of Eduard Bloch, with headquarters in Berlin, issued a series of cheap small pamphlets, "Poems and Jokes in Jewish Dialect—*Gedichte und Scherze in jüdischer Mundart*," which, to judge from the Yiddish phrases and esoteric pseudonyms they freely employed, addressed themselves to a purely Jewish audience. Their often biting and always crude jokes adopted anti-Jewish stereotypes without modification and without apologies: they ridicule the Jew's blatant passion for profit, his indecent bargaining, his parvenu's self-importance and ignorance—all types familiar from anti-Semitic myth-making. There is the Jewish theater-goer who, as his son falls into the orchestra from the top balcony, shouts after him, "Jacob, don't lose me the watch!" There is the Jewish "lady" in the dry goods store asking the price of some material she fancies and who, told "sixteen groschen per ell," muses to herself: "He wants sixteen groschen—so he means twelve—he'll give it to me for ten—it's worth perhaps eight—at most I'd like to give him six—so I'll offer him four groschen." And there is "Commercienrath Nathanson" telling "Commissionsräthin Philippsthal" that he has just bought an "old Rubens" at auction, only to be reproached by his hostess for penny-pinching: "Come now, you're rich enough to buy *new* pictures!"[37] The physiognomies of the dreary stick figures who

37. The full collection of pamphlets is at the Yale University Sterling Library.

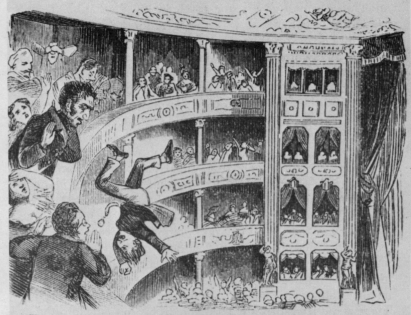

"Nathan Tulpenthal": father and son at the theater. Title page of *Schmonzes-Berjonzes* (1880s).

"David Hamanklopper": haggling at the cloth-merchant's. Title page of *Schlachmonaus zu Purim* (1880s).

211

"Mortche Omeinsager": a conversation about art. Title page of *Was meinen Sie, wie gesund ist das!* (1880s).

speak these sophomoric lines, and the lines themselves, have nothing to do with the self-respecting, liberating Jewish humor, for its part not free of self-criticism, that Sigmund Freud was to celebrate and analyze in his *Jokes and Their Relation to the Unconscious.* Identification with the aggressor could hardly be more complete than this.

Humor such as that retailed in Bloch's pamphlets was on a level far below any to which Hermann Levi could sink. But the two had this much in common: both took over and idealized the standards of the dominant culture, including its prejudices, valuing what it valued and despising what it despised—which happened to include them. Such a commitment to Germany expressed itself, of course, not merely in this negative way. Like practically all German Jews, Hermann Levi was an irreproachable patriot. Around 1864, when still a young conductor, he rejected a call to Paris on the ground that it seemed to him as though "I am rooted, as *musician,* in Germany with my whole being." In France he thought he would miss "what is no less essential to me—German musicians. . . . Up to now no *real* German musician (I take this attribute as my own not for my ability but for my aspiration) has felt comfortable on foreign soil."[38] But Hermann Levi was more than a good German, he was also something of a chauvinist and an anti-Semite. He liked to quote the Talmud—or rather the few crumbs he had picked up from his father—but found it possible to deride his own relatives simply for being what they were: from a trip he reported back to Munich in casual telegraph style, "Family clan. Bankers. Each, seen

38. The draft is in Leviana, I, 47, 7. H.A., Stabi. A much later draft, of 1892, of a letter to his Intendant, von Perfall, documents how strong and persistent this patriotic feeling was in Levi: he called attention to the damage done German opera houses by "our import of alien operas," fostered by the "worrisome taste of the public." Always the diplomat, Levi quickly disclaimed any criticism of Perfall; he was *not* charging "His Excellency" with being "sicklied o'er with alien tastes," but "naturally" means Vienna, "with its cult of Massenet," and Berlin, "with its premières" and "its chasing after Mascagni, Leoncavallo and Bizet." Leoncavallo is an afterthought; Levi added the name in pencil. (Leviana, I, 45 [Perfall, 5]. H.A., Stabi.)

as an individual, tolerably intelligent and sensible. In corpore—Jews."[39]

Towards the end of his life, in an unusually acerbic letter, he managed to equate "un-German," which was to say "detestable," with "Jewish." Criticizing an opera score by the English composer Carlowitz-Ames, he denied it all "true feeling and simplicity," and denounced it as a mere search for effects in which "everything is superficial, in short, to my taste, abominable." But, he concluded, giving Carlowitz-Ames his *coup de grâce*, "I am surely not the right man to judge such un-German, Romanic-Jewish products."[40] And the long-time Munich critic Alfred von Mensi-Klarbach, who knew Levi well and liked him greatly, recalled that "once, Levi went so far as to reject a competent and pretty Jewish singer, unconditionally, for a certain role, because that role absolutely required an authentically Germanic performer." He even espoused the view, Mensi-Klarbach added, that "while in artistic matters the Semite could, like everyone else, reach the greatest heights in reproduction, he could never produce anything immortal."[41] Wagner could not have said it better; the prey thought that, on the whole, the hunter was right.

2. A LIFE OF SERVICE

This, then, was the man who could, in the 1870s, say respectful things about Wagner's scurrilous if imaginative essay, *Das Judentum in der Musik* and, in the 1890s, take the trouble to write a grateful letter to a reviewer who had praised Houston Stewart Chamberlain's pernicious speculations.[42] He could exalt others

39. Levi to Heyse, July 22, 1875. Heyse-Archiv, VI (Levi, 7). H.A., Stabi.
40. Levi to Heyse, June 20, 1899. Heyse-Archiv, VI (Levi, 41). H.A., Stabi.
41. *Theater-Erinnerungen*, 93. According to Mensi-Klarbach, Levi's low esteem for such "Jewish" composers as Meyerbeer, Halévy, or Mendelssohn was not a product of his infatuation with Wagner, and antedates the Wagner years.
42. See Levi to Karl von Krumbacher, a Byzantinist and Professor at the University of Munich, September 23, 1899(?). (Krumbacheriana, I. H.A., Stabi.)

because he debased himself. The public obeisance that the Master liked to receive graciously did not embarrass Hermann Levi. Mensi-Klarbach remembered seeing Levi rushing up to Wagner in the intermission of a concert he was conducting and kiss his hand humbly, a homage that Wagner "accepted as a matter of course." It was, the honest witness adds, "not an elevating spectacle."[43]

Levi's respect for his friends bears a family resemblance to his adoration of his Master, but with Wagner it achieved a special pathos. Felix Weingartner observed that Levi did not appear to advantage in the company of the Wagner clan. "There was a continual spiritual and physical bowing that I found painful." He found it particularly painful to see the "members of the Wagner family, scarcely troubling to conceal themselves behind the smiling mask of friendship, quietly sneering at him". One day Weingartner, gathering up his courage, asked his friend why he permitted even the Wagner children to be impudent to him, and in public, without protest. Levi gave him a grim look and "stammered in a rough voice: 'Of course, it's easy for you in this house, you—Aryan!' "[44]

The pathos of Levi's obsequiousness does not end here. By the 1870s, Wagner stood in the German cultural landscape like an outsized, garish monument. One could worship him or detest him, think him a prophet or a tempter; indifference was practically impossible. In a persuasive essay, Bryan Magee has suggested that Wagner's immense power to arouse emotions lay in his capacity to present in his music dramas what most men found it necessary to repress, particularly impermissible erotic fantasies. The thesis has much to commend it.[45] Certainly the energetic but discriminating rejection of Wagner that Brahms and Hanslick voiced was rare, not in being a rejection but in being discriminating.[46]

Whatever the reasons, the debate over Wagner caused wide-

43. *Theater-Erinnerungen*, 92.
44. Felix Weingartner, *Lebens Erinnerungen*, I (2nd ed., 1928), 264–65.
45. Bryan Magee, *Aspects of Wagner* (1968); this is not merely the most persuasive defense of Wagner, but also the shortest.
46. For Hanslick on Wagner, see below, "For Beckmesser."

spread and impassioned dissension, and divided old companions. Here was a new source of anguish for Hermann Levi: he of all people, who lived through friendships, was forced to choose, more than once, between his Master and his friends. In despair, but without hesitation, he chose Wagner. Richard Wagner cost Levi the friendship of his old teacher Vincenz Lachner, who thought Wagner a vicious man and a disaster for music, and who said farewell to his favorite pupil in a long, affectionate, unanswerable letter.[47] Wagner cost Levi the equally valued friendship of Johannes Brahms who, reserved as he was, had admitted Levi to his intimate thoughts. There was no ringing last letter here; Brahms simply let his correspondence with Levi die out in the late 1870s with some cordial, businesslike notes.[48] And Wagner almost cost Levi the friendship of Paul Heyse. In one of his New Year's letters, Levi recalled his earlier breach with Lachner in order to prevent a breach with Heyse: "A year ago today I wrote a letter which was far harder for me to write than this one, since I knew for certain that it was to be the last. It was addressed to a friend to whom I owe everything that I am and have, and who renounced me because he could have nothing to do with a Wagnerian. That was the most painful experience of my life." Until recently he had thought that one lost one's intimates only through death, but he had learned "to weep for the living dead, and you may believe me that for these my tears flow more copiously than for the truly dead." He was afraid that he might lose Heyse for the same reason that he had lost Lachner, and was resigned to it. But he thought it might be useful to explain why he had avoided Heyse in recent weeks: "I have not come to see you during Wagner's three-weeks' stay because I was as if intoxicated—*wie in einem Rausch lebte.* You have known for a long time that I am addicted to that man body and soul—*diesem Manne mit Leib und Seele verfallen bin.*" He insisted that he did

47. Lachner to Levi, January 3, 1880. *Briefe Lachners an Levi,* 35–38. The whole long letter is a moving document.

48. Leopold Schmidt, the editor of the Brahms-Levi correspondence, notes in his introduction that Levi had told him how "melancholy" this separation had made, and still made him. (*Brahms im Briefwechsel mit Levi,* 4.) It had been a close friendship.

not judge his friends by their attitude to Wagner, and cited Wilhelm Busch and Franz von Lenbach as examples. "But in those November days it would have been impossible for me to listen to a single derisive or ironic word about W." The whole letter reads like a pathetic and affectionate declaration of a man willing to do anything for his friend except to renounce his addiction.

The medical terminology—Levi's and my own—is precise and justified. It underscores the morbidity of his great love and, at the same time, the neurotic's helpless awareness that he cannot— or, rather, that he does not wish to—overcome his affliction. "If you read the above to mean," Levi concludes his confession, "that I am very fond of you, you will gather exactly what I mean."[49] In the light of these lines, Weingartner's memory of Levi saying to him one day at Bayreuth, "Once I stop conducting here, I won't go on living,"[50] sounds plausible enough.

Service to Wagner was not always a matter of life and death. One reason it was possible for Levi, as for others, to serve Wagner was that Wagner himself professed to be a servant. He exploited his "faithful" by assuring them that he was merely an agent of a higher power, a passive instrument in the hands of cultural renewal.[51] Like Wagner's followers, Wagner himself (as they liked to put it at Wahnfried) was "enlisted in the Cause— er diente der Sache." The Cause was divine, but Wagner himself, that little man with his glasses, his unheroic Saxon speech, his coarse humor, his ostentatious display, and his boundless sense of self, was only human. But only just: if some indiscreet worshiper blasphemously mistook the prophet for his god, he was forgiven. Belief in the Cause alone mattered, and that belief im-

---

49. December 31, 1880. Heyse-Archiv, VI (Levi, 23). H.A., Stabi. Two years later, at the height of his agitation over *Parsifal*, Levi's despair at losing touch with Heyse became even plainer. "I brood in vain," he wrote, pathetically, "what the reason may be why you give me no sign. Can't you see me, or don't you want to see me? . . . Whatever it may be: I beg you for a word. . . . After we have gone about together for nine years, I think I am entitled to ask for truth and clarity. Give me a sign!" (Heyse-Archiv, VI [Levi 24], H.A., Stabi.) It took a while until the old cordiality was restored. Wagner's death in February 1883 may have helped.
50. Weingartner, *Lebens Erinnerungen*, I, 265.
51. See below, 226–27.

plied sacrifice of self, especially the self of others. Towards the end of August 1875, when the preparations for the first Bayreuth Festival were already far advanced, Levi told his father: "From the 9th to the 13th I was in Bayreuth, listening to the rehearsals of *Siegfried* and *Götterdämmerung*. Was completely overwhelmed by the impression of the works, the house, and the performance. I of all people, who became a Wagnerian by a very circuitous route and after many inner battles, have perhaps a relatively independent judgment. I am old enough not to fool myself any more—and I tell you that what is going to take place in Bayreuth next year will produce a radical upheaval in our artistic life."[52] In Bayreuth, the music of the future became the music of the present, and Levi thought it no small honor to be in the front rank of the revolutionaries.

But—the fact remained—Wagner was an anti-Semite and Levi was a Jew, and the son of a rabbi. Hence Levi found it necessary to reassure his father about Wagner's character over and over again. In April 1882, the year of *Parsifal*, when the elder Levi still hesitated, still wished he could like Wagner, Hermann Levi enthusiastically replied: "That you surely can, and must, do! He is the best and noblest of men. That his world misunderstands and libels him is natural; the world usually blackens the radiant; Goethe, too, went through the same thing." Even Wagner's struggle against what he called "Jewry" in "music and modern literature" springs from "the noblest of motives," and he is wholly free of "petty Jew-hatred—*kleinliches Risches.*"[53]

Wagner's anti-Semitism could not be so suavely exorcised. It was something more than the telling of a few offensive jokes or a certain social snobbery; it was a philosophy from which it was easy to derive a deadly program, a philosophy not casually held and marginal, but passionately believed and central to Wagner's notions about the world. In fact, Wagner and his clan liked to re-

---

52. August 30, 1875. *"Parsifal"* Program, 6.
53. April 13, 1882. *"Parsifal"* Program, 9. In the fall of 1878, when Levi lay ill, his father came to visit him, and, as Levi reported to Heyse on November 16, sat by him, tried to read the *Nibelungenlied*, and asked his son questions. A substantial portion of German-Jewish history is summed up in this little domestic scene. (Heyse-Archiv, VI [Levi, 18]. H.A., Stabi.)

mind Levi of his "tragic flaw," with a kind of obsessive meanness. When Wagner visited Munich toward the end of 1880 and, as the guest at one of Ludwig II's private performances, heard Levi conduct *Lohengrin*, he noted dozens of false tempi and (in the words of Glasenapp, Wagner's uncritical semi-official biographer) "did not neglect to enlighten Levi about them." Apparently, Wagner thought these errors of judgment somehow "racial" in origin, for he took the opportunity to discuss with Levi the "depressing, destructive influence of Jewry on our public affairs," and to warn him against it "emphatically."[54]

Neither Richard nor Cosima Wagner could leave this delicate subject alone. They knew that Levi suffered under his Jewishness and, with a smiling sympathy more wounding than candid scorn, they told him he was right to suffer. "Everyone," Cosima Wagner wrote to Hermann Levi in 1886, three years after her husband's death, "everyone dies as a Christian, for Christianity is true. Blessed are those who are permitted to be Christians in their lifetime."[55] On his frequent visits to Wahnfried or during his encounters with the Wagners at watering-places or in Munich, Levi had to tolerate Cosima Wagner's explorations of his melancholy

54. See Carl Fr. Glasenapp, *Das Leben Richard Wagners*, VI (1911), 400, 404. That "racial differences" were at the heart of musical understanding was a crucial point in the ideology of Bayreuth. Cosima Wagner touched on the matter several times in her letters to Houston Stewart Chamberlain. (See December 12, 1888, and March 20, 1890. *Briefwechsel*, 43, 144.)

55. Cosima Wagner to Levi, September 8, 1886. Leviana, III, 7 (Cosima Wagner, 6). H.A., Stabi. There are no fewer than 307 letters from Cosima Wagner to Hermann Levi in the Levi papers, ranging from insinuating flattery to cool condescension and back. Seen as a whole, they are a collective masterpiece of seduction, open and concealed. On August 29, 1886, she assured him: "My attitude toward you is unchangeable; I have told you this and repeat it now." (Leviana, III, 7 [Cosima Wagner, 5]. H.A., Stabi.) At times (see the letter of June 21, 1887 [no. 301]), she could try to cajole him in sisterly fashion; at other times, as in several letters of 1889 (nos. 113, 114, and others), she could give his Wahnfried nickname, "major," a confidential-Jewish cast by addressing Levi as "dear major-leben." That Cosima Wagner was far more complex, far less confident, than she appeared in this kind of correspondence, we now know from her published diaries. See Peter Gay, "A Guardian of the Shrine" [a review of Cosima Wagner's *Tagebücher*, I, 1869–77], *Times Literary Supplement*, January 28, 1977, p. 94.

and, it seemed, incurable situation. Not long before his death, when he was already visibly ailing, she could not refrain from telling him that while a Jew could become a Christian, he could never become a Teuton. Her consoling gloss, that she prized the Christian above the Teuton, was such a transparent prevarication that it did not make Levi feel any better.[56]

The incident of July 28, 1881, which throws a glaring light on this degrading symbiosis, has been canvassed before but deserves another exploration. Hermann Levi was then staying at Wahnfried, participating in the final preparations for *Parsifal*. He had taken a walk into Bayreuth and returned to Wahnfried to have lunch with the Wagner family, but arrived at the house a little late. As he entered, Levi reports, Wagner stood "in the hall, watch in hand, and said in a highly ceremonious, serious tone, 'You are ten minutes late! Unpunctuality is half infidelity! He who keeps others waiting is an egotist.' " This little lecture over, Wagner in his normal voice asked Levi to go to his room and read a letter he had put on his table. Levi, as usual, obeyed. What he read was an anonymous denunciation from Munich entreating Wagner "to keep his work pure, and not allow a Jew to conduct it." In addition, the letter threw "suspicions" on Levi's "character" and on his "relations to Wahnfried."

We know that these suspicions were the accusation that Hermann Levi was having an affair with Cosima Wagner. The charge was absurd, but talk of love affairs touched the Wagners at a sensitive spot. When Levi sat silent at lunch, "profoundly upset and indignant," Wagner, whose sadism was evidently not yet sated, asked him why he was being so quiet. Levi replied that he could not understand why Wagner had not simply torn up the libel without showing it to him. Wagner's response was shrewd, but is suspect: "If I had shown the letter to no one, had I destroyed it,

56. See Cosima Wagner to Houston Stewart Chamberlain, March 1, 1900. *Briefwechsel*, 589–90. She admitted to her correspondent that her concession to Levi had not been truthful. For Chamberlain's rather lofty yet respectful attitude to Levi, see his "Zur Einführung" to Richard Wagner's letters to Levi, *Bayreuther Blätter*, XXIV (1901), 13–17; and Chamberlain's polite letters to Levi himself. (Leviana, I, 53 [Chamberlain, 1–14]. H.A., Stabi.)

perhaps something of it would have rankled within me. But now I can assure you that not the slightest memory will remain with me." Abreaction, we know, is a satisfying form of discharge; abreaction at the expense of another must have been doubly satisfying.

In any event, Levi only waited to the end of the meal to pack his things and leave for Bamberg, "without saying farewell to the Master." From there he wrote to Wagner, asking to be relieved from conducting *Parsifal*. It is easy to visualize Levi's turmoil: he had sacrificed much for Wagner, but now, as if struck in the face by his idol, the best and noblest of men, he was ready instead to sacrifice an assignment that would guarantee him a conductor's immortality. Wagner replied with a pacific telegram; Levi persisted in his renunciation, and Wagner now brought all the batteries of his charm into play. He did not apologize, he did not justify himself; instead he threw the blame on Levi's brooding introspection: "With all respect to your feelings, you don't make things easy for yourself or for us!" He added that everyone at Wahnfried agreed "to tell the world all about this sh . . , but it's essential that you don't run away from us, which will only let people suspect some nonsense. For God's sake, turn around right away and at last get to know us thoroughly! Lose none of your faith, but add strong courage to it! Perhaps—there will be a great turning point in your life—but at all events—you are my Parsifal-conductor!"

Wagner was bold to allude to the libel about Cosima and Levi (the "nonsense"), and even bolder to hint, once again, at Levi's possible conversion (the "turning point"). Only an experienced and self-assured gambler would have taken such a risk. Only the piling up of dashes and exclamation points and the self-conscious obscenity hint at an attack, however fleeting, of bad conscience, or even of fear that for once the snake would not dance to the familiar sounds. Risky as it was, Wagner's appeal worked. The letter, Levi later noted, "of course" made him return to Bayreuth. And, in the following year, he became what Wagner had called him, half coaxing, half commanding: his "Parsifal-conductor."

The affair is not wholly transparent. That Wagner wanted Levi and no one else to conduct *Parsifal* simply because of Levi's talents is just not credible. We have, to be sure, no recordings of Levi's performances, though reviewers agreed on commending his precision and his gift for getting clarity without coldness from the largest orchestras. And, whatever presumed racial incapacities to understand the Master's works some Wagner idolators professed to hear, there is evidence that he took Wagner's music at the rapid pace that Wagner himself liked. Yet Wagner had hinted to his intimates that he saw something sinister about the defilement of Bayreuth's mysteries by Jewish invaders. He had certainly intimated as much to his beloved, or at least indispensable, patron Ludwig II. But, while Wagner's friends at Bayreuth might sagely nod in agreement, Ludwig II, whatever his other psychotic symptoms, did not, as I have said, number racial anti-Semitism among them. And Wagner was in the king's debt up to his eyebrows; moreover, he needed the support of the Munich Opera Company to make his *Bühnenweihfestspiel* a reality. Levi's "desertion" would have jeopardized the whole enterprise; "no Levi, no *Parsifal*" was a very real threat.[57]

One is driven to suppose that Wagner felt compelled to make a tactical retreat, to disappoint his anti-Semitic followers (who in any event would never desert him) and let "the Jew Levi" conduct *Parsifal* after all. After its first performance, Wagner made a little speech in which he paid tribute to "his friend Levi," to his "endurance," his "understanding," and his "enthusiasm."[58] He was lucky that his letter of the previous July had aborted Levi's rebellion before it became public and, with that, irrevocable. It is a depressing affair, but what is most depressing of all is Levi's conviction that, after that letter, he must return to Bayreuth as a matter of course. With that "of course," we stand before a frightening psychological abyss.

57. The incident is the staple of all the longer biographies. The account in Newman, *Wagner*, IV, 636–38, remains valuable. Wagner's relevant letters, with Levi's commentaries and Chamberlain's commentary on the commentaries, are gathered in "Richard Wagners Briefe an Hermann Levi," *Bayreuther Blätter*, XXIV (1901), especially 31–32, 40–41. A number of Wagner's acquaintances report his gloom at having to turn over his *Parsifal* to the Jew Levi.

58. See Glasenapp, *Wagner*, VI, 638.

While Wagner and his family touched Levi's wound over and over again, *Parsifal* was at the centre of his malaise. "I have the book of *Parsifal* before me," he wrote to Paul Heyse in 1878. In Munich, mutual friends were making jokes about it; Lenbach claimed to know that after this *Bühnenweihfestspiel* Wagner would produce a *Bühnenkirchenweihfestspiel*. But Levi saw nothing funny in the book at all. "I withhold my opinion of the text for good and sufficient reason. Its extreme Christian tendency troubles me. I'll have no alternative but to have myself baptized once I begin to work it through."[59] One might take the last sentence as a specimen of black humor, but Levi never joked about Wagner.

Despite Wagner's racial anti-Semitism, he was by no means consistent in his attitude towards Jews. On the one hand, he could heartily commiserate with Levi about the cruel destiny that had doomed him to be born a Jew, and congratulate him for retaining his obviously Jewish name. On the other hand, he could urge Levi to accept baptism. Injured and confused, Levi sought clarity by consulting gentile friends like Wilhelm Busch. But, not sharing his obsession, they could not resolve his difficulties, least of all a convinced skeptic like Busch, who refused to settle Levi's anguished questions about whether "the Christians are right." "Over there, at the other bank of the river," Busch wrote to Levi in December 1880, "stands St. Augustine. He nods to me earnestly: Here is the boat of faith, grace is ferryman; whoever calls urgently will be brought across. But I cannot call; my soul is hoarse; I have a philosophical cold."[60] That was nicely said, but it could hardly help Levi, who wanted to call, urgently, but did not know the right words.

Levi's suffering was not assuaged by the triumph of *Parsifal*,

59. January 1, 1878. Heyse-Archiv, VI (Levi, 14). H.A., Stabi.
60. Busch to Levi, December 13, 1880. *Briefe*, I, 214–15. The practice of kissing the "Master's" hand, which Mensi-Klarbach had observed (see above, 215), was one in which Levi often indulged. Glasenapp records an incident in which Wagner, as he so often did, needled Levi to accept baptism: "I wish I could find the formula to let you feel entirely one of us, entirely belong to us." When Wagner saw Levi's "veiled, darkened face," he desisted from pressing further, and responded to Levi's handkiss with "a cordial embrace." (Glasenapp, *Wagner*, VI, 427-28.)

which was partly his triumph. He quarreled with Julius Kniese, director of the festival choir at Bayreuth, one of the true fanatics among the faithful, over Kniese's articulate and incurable anti-Semitism.[61] And he was kept informed of the anti-Jewish machinations of the Wagner entourage, which only grew in virulence after Wagner's death. His emotions thus remained at boiling-point. His acts of piety designed to keep the festivals going after Wagner's death were grudgingly accepted, and resented as impudence. And what he did not hear from adversaries intending to wound, he heard from admirers intending to soothe. In 1892, the young composer and conductor Felix Weingartner, in whom Levi had taken a fatherly interest, sent Levi a gigantic letter indicting Bayreuth's anti-Semitism with passion and in detail. Precisely as an admirer of Wagner's music who knew the Bayreuth festivals from the inside, Weingartner despised the Wagner cult. A "worthy performance of *Parsifal*," he told Levi, "is possible, at least at present, *only* and *exclusively* when you are there." He recalled the Festival of 1888, when illness had kept Levi from Bayreuth, as scandalously inferior. And that was the year, he noted, when "word went out from Bayreuth that *Parsifal* at last has been delivered from 'Jewish hands' and given back to Christianity."[62] Levi was doubtless flattered to receive an accolade so obviously straining not to flatter. But it did not lessen his

61. Some of the most implacable Jew-hatred at Bayreuth goes back to Kniese and his friends. Levi had some credit even in this improbable quarter: on March 22, 1883, a month after Wagner's death, Kniese admitted to Karl Riedel, president of the Allgemeine deutsche Musikverein, that "the Jew Levi (?)" might well be among those to keep the Wagnerian tradition alive. He added a question mark to his conjecture, but the conjecture occurred to him. Julie Kniese, ed., *Der Kampf zweier Welten um das Bayreuther Erbe. Julius Knieses Tagebuchblätter aus dem Jahre 1883* (1931), 56. It is worth recording that while Kniese intensely disliked Levi, Levi permitted himself to reciprocate, and to show, the sentiment. He could evidently find it in himself to resent slights from underlings but not from the principal.

62. August 6, 1892. Leviana, I, 53 (Weingartner, 9). H.A., Stabi. Weingartner apparently liked his almost pamphlet-length letter well enough to print much of it in his bellicose brochure, *Bayreuth 1876–1896* (1897), and even, thirty years later, in his autobiography.

perplexity. His father, earnestly trying to like Wagner, was often in his mind.

Had Hermann Levi been alone in his worship of Richard Wagner, his spiritual odyssey would be of interest mainly to the student of psychopathology. But Levi was not alone; the Master gathered about himself a never-exhausted supply of acolytes and disciples and victims. Wagner, indeed, had, or rather made, many victims. The privileged few admitted to his intimate domesticity at Tribschen in the late 1860s and, later, at Wahnfried in the 1870s often found him a genial and companionable host; many of the performers who labored through exhausting rehearsals were moved by his infectious enthusiasm for their work, and for his own creations. Yet the list of those who suffered at his hands is long: the conductor Hans von Bülow, his loyal friend and early advocate, with whose wife Cosima he fathered children long before the Bülows were separated, let alone divorced; the tenor Ludwig Schnorr von Carolsfeld, who died shortly after creating the role of Tristan, a sudden, shocking death that Wagner himself, not without some complacency, attributed to the demonic effect of his music; King Ludwig II of Bavaria, whose infatuation Wagner exploited with the most shameless effrontery. There were many others—old friends whom Wagner chose to slight, public officials whom he thought it politic to attack, musical competitors whom he defamed in the grossest terms.

He was voracious, insatiable; as with other self-proclaimed mortal enemies of materialism, his greed for money was unappeasable, and grew with his prosperity. There is no point moralizing about such a natural force. Clearly, Wagner gave while he took. His worshipers obviously regarded it as an experience beyond price to be allowed to touch the hem of greatness, and to share, in however lowly a capacity, in making the music of the future. Strikingly, most of those whom Wagner victimized came back for more, attributing their misery to their own inadequacies rather than to the Master's actions. And some of the most tenacious of his victims were Jews.

We cannot therefore dismiss the cultural dimension of Hermann Levi's self-flagellation; the crowd of Wagner's Jewish abject followers is too large for that. *Selbsthass*, it seemed, was more than a unique, private aberration. Some of the Jews susceptible to Wagner's person, and his dramas, like the pianist Carl Tausig, perished early; others, like the writer Heinrich Porges and the impresario Angelo Neumann, survived to become indispensable to the Cause.

But not all musical Jews were obsequious Wagnerites, and not all obsequious Wagnerites were Jews. If Levi negotiated at Richard Wagner's request with Wagner's publishers to save the Master trouble, if he assiduously hastened to fulfil Cosima Wagner's request to hear *Tristan* in Munich, if he thoughtfully supplied Wahnfried with books which he thought might amuse them, he behaved precisely like Nietzsche, that hardworking, overburdened professor at Basle. Nietzsche (who, by the way, was responsible for bringing Levi and Wagner together), found time to shop for toys that would please the Wagner children, took tedious pains over Wagner's writings, and neglected his own work at the insistent calls from Tribschen. It was common knowledge that life with Wagner meant utter self-abnegation. The gifted conductor Felix Mottl, who knew the Bayreuth atmosphere from close exposure, gave the watchword: at Bayreuth, he said, "the only word is—*serve!*"[63] And it was service with a smile. Heinrich Vogl, the celebrated tenor who, with his wife Therese, created some of Wagner's most important roles, once complained privately, to Levi, that Wagner had irresponsibly promised the same roles to too many singers. "We are at fault," he wrote, angrily, sarcastically, and resignedly. "Unlike others, we do not tread the paths of flattery, which they like at Bayreuth all to well."[64] Still, he could not bring himself to blame the Master. It must be his entourage that was behind all this duplicity. The mechanism of exculpating the man at the top by blaming his followers is as old as the theory of medieval kingship and as modern as the mouthings of Nazi apologists; it was a characteristic quality of the Wagner mythology. In the end, the Vogls sang when, where, and what Bayreuth wanted them to sing.

63. Weingartner, *Lebens Erinnerungen*, I, 266.
64. Vogl to Levi, May 26, 1882. Leviana, I, 53 (Vogl, 2). H.A., Stabi.

There are moments when the cultists' masochism emerges into full view. "A marvellous testimonial to your vitality, *hochverehrte Meisterin*," Houston Stewart Chamberlain wrote to Cosima Wagner, "is the way you have of chastising someone, when he has deserved to be chastised."[65] In Bayreuth, there were many opportunities to be chastised, and it was part of the Bayreuth code to hold out one's hand to the rod without complaining.

The personal strategies that Richard and Cosima Wagner developed could therefore not be specialized for susceptible Jews; they must have general application. In speaking of strategies I am not hinting at some secret plot or even a long-range, coherent Wagnerian plan. The Wagners were more pragmatic than that; they used what worked and discarded what failed: self-inflation and self-denial were not permanent postures but adaptable instruments. The little speeches with which Wagner liked to reward his musicians (which would repay close study) are masterly performances. One such, given in Munich on May 11, 1865, after a dress rehearsal of *Tristan*, and preserved in the Levi papers, is a splendid representative of the genre. Wagner told the assembled musicians that he did not plan to conduct the premiere; first, because his health was not as strong as it looked, and, secondly, because he had become unnecessary. The company had taken possession of his drama and could now, as it were, give it back to him: "I can enjoy it in peace." The ultimate in beauty had been reached: "The artist can be forgotten in face of his work of art." Thus, with the great task accomplished, the artist had achieved deliverance: "To be forgotten! . . . How happily do I see myself forgotten!"[66]

It was pure demagoguery, but it worked. His listeners must

---

65. November 30, 1891. *Briefwechsel*, 255.
66. A copy of Wagner's little speech, in Eva Wagner's handwriting, is in the Leviana, III, 2. H.A., Stabi. The pose is no less impressive for being common: historians like Fustel de Coulanges and Leopold von Ranke, both Wagner's contemporaries, liked to insist that history spoke through them; and a little later, Gustav Mahler wrote to a friend about his third symphony: "Now I want you to think about such a great work, in which indeed the whole world mirrors itself—one is, so to speak, only an instrument on which the universe is playing." (Quoted in Wolfgang Schreiber, *Mahler* [1971], 68.)

have sensed that the man who told them he reveled in being forgotten wanted nothing more than to be remembered. But the contradiction was only apparent: the self-denying claim was a claim to greatness. For only the rarest of artists could so utterly identify himself with his work, so completely realize himself within it, that it, in a way, annihilated him. And there were other occasions, notably when he needed money, when Wagner sounded rather different.

Wagner's aims did not range as widely as his methods; they only grew more ambitious as success turned fantasies into reality. Wagner, Nietzsche wrote after his awakening, had turned into an Imperial German—"*reichsdeutsch.*"[67] But, in the derisive sense in which Nietzsche used the term, Wagner had been *reichsdeutsch* before there had even been a Reich. In crass contrast with the portrait of Wagner as an *"Unzeitgemässer,"* first proposed by Nietzsche and later assiduously spread by the propaganda machine of Bayreuth, the Master was anything but an "untimely man." He wanted what most Germans of the day wanted; the political radicalism of his early years should not obscure this point. Wagner gave the public gigantic and original music dramas, which he wanted to be treated as sacred works, not in the hyperbolical or metaphorical but in the literal sense.

In his voluminous writings he assimilated what he confessed to be his unique achievement to his nationality. His work was German because it was great, and great because it was German. The musical literature of the late nineteenth century, not excluding the technical periodicals, was extraordinarily chauvinistic everywhere, though, I think, more extravagantly so in Germany than elsewhere. The article of faith that coupled musical achievement with German national character was widely held, and Wagner's claims, like Wagner's work, gave it rich substance. Certainly Hermann Levi was a true believer. Berlioz, he thought, was an interesting composer, Sarasate a gifted violinist, but both, to his German ear, lacked, like all foreigners, German *Innerlichkeit.*

The apotheosis of Wagner drew on yet another element. Wagner lived the artist's life, acting out the extravagant fantasies of

---

67. *Ecce Homo, Werke,* 5 vols. (1972), III, 537.

the good bourgeois. In a century of heightened self-control, in which "civilization" increasingly tried to inhibit "nature" in the way people ate, talked, and made love, the artist played the part of the holy fool; he was allowed to tell the truth and follow his passions, free from the inhibitions of gentility. As Baudelaire and Oscar Wilde discovered, there were limits. But these limits were staked out far wider than those that the citizen of the new industrial age had set for himself. There were of course advanced painters, sculptors, and composers who lived as respectable people, keeping regular hours, saving their money, and being soberly monogamous; the domestic ideal had its attraction for artists just as the bohemian ideal had its temptation for merchants. But Wagner was his own law. Above all in his affair with Cosima von Bülow he offended, publicly and without apparent shame, the very rules that ordinary mortals assiduously obeyed or violated only in the strictest secrecy. When Wagner and his mistress invited the sister of their newly acquired friend, Friedrich Nietzsche, to Tribschen, she hesitated and asked for advice. But she went.

So did his other admirers. No one, after all, played the role of the unconventional artist with greater panache than Wagner. If in his last years the couple paraded as prophets of a new culture, and acted as though they had a monopoly not merely on *Kultur* but on morality as well, it only made them more interesting. They radiated, as Nietzsche had quickly noticed, the impression that what they did was natural and right. If they were entitled to judge others, others were not entitled to judge them. It was an attitude incredibly seductive to most of their contemporaries, who were, like most mortals, weaker vessels, ready to yield to the happy few who were blessed with utter certainty. That as late as 1881 the Wagners did not manage to be wholly indifferent to the accusation of infidelity—I am, of course, speaking of the anonymous letter linking Cosima Wagner with Levi—may suggest that they did not feel quite so superior to the world as they liked to appear. But they took care to reveal as few such symptoms of mere human weakness as possible.

All this would not have counted for so much if the idealization of the artist had not been so important in the nineteenth century.

For many, art had become something of a religion, and Wagner incarnated the role of priest to perfection. Wilhelm Busch drily took his distance from what he called "revelations through music,"[68] but he could hardly expect to gain Hermann Levi's assent to such ironic rationalism. It would have been worthwhile if Nietzsche, after his famous exploration of attitudes to history, had turned his mind to the uses and abuses of art in the nineteenth century.

Levi's deification of Wagner was thus more than a personal, or a German-Jewish tragedy, though it was both. It was part of a larger cultural tragedy, baleful for civilization at large but particularly destructive for Germany. It inhibited critical thinking at a moment when such thinking was imperative. But it was not a conductor's tragedy, because Levi's wide cultivation and elevated sense of his *Kapellmeister*'s responsibilities freed him from an exclusive devotion to the corpus of Wagner and that of his disciples. And yet it was precisely his infatuation that helped to make him a consequential figure in German culture in his day. To have mastered the Wagnerian repertory was to have become indispensable, almost irreplaceable. This mastery gave Levi whatever internal stability and external authority he commanded. When Richard Wagner was buried at Wahnfried on February 16, 1883, the Jew Hermann Levi was one of the pallbearers. He left the best part of himself in that grave. But the Cause lived on, and so did Hermann Levi—to serve it.

68. Busch to Lenbach, August 27, 1886. *Briefe*, I, 271.

V

AIMEZ-VOUS BRAHMS?
On Polarities in Modernism

The need to order experience through polarities seems to be deeply anchored in the human psyche; at least, it has long dominated the mental style of Western man. We categorize and generalize by pitting one class of things against another. Hot against cold, early against late, proper against improper, and dozens of other confrontations place our perceptions and orient our judgments. Most polarities are imprecise, unscientific, evasive, and distorting, but they appear indispensable. Historians, too, though enjoined to respect complexity and individuality (both inhospitable to simplistic categories) often find themselves governed, or guided, by them. They confront radical with reactionary, past with present, private with public; and, though they may manfully resist, often they cannot help confronting friends with enemies, good with bad. Their ways of thinking prove that, for all their professional training, historians are as human as everyone else.

Modernism seems at first glance to have escaped this kind of schematic thinking, escaped it by the paradox to which I alluded in my introduction: the Modernist's hatred of the modern. This defining perception certainly cuts through so insinuating a polarity as traditional against innovative by letting the Modernist be, quite simply, both. In detesting and combating what is most modern about the modern world—the machine, the metropolis, the mass man in mass culture—the Modernist has resorted to tradition without being mired in sheer revivalism, and experimented with style, with technique, with claiming new terrain for permissible subject matter, without committing himself to the political and social novelties around him. The letter that Hermann Levi wrote to his father about the forthcoming first Bayreuth Festival is an arresting instance of how the paradox of Modernism can confound received modes of thought: "The works of Wagner," Levi wrote, "may perish, but not his reforming, or, rather, reactionary ideas. I say 'reactionary,' because he has once again assigned to music the proper station that it already had before, with Gluck."[1] And this much I concede: to the extent that it has enabled us to see the world as something more than a simple, single combat, the paradox of Modernism has proved an instrument of intellectual clarification.

At the same time, though, Modernists, dragging their historians behind them, pay tribute to polarities of their own, just as invalid as the polarities they have rejected. I have listed these polarities before: the alienated artist against the complacent bourgeois, the avant-garde against the academy, the outsider against the establishment. Modernists and their historians have, in short, seen the world from the mid-nineteenth century onward as a world riven in two, a culture in civil war.

That there is something in this, that some self-appointed *poètes maudits* were damned souls and many accused of philistinism true philistines, I have no reason to doubt. Nor do I have the slightest intention of minimizing the importance of conflict in human affairs: it marks the mental life of the individual as it helps to shape the course of political and economic life. But conflict is neither so continuous, nor so simple, as customary thinking, thinking in polarities, would have it. Strife is succeeded by intermissions of calm; peace is disrupted by sudden war. Brothers turn into enemies; enemies into brothers. Nationalist efferves-

1. August 30, 1875. Bayreuther Festspiele, 1959, *"Parsifal" Program*, ed. Festspielleitung (1959), 6.

cence silences class struggles; adversaries become allies because both have discovered a common object of hatred and, conversely, alliances collapse once the occasion for alliance has been removed. Individuals want incompatible things: public renown and professional respect, power and affection. Interests shift; ambivalence underlies the most loudly proclaimed, most firmly held sentiments. All this is true, commonplace—and forgotten, even by historians. This essay on the surprising history of Brahms's reputation should serve as a reminder. Brahms, in his aspirations, his culture, above all his compositions, embraced, without strain, many of the polarities we have been taught to see as unchangeable, and unchangeably opposed to one another. The lesson of his reputation is the urgent need to restore our sense of complexity about Modernism.

1. THE DIFFICULT EPIGONE

I begin with a scene from one of Françoise Sagan's cool and meretricious fictions. Paule, the worldly, aging protagonist of *Aimez-vous Brahms?*, receives a letter from a younger man, a recent, promising acquaintance, inviting her to a concert and asking her, in passing, "Do you like Brahms?" Puzzled and intrigued, Paule hunts among her records to find, back to back with a Wagner overture she knows by heart, a Brahms concerto she has never listened to. The coupling is improbable, but, whatever the probabilities, Paule puts on the Brahms concerto, and does not listen to the end. Its very opening repels her, she says, as too "romantic." For her, a knowing, modern woman, Brahms is *passé*.[2]

Paule speaks for the general public, the public certain that Brahms was a musical reactionary, too "romantic"—which is to say: sentimental, low in emotional appeal, a museum piece on the order of antimacassars, china sculpture, and virginal brides. Brahms is a dusty relic from those old days. His symphonies and

2. *Aimez-vous Brahms?* (1959).

concertos are staples of our musical repertory; the reviewer scribbling his hasty verdict on a program including Brahms's Fourth Symphony or Second Piano Concerto finds the temptation irresistible to call them "war horses." He is more likely to assess the performance than appraise the music—a tribute to its familiarity.

It is a tribute concealing derision. Familiarity has always bred contempt, and our sensibility has elevated the contempt that familiarity breeds into an article of faith. The atmosphere of high culture that we have been inhabiting for nearly a century is rather like the Hell that George Bernard Shaw's John Tanner visits in his dream: a place where all is reversed. Here, unpopularity is the precondition of popularity, at least among the sophisticated consumers of the arts. And the obverse holds just as true: popularity engenders unpopularity, again among the sophisticated. In our high culture, as in Don Juan's Hell, one must be damned to be saved, and the saved are damned.

If this is a paradox, it is not a cheap one. It is, in any event, not mine. It pervades the performing arts, literature, and thought. Since the Impressionists first defied the French Academy, painting has produced a parade of movements, each more esoteric than its predecessor. Since the Symbolists first shut themselves into their exclusive enclaves, poetry has spawned schools of increasing difficulty. Since in his late years Henry James designed monuments of discrimination making severe claims on their public, the novel has ventured into formal experimentation, linguistic adventures, and planned incoherence. Sculpture, architecture, philosophy, and, more recently, literary criticism have been conquered by avant-gardes going their solitary way, despising not merely the common but even the educated understanding, looking over their shoulder with a curious mixture of self-pity and truculence. And modern music has gone as far as it is possible to go in the cultivation of incomprehensibility, its surrender to the machine, or to chance. It is composed by the very few, for the very few. A handful of true believers apart, to attend a concert of contemporary music is to document one's membership in a coterie, or to race, desperately, after a cultural train that left the station long ago.

The recent counter-attack of common-sense traditionalists, often virulent and generally obtuse, is doubtless more pernicious than the aberrations it professes to combat.[3] But our distaste for this vulgar, even unsavory reaction cannot compel us to treat aberrations as masterpieces. And these aberrations are only the most egregious exemplars of that pervasive Modernist characteristic: the will to fail. High culture has become an industry of self-fulfilling prophecies. Anticipating, indeed craving, misunderstanding, bafflement, and rejection, Modernists have manufactured artifacts bound to be misunderstood, baffling—and rejected. In its code, to succeed—to be understood by the public, praised by the reviewer, subsidized by the patron—is to fail where it really matters: in one's art or one's thought. To sell is to sell out. To make matters worse, many critics and historians, at once uncritical and unhistorical, have taken the Modernists at their self-destructive—which is to say, self-serving—word; they have professed to recognize Modernist artists, writers, and philosophers by two essential, distinct but related, qualities: alienation and difficulty. With a few exceptions, they will insist, the Modern is the disruptive stranger.

Brahms, on this definition, fails to qualify as a Modern. He is a classic and seems, from our perspective, to have been born that way—a composer who was never young. He appears not alienated but conformist, not difficult but accessible. To begin with: he scarcely sounds like an alienated experimenter. His symphonies have the expected four movements. His chamber music moves within the predictable confines laid down by his classical predecessors. His lieder march in the paths marked out by Schubert and his followers. It is not an accident that for all his repeated but half-hearted explorations, Brahms never ventured into the musical genre which, in the nineteenth century, offered troublemakers their finest opportunity: the opera. The familiar anecdotes that cluster about him only underscore the impression that he looked to the past for his inspiration, and to the past alone. Brahms studied earlier music with the earnestness of the devout

3. In a brilliant polemic, Hilton Kramer has called this counter-attack "The Revenge of the Philistines." See *Commentary*, CIX, 5 (May, 1975), 35–40.

conservative, and put the seal on his antiquarian passion by collecting musical autographs of the composers he most admired: Bach, Haydn, Mozart, Beethoven.

Brahms's musical politics express the same style of thinking. He led, or (which is much the same thing) was widely thought to lead, the party that opposed Liszt, Wagner, and Bruckner—the self-proclaimed Musicians of the Future. And, by definition, the musician who rejects the Music of the Future must speak for the Music of the Past. Perhaps the most damaging piece of evidence convicting Brahms of conformism is the long, tormented gestation of his First Symphony. It is a familiar but true story: Brahms carried the idea of a symphony about with him for many years. As early as January 1854, he could tell his mentor, Robert Schumann, that he had already orchestrated the first, and composed the second and third movements. In the 1860s, he punctuated his letters to his closest friends with allusions to that symphony. But instead of completing the composition so slow in the making, he adopted a series of strategic retreats: the First Piano Concerto of 1859, the First String Sextet of 1862, the Piano Quintet of 1865. And as late as the early 1870s, he could sense the oppressive presence of Beethoven: "I'll never compose a symphony," he is reported to have said. "You have no idea how the likes of us feel when we keep hearing such a giant behind us."[4] It was not until 1877, when he was forty-four, that he dared step before the public with his First Symphony, a delay so emphatic that it eloquently speaks of an unsurmountable respect, an invincible humility, before the classics of his craft.

Brahms's way of life seems perfectly consistent with such timidity. The mildest of debauches apart, he lived soberly, modestly, solemnly; his lifelong bachelorhood is a symptom of bourgeois cowardice rather than a badge of bohemian freedom. There was no madness in his life, as in that of his beloved Schumann; he provoked no salacious scandals such as those marking the life of Liszt; he made no move to compete with Wagner in prophesying a new religion of art. Brahms sought financial security, practiced

4. Reportedly a remark made to Hermann Levi, quoted in Kurt Stephenson, "Der Komponist Brahms im eigenen Urteil," *Brahms-Studien*, ed. Constantin Floros (1974), I, 15.

innocent pleasures, enjoyed decent company; he was a slave to the ethic of work, much like a bank clerk or a shopkeeper. He had been a young man of almost ethereal beauty who entered— almost fled into—middle age behind the appropriate disguise of a bushy beard, the very emblem of respectability.

More important: Brahms is not difficult but easy. He strikes the modern ear, in fact, as all too easy, with those long yearning melodies announced by the cello, and the thick resounding tutti produced by his sizable orchestra. Even his chamber music—that demanding, spare genre that reveals all—often sounds oddly symphonic. Much of it lacks the acerbity, the dry wit, the intimacy of classical chamber music; with its all-too-pleasing themes and sonorous scoring, it approaches at times the kind of music played by a discreet ensemble in resort hotels to the clatter of spoons and the hum of conversation. Possibly the most devastating portrait of the "easy" Brahms comes from George Bernard Shaw, the perfect Wagnerite. Comparing Brahms with Elgar, Shaw thought Brahms to have been, "with a facility as convenient as Elgar's," a "musical sensualist with intellectual affectations," who "succeeded only as an incoherent voluptuary, too fundamentally addleheaded to make anything great out of the delicious musical luxuries he wallowed in."[5] It was bad enough to be a voluptuary, but to be an incoherent voluptuary was to throw worse emotions after bad.

The literature of condescension that has collected around Brahms the "romantic classicist" is too familiar to require recital. I want to recall only one telling instance. In his *Steppenwolf*, Hermann Hesse has his narrator amble his way through a fantastic dream theatre; there he encounters Mozart and, as the two talk about music, glimpses a mysterious scene. In a distant valley, obscured by fog and clouds, he sees a procession led by a dignified old gentleman with a long beard and a melancholy expression, followed by a train of about ten thousand men, all in black; Mozart identifies him: "You see, that is Brahms. He strives for salvation, but that will take quite some time." And the narrator learns

5. "Sir Edward Elgar," first published in *Music and Letters*, January 1920; collected in George Bernard Shaw, *How to Become a Musical Critic*, ed. Dan H. Laurence (1960), 312.

that those thousands of men in black are the musicians who had been compelled to play all of those superfluous Brahmsian notes. "Too heavily orchestrated," says Mozart, "too much material wasted."[6] These are the sounds we have come to call—loosely, in fact inaccurately—"romantic." To be sure, Hesse consigns Wagner to the same predicament; Wagner, too, drags a black-coated train of weary musicians behind him. Rather like Françoise Sagan, Hermann Hesse yokes these two adversaries together. But it is Brahms who is the model of those we may call, adapting Brecht, culinary composers. Whatever stature we assign to Hesse as a writer, he is a prince among Modernists, and it is chilling to see how pitilessly he places Brahms in the camp of the enemy, the anti-Moderns. That, not long after the *Steppenwolf* was published, Arnold Schoenberg should write an essay entitled "Brahms the Progressive" would appear to be little more than a bit of personal perversity.

These are the current convictions about Brahms. Their resemblance to historical realities is, however, purely coincidental. In 1874—that is, fifteen years after its first performance—the Viennese music critic Eduard Hanslick listened to Brahms's First Piano Concerto. Hanslick was a dependable friend and consistent supporter of Brahms, yet he found himself reflecting that "Brahms is not among those who obligingly meet you halfway. He needs to be thoroughly known, devotedly studied. But then," he added, Brahms "amply repays our efforts and our confidence."[7] Six years earlier, the composer Max Bruch had angrily reproached his friend, the conductor Hermann Levi, for being "an exclusive fanatic for Brahms's music." And Bruch had boasted, with a mixture of pride and anxiety, that people loved *his* compositions; they "do not wonder at it from a cold distance, as they do with some of the works of *your* idol."[8] This cold distance persisted. Shortly

6. *Der Steppenwolf* (1927), 271.
7. Hanslick, *Concerte, Componisten und Virtuosen der letzten fünfzehn Jahre. 1870–1885* (2nd ed., 1886), 111.
8. Bruch to Levi, April 26, 1868. Quoted in Wilhelm Lauth, "Entstehung und Geschichte des ersten Violinkonzertes op. 26 von Max Bruch," in *Max Bruch Studien*, ed. Dietrich Kämper (1970), 63.

after Brahms's death, "J. B. K." wrote to the London journal *Musical Opinion* from Berlin that "Brahms is very much *en évidence* this season: the usual fate of composers who wrote 'over the heads' of their contemporaries."[9] Three years later, an anonymous critic noted in the same periodical that while there were some who thought highly of Brahms, in general his "position among the great composers is still a matter of debate among musicians. Some can see neither beauty nor emotion in his music, and declare that he is never likely to reach the average music lover except in one or two of his songs."[10] A review of the literature amply proves those unable to find either beauty or emotion in Brahms's music to be a sizable majority in those years.

In short, the public found Brahms difficult. And serious critics, like professional musicians, agreed with amateur performers or listeners that Brahms *was* difficult. In 1872, Hans von Bülow recommended Brahms's Variations on a Theme of Haydn, a work that presents us with no puzzles whatever, as a composition he had "grown to love gradually," but one he still thought to be "terribly difficult—*furchtbar schwer*."[11] Two years later, writing to Frits Hartvigson, a pianist he respected, Bülow described Brahms's First Piano Concerto as "very beautiful indeed," but added that it "was not really a piano concerto proper." And he thought it less likely to please the public than the piano concerto of Hans von Bronsart, a composer now wholly forgotten.[12] In February 1889, a correspondent wrote from Leipzig, that great musical center, that the thirteenth concert of its Gewandhaus Orchestra had been comparatively ill-attended, and "the unreserved seats empty," possibly because its program had included "such heavy dishes as Brahms's First Piano Concerto and d'Albert's Overture to *Esther*." He conceded that d'Albert had played the Brahms "so exquisitely" that it had made a "deep impression," but that impression was not one of uncomplicated delight;

9. *Musical Opinion and Musical Trade Review*, XXI, No. 243 (December 1, 1897), 200.
10. *Musical Opinion*, XXIII, No. 272 (May 1, 1900), 554.
11. Bülow to Frau Laussot, December 13, 1872. Hans von Bülow, *Briefe*, ed. Marie von Bülow, V, 1872–1880 (1904), 107n.
12. April 10, 1874. *Briefe*, V, 161.

echoing Bülow, no doubt unwittingly, he pronounced the Brahms piece to "exceed in every way the legitimate limits of a concerto." Audiences appreciated the virtuosos who managed to play all of Brahms's notes more or less correctly. And they admired the sheer ingenuity of the composer for exploring the frontiers of such traditional forms as the variation. But the kind of unreflective emotional surrender, the tributes of pious silence or swooning assent, that would greet truly "romantic," genuinely popular composers, were not for him. They were reserved for Richard Wagner—or for Robert Volkmann, a composer now a name to specialists alone. At the eleventh Gewandhaus Concert of the 1888–89 season, Volkmann's D-Minor Symphony "formed," the reviewer reported, "a fitting climax" and aroused "great enthusiasm"—"as," he took care to add, "it always does." It was precisely great enthusiasm that Brahms rarely aroused.[13]

So innovative, so self-consciously modern a composer as Richard Strauss found Brahms's music inaccessible. In January 1884, after listening to a rehearsal of Brahms's Third Symphony in Berlin, he wrote to his father, a distinguished professional musician, that his head was still "buzzing with all this obscurity. I candidly confess that I haven't yet understood it, but it is so obscure and miserable in its instrumentation, that in the first and last movement I could make out only two connected ideas of four bars each."[14] He added that he was keeping this opinion within the family, since there was, in Berlin, something of a Brahms cult—a cult, I might interject, largely confined to Brahms's old friend Joseph Joachim and Joachim's pupils. Interestingly enough, Strauss changed his mind on repeated hearings: on February 1, he could report home that he had by now listened to the new Brahms symphony three times, "and liked it better each time, so that I

13. See, for both concerts, *The Monthly Musical Record*, XIX, No. 218 (February 1, 1889), 31. It is fair to add that *at times* Brahms had reason to take pleasure in his audiences. In that very season of 1888–89, the premiere in Vienna of Brahms's Double Concerto for violin and cello brought him "the cheers of an enthusiastic audience," while, in Budapest, the first public performance of his Third Violin Sonata produced an "ovation." "Music in Vienna," *Monthly Musical Record* (February 1, 1889), 32.

14. January 6, 1884. Richard Strauss, *Briefe an die Eltern, 1882–1906*, ed. Willi Schuh (1954), 32.

am now almost enthusiastic"[15]—that "almost" haunted Brahms all his life. Brahms, it would seem, did not merely *deserve* rehearing, as Hanslick had observed; he *needed* rehearing.

If even Germany found Brahms difficult—Germany, the country of Brahms, which took inordinate pride in its developed musical taste and unequaled musical production—other countries found him no easier. England, which in fact early gave Brahms a sensitive and generous hearing, incorporated him into its repertories with marked reluctance. When in March 1891 (fifteen years after its publication) the Shinner String Quartet played Brahms's Opus 67 for the first time in Birmingham, a reviewer noted that its "clearness and beauty" were "at once recognized and appreciated," but he immediately qualified this praise by adding a caution that was becoming a topos in Brahms criticism: "it is obvious that further repetition is needed to understand all its artistic import."[16] Two years before, a London reviewer had singled out Brahms's Second Piano Concerto as a "difficult work,"[17] and by "difficult" he did not mean the soloist's virtuoso part.

It is true that Brahms had his partisans among critics and conductors, but their support produced the kind of mutual alienation between the professional and the public that we normally associate with performances of avant-garde work. A typical review of a Brahms work would describe it not merely as "difficult" but also as "neglected." In Vienna, in 1889, when the Akademische Gesangverein produced Brahms's somber Begräbnisgesang, a reviewer called it "noble" (scarcely an epithet denoting a joyous yielding to the music) and added that it was "too-seldom-heard."[18] There were at least some critics who wondered out loud whether perhaps the resistant public showed a taste superior to

15. *Briefe an die Eltern*, p. 38. There is an excellent survey of German Brahms criticism in one influential periodical during Brahms's most creative period: Imogen Fellinger, "Das Brahms-Bild der *Allgemeinen Musikalischen Zeitung* (1863 bis 1882)," in Heinz Becker, ed. *Beiträge zur Geschichte der Musikkritik* (1965), 27–54.

16. *The Musical Times*, XXXII, No. 578 (April 1, 1891), 222.

17. *Musical Opinion* (September 1, 1889), 576.

18. *Monthly Musical Record*, XIX, No. 221 (May 1, 1889), 103.

that of conductors who forced the noble Brahms on it.[19] But in general, reviewers wanted to hear Brahms more often than his notorious angularities induced conductors to perform him. George Bernard Shaw, who, as we know, had a "poor opinion of most of Brahms's music,"[20] spoke for a minority in the critical fraternity. More representative was the London reviewer who found, in the 1888–89 season, that George Henschel's conducting Brahms's Second and Third Symphonies had not sated his appetite; why not, he asked, put the First and Fourth on the program as well, thus completing the "remarkable series"? He was glad to have attended a "good performance" of the Second, the "most cheery" of Brahms's four symphonies, and thought that it, too, was "too rarely heard."[21] In like manner, a colleague, who had objected to Henschel's inadequate rehearsals and hurried tempi, described Brahms's Third Symphony, "the most concise and genial" of his four, as a composition that was "strangely neglected."[22] Later in the same year, commenting on Brahms's much-debated First Piano Concerto, a correspondent in London called it "a strangely

19. When in Vienna, in 1889, the audience found Brahms's Gesang der Parzen supremely uninteresting, one reviewer openly sympathized with its demonstrative displeasure; "perhaps," he wrote, the public had "been right" to reject the composition so frankly. Neue Zeitschrift für Musik, LXXXVI (1890), 319.

20. How to Become a Musical Critic, p. 209. Shaw was an intelligent if doubtless deliberately provocative critic, and his musical criticism invites sober reflections about the instability of reputation and the ingratitude of posterity. On November 22, 1893, he reported on a symphonic concert in which Hermann Goetz's Symphony in F Major had been "the gem." In his judgment, this was "the only real symphony that has been composed since Beethoven died." Goetz, Shaw wrote, "has the charm of Schubert without his brainlessness, the refinement and inspiration of Mendelssohn without his limitation and timid gentility, Schumann's sense of harmonic expression without his laboriousness, shortcoming, and dependence on external poetic stimulus. . . ." As for Brahms: "Brahms, who alone touches him in mere brute musical faculty, is a dolt in comparison with him." (Music in London, 1890–94, 3 vols., III [ed. 1932], 94.) Needless to say, Goetz's symphony has disappeared from the repertory, while the dolt Brahms is doing well; probably the only composition of Goetz still widely performed is the overture to his opera, The Taming of the Shrew.

21. Musical Opinion (March 1, 1889), 276.

22. Musical Times, XXX, No. 551 (January 1, 1889), 22.

neglected work."[23] That was the principal tone sounded in the musical criticism of the day: Brahms was not just neglected, he was strangely neglected.

It is apparent, then, that difficulty did not preclude esteem. But with Brahms it was esteem chilled by a sense of duty. Most of his contemporaries ingested Brahms like some nutritious but unpalatable diet: he was good for one. Brahms saw this quite unsentimentally. Near the end of his life, talking with his friend and eventual biographer, Max Kalbeck, he asked: "My God, what do you want? I have got far enough. People, friends and opponents alike, respect me. Even if people don't love me—they respect me, and that is the main thing. I don't ask for more."[24] And, of course, neglect, strange or otherwise, is a relative matter. Brahms was performed, but less consistently than his present-day stature would lead us to expect. Consider the Hallé Orchestra of Manchester, prominent among symphony orchestras in Europe, owned, managed, and conducted by Sir Charles Hallé, as receptive to music from his native Germany as he was to that of his adopted England. In his twenty-concert season of 1890–91, Hallé drew, as usual, heavily on German composers: he put on his program Volkmann's cello concerto, Reinecke's suite *From the Cradle to the Grave*, and Raff's *Lenore* Symphony, offered many selections from Wagner's music dramas, and spread out—as did every conductor, everywhere—a rich diet of Beethoven: three of Beethoven's nine symphonies, two of his five piano concertos, the violin concerto, three overtures, the choral fantasia, a song, a piano sonata, and the Missa Solemnis. In the same season, Hallé's Orchestra performed three of Brahms's lieder and the German Requiem, but none of Brahms's symphonies, overtures, and sere-

23. *Musical Opinion* (September 1, 1889), 576. The reviewer was willing to forgive Brahms "the notorious reminiscence from the Ninth Symphony in the opening subject," because the concerto "reflects the spirit of Beethoven." He thought the work "remarkable for genuine grandeur of style and a wealth of ideas seldom equalled in compositions of the present day, and without which no virtuoso's *repertoire* should be considered complete." England, as I have said, gave Brahms a generous hearing fairly early, but these are accents rare even for England.

24. Quoted in Stephenson, "Der Componist Brahms im eigenen Urteil," *Brahms-Studien*, I, 14.

nades, and neither of his piano concertos. While Hallé found occasion to offer the violin concerto of Brahms's old friend Joachim, he found none for Brahms's own.

This was typical. In 1891–92, an adventurous season in which Hallé experimented with an all-Mozart evening and a program consisting entirely of the third acts of *Lohengrin* and *Tannhäuser*, Brahms was represented by two lieder and one Hungarian dance. Like other conductors intent on filling their halls, Hallé could not afford to affront his public too often. However independent in spirit, however didactic his purposes, his programming had to reflect public opinion, and public opinion was tepid about Brahms.

Public opinion changed over the years, and public performance changed with it. But not drastically. In the decade dating from Brahms's death in 1897 to the year 1906, the Hallé Orchestra played his First Symphony (performed only once before) three more times. The Second, widely thought the most cheerful—or, the least depressing—among Brahms's symphonic works, enjoyed somewhat greater acceptance: it had been played five times before and was now played four times more. The Third and Fourth Symphonies, on the other hand, considered far more formidable, were each played only twice in that decade. Wagner and Beethoven were performed far more often, both before Brahms's death and after. While Brahms was scarcely a forgotten composer, he was anything but a popular favorite. Audiences did not mind hearing him, but did not ask for more: if Hallé was induced to repeat his *Lohengrin-Tannhäuser* program within the same season, no similar requests for Brahms are on record.[25]

25. Computed from printed programs and a handwritten "Complete List of Works Performed 1858–1907," Henry Watson Music Library, Manchester. And Michael Kennedy, *The Hallé Tradition: A Century of Music* (1960), adds useful statistics. Incidentally, the demand for Wagner was so stormy that Hallé repeated that *Lohengrin-Tannhäuser* evening once more in the following season, in 1892–93. In the last decade of Brahms's life, from 1887 to 1896, the Hallé Orchestra played Brahms's compositions 38 times, Wagner 90 and Beethoven 112 times. In the following ten-year span, from 1897 to 1906, the figure for Brahms rose from 38 to 59, while that for Beethoven declined slightly to 110; Wagner rose to 148.

The performance record of the Philharmonic Orchestra of Berlin confirms the impression gleaned from the Hallé. Berlin is an interesting test city for Brahms. It was here, on March 4, 1889, that the great Hans von Bülow had brought his good friend to conduct his own D-Minor Concerto, with Bülow at the piano: to complete the triumphant evening, Brahms had conducted the Academic Festival Overture with Bülow performing creditably at the drum. Moreover, as a private orchestra of recent foundation, the Philharmonic had, from its beginning in 1882, rapidly played itself into the forefront of European ensembles. In 1895, after the short reigns of such charismatic conductors as Bülow, there began the principate of Arthur Nikisch, who was to establish his unquestioned authority over players, audiences, and critics alike. And Nikisch played Brahms, less frequently than Beethoven but more frequently than Wagner. In the first twenty years of his tenure, faithful subscribers could count on hearing all of Brahms's symphonies and concertos several times, as well as his overtures and a number of his choral compositions. Even less than at Manchester, Brahms was scarcely a forgotten man in Berlin.

It is hard to know how to interpret such figures. As Nikisch himself noted, he was in no position to dictate to visiting virtuosos, and in those days, in Berlin as elsewhere, no symphony concert was complete without at least one soloist.[26] Besides, however unchallenged Nikisch's authority might appear, he was only one element, if a powerful one, in a complex field of force, involving intricate accommodations and mutual concessions among conductors, players, soloists, critics, rival orchestras, highly placed bureaucrats, and the public—or, rather, publics. Moreover, whenever Nikisch performed Brahms, did he perform him as a classic

26. In a reply to a critic accusing Nikisch of vastly over-valuing Tschaikowsky (only published after his death), Nikisch made the point that statistics of performances do not wholly reflect the conductor's taste, since "we are seldom in a position to influence a soloist's choice of programs." See Ferdinand Pfohl, "Arthur Nikisch," in *Arthur Nikisch: Leben und Wirken*, ed. Heinrich Chevalley (1922), 81. The rage for soloists was general; Michael Kennedy, the historian of the Hallé Orchestra, explicitly notes that the 1901–2 season "began with an innovation—a purely orchestral concert." *The Hallé Tradition*, 149.

or as a rebel?[27] The category of the "classical" differed markedly in those days from our current definition: the classical fare we expect to encounter often—Haydn symphonies and Mozart piano concertos—were almost wholly absent from Nikisch's programs. In contrast, he gave hospitality to German composers like Alexander Ritter, Felix Draeseke, or Xaver Scharwenka, though normally for a single appearance. But they and their kind figure far more prominently than a foreign radical like Claude Debussy, who, in those twenty years between 1895 and 1914, appears in a Philharmonic program only once, with a single performance of his *L'Après-midi d'un faune*. In contrast a German experimenter, Richard Strauss,[28] was in the ascendant: it is a commentary on the state of musical taste in Berlin at the turn of the century that the Philharmonic should have played Strauss more often than Mozart, and more than twice as often as Haydn. Brahms, then, was comfortably—or, rather, uncomfortably—lodged between the ancients and the moderns: not ancient enough to be, like Haydn, slighted; not modern enough to be, like Strauss, titillating. It was a critic in London who, in 1890, placed his position most precisely. Comparing Brahms's Tragic Overture with Liszt's Dante Symphony, he found the two works "very widely contrasted, though each belongs to the modern school; but Brahms adheres to classic precedents, whereas Liszt casts them aside. . . ."[29] Brahms was a conservative difficult modern classicist.

Most of Brahms's contemporaries, then, thought him unimaginative and solid, a technician who was, at best, an apt disciple of his betters. One widely read German musical historian, Professor Emil Naumann, listed Brahms among the followers of Schu-

27. In the passage I have just quoted (see note 26), Nikisch instructively calls Brahms a composer whom "I am already counting" among "our classics." The "already" suggests Brahms's transitional status. I intend to explore what I here call "fields of force" in the second projected part of "Imperial Culture."

28. It is interesting to note that even Hermann Levi, toward the end of his life, had to admit that for all his commitment to the Music of the Future, he could no longer fully understand Richard Strauss: Levi to Paul Heyse, ca. December 1899 (half a year before Levi's death): "*Auch ich vermag Strauss nicht mehr zu folgen.*" (Heyse-Archiv, VI, [Levi, 44]. H.A., Stabi.)

29. *Musical Times* (July 1, 1890), 407.

mann, in the company of Albert Dietrich and Robert Volkmann, and devoted less space to him than to Raff.[30] Another
German critic, surveying the condition of chamber music in
1890, praised Brahms, but for understanding Beethoven best and
following him most closely.[31] The year before, Brahms's one-time
friend and admirer Hermann Levi, long after the friendship had
soured and the admiration lapsed, put it more economically and
more brutally when he called Brahms an "epigone."[32] It was a
word, it seems, that came easily to the pen. In the midst of an
appreciation, the once-famous critic Paul Marsop called his favorite among all of Brahms's compositions, the German Requiem, a derivative piece: "the tribute that an epigone presents
to the immortals."[33] In short, the nineteenth-century reputation
of Brahms embraced two conflicting elements: he seemed at once
traditional and difficult, the most surprising, certainly, of all
epigones.

2. THE CEREBRAL SENTIMENTALIST

Not all tributes to Brahms were condescending. One English amateur poet published in 1891 a sonnet that reflects a sunnier view:

Brahms, strong, self-governed soul, be this thy praise,—
That in a fitful age thou didst refrain

30. Naumann, *Deutsche Tondichter* (5th ed., 1882), chapter 12, "Die
Gegenwart," 346–77 passim. This low estimate dates from the first edition
of 1871, when Brahms had already published a great deal of distinguished
music; by 1882, he had added the violin concerto and his first two symphonies, but none of these works caused Naumann to revise his verdict. For
a survey of the minor composers, see Rudolf Louis, *Die deutsche Musik der
Gegenwart* (rev. ed., 1912).
31. To translate: Brahms's eminence in chamber music lay in his capacity
to imitate. "He, too, has not carried the chamber music style forward. We
still stand where we stood sixty years ago." (*Neue Zeitschrift für Musik*,
CXXXVI [1890], 556.)
32. Levi to an unidentified correspondent, December 15, 1889. Autograph
195/46. H. A., Oesterreichische Nationalbibliothek, Vienna. For Levi, see
above, 189–230.
33. "Johannes Brahms," *Musikalische Essays* (1889), 194.

From methods false, from liberties profane:
For thou hast gathered in tradition's ways
The flowers of full-blown thought that crown thy days.
Hark, in thy mellow music, strong and sane,
Beethoven's harmonies vibrate again,
And fill our listening spirit with amaze.

His mantle rests upon thee. Art not thou
High Priest of Music's mysteries in his stead,
The jealous guardian of the law divine?
So men shall call thee Master; even though now
They follow after other gods than thine,
And trample out the footprints of the dead.[34]

However limited the value of this sonnet as poetry, it helps to resolve the paradox of how Brahms could be a mere imitator and
hard to understand at the same time. Brahms, the poet tells us,
has "gathered in tradition's ways / The flowers of full-blown
thought." Similarly, an English review called Brahms's Fourth
Symphony, in 1890, "one of *the most abstruse* and least inspired
of the composer's larger works."[35] In the same tenor, Brahms's intimate friend, the distinguished surgeon and gifted amateur pianist Theodor Billroth, criticized Brahms for having "too little
sensuality—*zu wenig Sinnliches*—in his art, as composer and performer alike."[36] Phrases like "calculating intellectuality," "mathe-

34. *Musical Times*, XXXII, No. 578 (April 1, 1891), 210.
35. *See Musical Times*, XXXII, No. 581 (July 1, 1890), 407. Italics mine.
The reviewer does exempt the slow movement, "a gem," from this general
stricture. The charge of intellectuality runs through the Marsop essay I have
just quoted. Brahms was "a restless student—*ein rastloser Lerner*"; with a
few exceptions there is "always something dull and dry—*etwas Dumpfes und
Trockenes*—in the Brahmsian orchestration"; there is "always something
deliberate, intellectualized—*Gewolltes*—in Brahms's tragic vision—*Tragik*."
And so forth. Though, at the same time: "This scholar and thinker in sound
was, at the same time, a poet—*ein Dichter*." "Johannes Brahms," *Musikalische
Essays*, 184–95 passim.
36. This in the midst of a paean to Brahms. Billroth, agreeing with Hanslick,
to Professor Lübke, December 24, 1867. *Briefe von Theodor Billroth* (8th
unchanged ed., 1910), 73. By linking Brahms to Bach and Beethoven in this
complaint, Billroth only confuses matters further; in any event, he thought
Brahms's intellectualism not some defect in sensual powers but the consequence of a deliberate policy.

matical music" and "dry pedantry," "abstruse, intellectual" and "unintelligible, dry, deliberate and uncongenial," "emotional impotence" swamp the critical literature. Brahms was the Browning of music.[37] Even Brahms's Double Concerto for Violin and Cello, which it would take some imaginative effort to find ungrateful to the imagination, aroused the *Manchester Guardian* to precisely that reflection: "Those who look upon music for the expression of emotion will find little . . . to arouse the feelings."[38] The same newspaper, reporting on the first Manchester performance of Brahms's Third Symphony in November 1884, found critic and audience alike paralyzed by the obvious question: " 'How do you like the symphony?' " The reviewer, George Fremantle, concluded that "The symphony gave us all the mental occupation we could desire."[39] The most devoted followers of Brahms could not deny the cerebral quality of his compositions: "Enjoy Brahms in the Wagnerian or Chopinesque sense of the word one cannot," Rutland Boughton admitted, "but one can listen in admiration at his grandeur, and marvel at what he tells us, for it is all true and great."[40] Brahms was work—brain-work.

This is the line, too, on which French musical opinion united in confronting Germany's most considerable composer, certainly since Wagner's death in 1883. While Brahms's choral and chamber works enjoyed a measure of specialized favor among French musicians, leading conductors discovered him late and played him little. Brahms's Fourth Symphony came to Paris in 1890, five

37. The first quotation is from *Musical Opinion* (April 1, 1891), 255; the others, in order, from the Boston *Gazette* (January 24, 1878); Boston *Daily Advertiser* (October 31, 1882); Boston *Gazette* (November 8, 1884); J. F. Runciman, [Boston] *Musical Record* (January 1, 1900); *New York Times* (February 28, 1896), all quoted from Nicolas Slonimsky, ed., *Lexicon of Musical Invective: Critical Assaults on Composers Since Beethoven's Time* (ed. 1965), 68, 70, 71, 79, 182. The *Lexicon*, a shrewdly gathered treasure, contains insults to other composers as well, though few have had so singleminded a group of assailants as Brahms.
38. Kennedy, *The Hallé Tradition*, 60.
39. Kennedy, *The Hallé Tradition*, 55; see also 45, 49, 57. Fremantle, as Kennedy records (64–65), also found parts of Tschaikowsky's *Symphonie Pathétique* baffling and obscure.
40. "Brahms' Variations for Piano Solo," *Musical Opinion*, No. 254 (1898), 109.

years after its first performance; the Third not until 1895, twelve years after *its* premiere. The principal, certainly the ostensible, reason for this resistance was Brahms's dryness, his intellectuality. Arthur Pougin, the regular critic for *Le Ménestrel*, refused to credit Schumann's enthusiastic verdict that Brahms was a genius, and thought rather that Brahms lacked the stuff of greatness which leaves "its brilliant and luminous trace." Listening to the Paris premiere of the Fourth did not induce Pougin to change his mind: doubtless the symphony was "important" and displayed "solid and powerful qualities." But, he thought, it sadly lacked "inspiration" and "personality"; the "elegance" and occasional "grace" of its dress barely concealed its "aridity—*sécheresse*." Its orchestration, though "solid," was equally disappointing: "it is the excellent exercise of a good student—*excellent devoir de bon écolier*," a Gallic circumscription for that curter curse, epigone.[41]

Five years later, attending the first Paris performance of Brahms's Third, Pougin copied his earlier review almost word for word. He found this symphony, like the Fourth, "important," though in no way comparable to some fine early Brahmsian works like the Requiem, the string sextets, and the Second Symphony. And just as he had thought the Fourth Symphony a "cold" composition, from which both "originality and the heat of inspiration were absolutely absent," so Pougin now found the Third lacking in "inspiration," and the work as a whole, "gray."[42] Need I add that gray is the color of the brain?

Pougin was speaking for his colleagues: Brahms did not rank very high with French critics. In April 1892, reflecting on the concert season just past, Hyppolite Barbedette criticized the two leading conductors in Paris, Charles Lamoureux and Edouard

41. "Revue des grands concerts," *Le Ménestrel*, 56th Year, No. 3 (January 19, 1890), 21. French composers seem to have agreed: Vincent d'Indy, for one, held that Brahms "did not understand how to benefit by the valuable lessons" that Beethoven had left "for future generations, and his weighty symphonic luggage must be regarded as a continuation rather than as a progress." (*César Franck* [1906, tr. 1910], 87.)

42. "Revue des grand concerts," *Le Ménestrel*, 61st Year, No. 5 (February 3, 1895), 36.

Colonne, for their timid programming, and proposed that they play more Haydn and seek out the minor works of Beethoven or Mendelssohn. Then, moving down to a lesser rank, to "Niels Gade, Brahms, Rubinstein, Raff," Barbedette suggested that they, too, might have some interesting overtures or symphonic works worthy of resurrection. The company into which Barbedette, an articulate anti-Wagnerian critic for *Le Ménestrel*, placed Brahms is, from our perspective, astounding but from his own perfectly natural.[43] Not even the pious hyperbole that marks, and mars, most obituaries could wholly erase the dutiful appreciation that French music critics brought to Brahms, the intellectual. Writing in *Le Ménestrel* in mid-April 1897, just after the news of Brahms's death had reached Paris, O. Berggruen noted his "rare intellectual cultivation." But even Brahms's prolific output of songs, Berggruen thought, could not equal the quality of Schumann's, or even Robert Franz's, lieder: "To tell the truth, at most a dozen or so of his songs have become popular." The German Requiem, which had made Brahms famous, was a work he never surpassed; his vocal music shows him to have been an "inquiring and abstract spirit." Brahms's instrumental music displays the same character: rarely a truly flowing melody anywhere. Berggruen conceded that one must admire Brahms's gift for making combinations, his powers of construction, and his sovereign control of the means of musical production—all qualities of an intellectual craftsman.[44] The French shared and underscored the opinion of Europe: Brahms was a cerebral composer.

3. THE ALIENATED CONFORMIST

I have submitted sufficient evidence, I think, to substantiate my argument that our favorite commonplace about Brahms, his easy

43. *Le Ménestrel*, 58th Year, No. 16 (April 17, 1892), 127.
44. "Nécrologie," *Le Ménestrel*, 63rd Year, No. 15 (April 11, 1897), 113–15. Berggruen concedes that some of Brahms's late chamber music, like the clarinet works written for his friend Muhlfeld, are "ravishing"; for the rest, Brahms is "laborious and solid," deserving respect, no more.

romanticism, was not held by more than an insignificant minority in his lifetime and for some years after his death. The other commonplace, his conformism, is at least open to question. We are told that the distinguishing mark of the avant-garde is to be at odds with the "bourgeois civilization" of its age. Now, Brahms was distinctly at odds with his age. Compared to the giants of the eighteenth and early nineteenth centuries, he would insist, over and over again, the musicians of his time were vulgarians: uninventive imitators or brash eccentrics: "I don't like us," he said. "*Wir gefallen mir nicht.*"[45] His own way of confronting the depressing situation of modern music was to compose with that mixture of respect and disrespect, of adaptation and independence, that characterizes the true cultural innovator.

Even Brahms's choice of texts for his copious vocal compositions provides clues to depths unsuspected and unexplored. An earnest if unsystematic reader, he drew his inspiration from unpredictable masses of printed materials ranging from the insipid to the profound, from the sentimental to the experimental. And at least two of his most moving works for voice and orchestra, the Song of Destiny and the Alto Rhapsody, utilize texts strikingly superior to the workaday poetic tastes of most nineteenth-century Germans. Brahms's Schicksalslied is a setting of a poem that Hölderlin inserted into his novel *Hyperion*. With its painful and yearning contrast between clear-eyed, unchanging Greek gods and restless, ever-suffering humanity, it was more than conventional nostalgia; when Brahms came upon Hölderlin in 1868, his poetry was little known and his message uncertain.[46] And when soon after Brahms decided to compose portions of Goethe's dark *Harzreise im Winter*, he fell upon a text which, though by Germany's most celebrated *Dichter*, was, like Hölderlin's verse, far from being a popular poem. Brahms's setting of Goethe's lines,

45. See Stephenson, "Der Komponist Brahms in eigenen Urteil," *Brahms-Studien*, I, 11–13.
46. Consider the brief treatment in Hermann Hettner's classic volume, *Literaturgeschichte der Goethezeit* (3rd ed., 1876; reprinted with unaltered text, 1970), 591–99; appreciative but rather perfunctory. Interestingly, the little essay ends with the very lines that Brahms set to music.

with its splendid interweaving of contralto, orchestra, and late-entering chorus, is unforgettable: the lonely traveler of Goethe's poem is estranged from the world, in danger of transforming self-hatred into hatred of others, eating himself up and appealing to a divinity to show him the way out. Such choices, and the music Brahms composed, seem like prophetic anticipations of the Modernist malaise and the Modernist sensibility.

This is the point of my essay. It is doubtless interesting and useful in itself to document the dramatic shift in Brahms's reputation, but *that* story holds few surprises. The history of taste is, after all, full of such shifts to which not even Dante, not even Shakespeare, have been immune. Only stability needs explaining. But more went into the making of the twentieth-century Brahms than this. What changed was not merely a judgment but a *mode* of judgment. Brahms the frigid intellectual has become Brahms the sultry sentimentalist. This is more than a widening appreciation, it is more than an act of learning. It warns the historian that not evaluations alone, but even presumably stable categories, are far from permanent or absolute. It is not simply that we have come to like—or detest—what once mainly puzzled our elders, but rather that what one century saw as the product of intellect another century has come to see as the product of emotion. Psychologists have long thrown doubt on the proposition that the mental activities we call "reason" and "passion" are mutually exclusive and wholly unalterable, and historians will do well to take their point and relativize their perception of these psychological forces.[47]

I can illustrate both what has happened to Brahms in particular and the chameleon nature of "reason" and "passion" in general by alluding to the analogous history of Impressionist painting. The Monets and Renoirs that today, in cheap reproductions, adorn the walls of teenagers just past puberty, were scorned only a century ago as offenses to good taste and violations of nature. Degas, the misanthrope, with his awkward, sweating ballerinas, exhausted jockeys, and depressed prostitutes, has been

47. For a specific application of this idea to the psychology of music, see Leonard B. Meyer, *Emotion and Meaning in Music* (1956).

victimized by a change in sensibility that has trivialized his beautiful ugliness to mere prettiness. If we read Schoenberg's essay, "Brahms the Progressive," with such shifts in mind, we will read it with new comprehension. The radical innovations in harmony and rhythm that Schoenberg discerns in Brahms's work have been absorbed into the mainstream of taste with the passage of time; what once mystified and alienated listeners now lies comfortably, almost lazily, in our ear.

But I am offering the history of Brahms's reputation to sustain an even larger argument. I want to argue that the material I have presented invites us to revise the current account of how our Modernist sensibility arose, and that in two ways. We must rethink the distance of the avant-garde from its comtemporary Establishment, and the relative share of the past in its aggressive work. That mysterious activity we call creation, which has fascinated and defied so many investigators, is always an act of fusion. However urgent the impulse of defiance or the assertion of originality, there are elements in the creator's world that he accepts and incorporates. What he sees as his "world" is, after all, not an undifferentiated mass of stupidity, ineptitude, and hostility, but a series of environments of which at least some are admirable or prove inescapable. The rebel's individuality can never be as total as he would like to think. The modern cant word *creativity*, with its resonance of a divine power making something out of nothing, is, however flattering, profoundly misleading. Inspiration depends on knowledge and technical competence as much as it does on some private alchemy unique to the creator; he builds at least partly with bricks he has got from others.

The creator is quite as enmeshed in the tradition. We would see this more plainly than we normally do if we used comprehensive terms like *present* and *world*, or *tradition* and *past*, in the plural. Nor, for that matter, are presents and pasts insulated from one another: Manet quoted seventeenth-century Spaniards to discomfit nineteenth-century Frenchmen just as, a hundred years before him, Diderot had exploited ancient pagans to assail contemporary Christians. To turn to the past—or, rather, one past—may be the most effective way of preparing the future. I am far from disparaging the daring of the innovator or denying the reality of innovation.[48] I am only trying to give a realistic account of both.

I return to my starting point. Brahms was both a traditionalist and an innovator, both a conservative and a radical, both a craftsman and a creator; he was an emotional intellectual, without crippling conflicts, without paradox. Only a handful of critics have discerned this compound of qualities in Brahms. An anonymous reviewer, writing in the Boston *Daily Advertiser* in 1878, was disturbed enough by the First Symphony to define Brahms as "a modern of the moderns." His "C minor Symphony," he added, "is a remarkable expression of the inner life of this anxious, introverted, over-earnest age," a shrewd, if tendentious appraisal.[49] Billroth, of course far more appreciative, called his good friend "our most modern composer,"[50] while as early as 1869 an obscure critic, P. Kleinert, perceptively suggested that while Brahms had listened to the old masters closely and intelligently, he had by no means imitated them, but had, rather, absorbed what they had to teach and gone his own way: "We are confronted with modern music."[51] These were isolated voices, and they have remained isolated; in our day it has been Schoenberg who said of Brahms, "he would have been a pioneer if he had simply returned to Mozart." And he immediately adds: "But he did not live on inher-

---

48. I have dealt with Diderot's (and the other philosophes') strategies of exploiting what I have called "the useful and beloved past" in *The Enlightenment: An Interpretation*, Vol. I, *The Rise of Modern Paganism* (1966); and with Manet's in my *Art and Act: On Causes in History—Manet, Gropius, Mondrian* (1976).

49. January 18, 1878, quoted in Slonimsky, *Lexicon*, 68.

50. In a freely rendered but doubtless largely authentic conversation that Hanslick records holding with Billroth, in Hanslick, *Aus meinem Leben*, 2 vols. (1894), II, 302. Marsop is rather more half-hearted: "Brahms too belongs among the discoverers of the modern. Only we must group him among those who, rather than blazing paths into yet unknown lands, demonstrate hitherto neglected beauties and charms among old familiar things." *Musikalische Essays*, 191.

51. Quoted in extenso in Max Kalbeck, *Johannes Brahms*, 4 vols. in 8 (1904–14), II, 1, 273–74. Kalbeck's biography, despite its patent Brahms-worship, remains the classic.

ited fortune; he made one of his own."[52] I have written this essay
to show that Schoenberg was right in both of these assertions,
and that the consequences of his being right are, for the historian,
nothing less than momentous.

52. "Brahms the Progressive," (1933, revised in 1947), in *Style and Idea*
(1950), 99. The whole essay (52–101) is of central relevance to this subject. In preparing it, as a lecture, Schoenberg wrote to Hans Rosbaud on
January 7, 1933: "Would you be interested in a lecture on Brahms? I think
I might have something to say on that subject that I alone can say. To be
sure, my contemporaries and those who are older than I am have lived
through the age of Brahms—*Brahmszeit*—, but they are not 'modern.' And
the younger Brahmsians no longer know the Brahms tradition from their own
experience and are also for the most part 'reactionary.' But: I am thinking
of the theory of composition, anecdotes!" (*Arnold Schoenberg, Briefe*, selected and edited by Erwin Stein [1958], 185–86.) On March 18, 1939, he
explained to Alfred Frankenstein that he had orchestrated Brahms's Piano
Quartet in G-minor because he loved the piece, and had known Brahms's
style for almost fifty years. (*Briefe*, 223.) I do not want to overstate the isolation of Schoenberg's perception of Brahms (and, with that, my own originality). I record my indebtedness to a long essay by Donald Francis Tovey,
"Brahms's Chamber Music," 1929, conveniently reprinted in a generous collection of his essays, *The Main Stream of Music and Other Essays*, ed.,
Hubert Foss (1949; ed. 1959), 220–70. Brahms's problematic modernity is
also noted, briefly and perceptively, in Ivor Keys, *Brahms's Chamber Music*,
BBC Music Guides (1974).

VI
FOR BECKMESSER
Eduard Hanslick, Victim and Prophet

In 1862, Johannes Brahms came to Vienna for the first time, and at least one of his new acquaintances, the music critic Eduard Hanslick, found the visit memorable. More than thirty years later, recalling a lifetime of inky combat, Hanslick spoke of the encounter in accents of pure delight. When Brahms arrived in Vienna, Hanslick remembered, his compositions were familiar to a restricted circle; the general public knew of him only through "Schumann's prophetic commendation," that celebrated open letter of 1853, which had forecast a brilliant future for the young, still wholly unknown composer. Hanslick himself had found Brahms's early piano pieces, with their stunning boldness and their artful harmonies, highly interesting, "but more interesting than satisfying"—a verdict that recalls the contemporary view of Brahms as a composer who piqued his listeners' curiosity and impressed their intellect, but failed to gratify their emotions.[1] He was, at that moment, "a young Hercules at the cross roads," facing the path of extreme romanticism or that of the classical masters. He chose, of course, classicism. By the time he had introduced his first Viennese audiences to his Variations on a Theme of Händel and his G-Minor Piano Quartet, there was no question left, at

1. For other instances, see above, 247–51.

least in Hanslick's mind: this was no longer a promising genius, but a "master in the noblest sense of the word," a master "who could shape unique, modern content in classical form."[2] And Hanslick remembered one evening, "as we listened to his B-flat major Sextet, after Wagner had, in the afternoon, performed various fragments from the Ring and from Tristan. We thought ourselves suddenly translated into a world of pure beauty—*eine reine Welt der Schönheit*. It sounded like a kind of redemption—*eine Erlösung*."[3] Doubtless, Brahms's music gained, for Hanslick, from the contrast with Wagner's showy and emphatic performances, but it provided, on its own, access to that most remote of realms, a world of pure beauty. If Richard Wagner was a threat worth fighting against, Johannes Brahms was a cause worth fighting for.

1. A NEW AGE OF CRITICISM

I have spoken of music criticism as if it were a species of combat. My metaphor is trite with repetition, but that is precisely its virtue: it transports us back to the nineteenth century, to the age of Hanslick, for which the activity of the critic seemed something like a boxing match, a political maneuver, or a military campaign. Hanslick certainly relished the pugilistic side of his work. At the same time, he took a larger view. "Criticism," he wrote in 1894, in the very autobiography in which he recalled his first meeting with Brahms, "criticism does not exist to praise everything, but to tell the truth."[4] If the truth was unpleasant much of the time the critic often—well, sometimes—found reasons for satisfaction and grounds for celebration. In any event, Hanslick gravely wrote, "I consider it the critic's duty not to discourage

2. This, too, is a common contemporary verdict: beautiful new wine in unmatched old bottles. See above, 233–47.

3. Eduard Hanslick, *Aus meinem Leben*, 2 vols. (1894), II, 14–15.

4. *Aus meinem Leben*, II, 49. For some instructive nineteenth-century instances of combative language, see Imogen Fellner, "Das Brahms-Bild der *Allgemeinen Musikalischen Zeitschrift* (1863 bis 1882)," in Heinz Becker, ed., *Beiträge zur Geschichte der Musikkritik* (1965), 30, 41–43.

production, to recognize the truly felt and the naturally witty—
ungesuchte Geistreiche—and not to denigrate them in contrast to
some 'vanished golden age.' "[5]

This is a responsible, even an exalted definition of the critic's
function. It speaks of more than Hanslick's sense of himself; it
reflects a consensus among a sizable and steadily growing profession. Modernist culture had emerged, and was flourishing, in an
atmosphere of frank, uninterrupted, sometimes hysterical criticism of all kinds—social, cultural, literary criticism, criticism of
painting, of architecture, of music. When, around 1890, Oscar
Wilde paradoxically asserted that criticism is an act of creation
and hinted that the maker of art really served the critic, he was
saying, in his usual manner, something penetrating by saying
something that was not wholly true. It is not too much to argue,
I think, that Modernism was the creature of criticism, in Germany as everywhere else. And Modernism was a creature, in part,
even of such noted conservatives as Eduard Hanslick. This is not
the first time I have observed that Modernists forged alliances
which only later historians, applying their ready-made categories
and confrontations, would decide to find incongruous.

Criticism was, of course, not an invention of the mid-nineteenth century. A century earlier, the men of the Enlightenment
had produced original and powerful social and aesthetic criticism; the most enduring critics among them—Diderot, Voltaire,
Hume, Lessing, Kant—had also been the Enlightenment's most
accomplished poets, playwrights, and philosophers. It was Kant,
the most philosophical among the philosophes, who had named
his century, without a hint of apology, an Age of Criticism. And
there were wide currents of influence running from the age of the
Enlightenment to the age of Modernism, continuities sometimes
explicitly acknowledged but in general quite simply accepted as
part of the nineteenth-century cultural experience. Baudelaire
looked back appreciatively to Diderot; others, great unmaskers
like Marx and Nietzsche, owed much to Enlightened critics like
Gibbon and Adam Smith and Voltaire; German nineteenth-century criticism reads much like an interminable debate with the

5. *Aus meinem Leben*, II, 308.

shade of Lessing. And the Modernists accepted that fundamental proposition of Enlightenment thought that Voltaire had formulated most felicitously for himself and his fellow-philosophes: it was necessary to destroy before it would be possible to build.

It seems an unproblematic saying, but it requires interpretation. The philosophes themselves did not sharply separate demolition and construction: the two were related aspects of a single activity —the exercise of intelligence. Their great achievement had been to recognize that everything lay open to rational inquiry.[6] And it would be unrewarding to divide the making of Modernism into two phases, a destructive followed by a constructive one. It is impossible to sort out critical from constructive energies; in the nineteenth as in the eighteenth century, they were inseparable, and often indistinguishable, from one another. It is striking to note in this connection that in this very age of specialization many first-rate poets, novelists, and painters were also important critics: I think of Charles Baudelaire, Henry James and T. S. Eliot, of Gustave Courbet, Vincent van Gogh, and Georges Seurat; I think of Germans like Theodor Fontane, Thomas Mann, and Max Liebermann. Nor were the composers any less active in this dual capacity: Hector Berlioz, Richard Wagner, and Claude Debussy would have made substantial reputations as writers on music even if they had never composed a line. All these artists, and others, applied the critical intelligence at their command to place the tendencies of their day, the work of fellow-artists and their own; to identify moments of excellence, discriminate the first- from the second-rate, secure distance from stifling aesthetic habits and from themselves, thus to discipline their talents in the service of their creative labors. Hanslick's sense that it was his duty as a critic to assist and encourage the artist is part of this mission to understand. If Kant could speak of his own time as an age of criticism, the years of Hanslick were a second age of criticism.[7]

6. I have dealt extensively with this view of the Enlightenment in *The Enlightenment: An Interpretation*, 2 vols. (1966, 1969), esp. I, 130–31. The formulation of "two aspects of one activity" is best expressed in Ernst Cassirer, *The Philosophy of the Enlightenment* (tr. 1951), 275.

7. I have learned much from René Wellek's authoritative *History of Modern*

It was inevitable that amid all this clamor one chief topic of criticism should come to be criticism itself. As the outpouring of feuilletons, pamphlets, brochures, books ever increased, discrimination was bound to suffer and standards were bound to decline. Henry James was only one among several serious critics to lament the proliferation of opportunities for self-expression, and to establish boundaries between reviewing and criticism.[8] But, if we abstract for a moment from its quality, the sheer quantity of criticism, though often depressing, also had something exhilarating about it. The public rehearsing of available alternatives in art, literature, and politics, the dramatic eagerness to question received truths, subvert long-standing traditions, and affront reigning conventions, were signs of health more than symptoms of decay. They were, with all their faults, a glory of liberal culture. And all the partisanship, all the exuberance and anxiety generated by so much innovation, all the diverse positions that gave nineteenth-century culture its immense vitality, turned critics, whatever else they wanted to be, into combatants. The second age of criticism was alive with manifestos, letters to the editor, indignant resignations, alive with the noise of dissension, advocacy, and denigration. It was in this spirit that Hanslick quoted Scripture: "In my father's house are many mansions."[9]

Criticism, 4 vols. so far (1955–65); while it concentrates on literary criticism, the *History* is immensely suggestive for other kinds of critical activity as well. Surveying the late nineteenth century, Wellek comments, in some astonishment, on "the incredible bulk of the criticism of the time," the "expansion of its claims," the "proliferation of its methods and materials," and, not least, the "increase of its prestige." While later decades have come to think less well of its work, in its time the late nineteenth century "appeared as the golden age of criticism"; if it was less than that, it remains "a laboratory of criticism, with an enormous, ceaseless debate in which every possible position was pushed to its extreme." "Introduction to Volumes 3 and 4," in *History of Criticism*, III, xi–xiv.

8. See especially his brief, powerful essay "Criticism" (1893), accessible in *The Art of Fiction and Other Essays by Henry James*, with an introduction by Morris Roberts (1948), 215–19. Tellingly, poignantly, James, when he deals with reviewing, uses metaphors from commercial life; when he moves to criticism, nothing less than metaphors from chivalry will do.

9. *Aus meinem Leben*, II, 305.

2. A PLEA FOR BECKMESSER

Criticism, then, including music criticism, was a risky business. Making and breaking reputations, fostering one school and maligning another, critics intervened in the lives of the makers, performers, businessmen, and consumers of culture. No wonder they got the reputation of being men who kill people for money. As professional assassins, theirs proved a dangerous calling, for they invited counterattack. The duels between creators and critics therefore occupy a prominent, if rarely edifying, place in the history of Modernist culture. Often, the critic survived the encounter he had provoked mainly as a warning to others: it was less his generosity or his prescience that was likely to preserve his name for posterity than his lapses. This is the way that Eduard Hanslick has survived, and not even under his own name. He is known, if he is known at all, not as Hanslick but as Beckmesser.

It was, of course, Richard Wagner who gave Hanslick this unwelcome sort of immortality by fixing his image as the egregious "Merker" who stumbles through the *Meistersinger*, the embodiment of the critic as conceited and incorrigible fool. Beckmesser, the pedantic and assertive guardian of high standards and judge of talents, proves himself to have neither; and opera-goers, exhilarated by the spectacle of a victim who deserves to be victimized, by a legitimate target for their free-floating aggressions, laugh, approve, and ask no questions.

Hanslick was admittedly vulnerable, but his vulnerability was less a quality of his person than of his position. By the 1860s, when Wagner completed the *Meistersinger*, Hanslick was an influential music critic writing for authoritative newspapers, in a city that was widely recognized as the musical capital of Europe. Vienna was a goal to which musicians aspired, a test that musicians feared. When Wagner chose to make Hanslick into his public victim, he knew what he was about; he was acting as the recognized leader of a musical party seeking to strike down a recognized leader of the opposition. His invention of Beckmesser, private as it may have been in its inception, had more than private implications.

By 1868, when the *Meistersinger* had its premiere in Munich, Hanslick and Wagner had been mortal enemies for several years, but their professional lives had been entangled for much longer than that. As early as 1846, the year that the young Hanslick moved to Vienna from his native Prague, he wrote an extensive appreciative essay on Wagner's *Tannhäuser* for the *Wiener allgemeine Musik-Zeitung*[10] and reviewed the career of Wagner, his casual acquaintance, at some length. Wagner, who had already drafted a *Meistersinger* poem containing the part of a self-important musical "censor," had no cause to be dissatisfied with Hanslick, and no reason to aim his satire at him. Even in 1854, when Hanslick explicitly and publicly rejected Wagner's call for a music-drama, the two men did not feel—certainly nowhere voiced —any mutual antipathy. All this was to change: in November 1862, Wagner came to Vienna and gave several readings of his *Meistersinger* libretto, in the version which permitted no doubt that Beckmesser was a scarcely disguised caricature of Eduard Hanslick—"the dangerous reviewer."[11] Hanslick was more than a dangerous reviewer by then; the feared music critic of the *Presse* was also a learned lecturer on music at the university, and the sociable acquaintance of everyone who was anyone in music. To affront him was to affront a person of consequence.

The hosts for one of Wagner's private readings—on this at least the autobiographies of Wagner and Hanslick agree—tactlessly invited Hanslick to attend. Wagner later recalled that Hanslick "grew paler and more depressed in the course of the recitation," and could not be induced to stay. "My friends," Wagner innocently comments, "were agreed that Hanslick looked upon the whole libretto as a lampoon directed against himself," and

10. "Richard Wagner, und seine neueste Oper 'Tannhäuser.' Eine Beurtheilung," reproduced in full in Helmut Kirchmeyer, ed., *Situationsgeschichte der Musikkritik und des musikalischen Pressewesens in Deutschland . . .* Part IV, *Das zeitgenössische Wagner-Bild*, vol. III, *Dokumente 1846–1850* (1968), cols. 147–84.

11. Richard Wagner, *Mein Leben*, 3 vols. in one (ed. 1915), III, 341.

he adds that from then on Hanslick's attitude toward him grew markedly more hostile.[12] Hanslick, for his side, reports no pallor and no depression, points to his discriminating judgment of the *Meistersinger*, and gives cogent reasons for his detestation of Wagner's character and dislike of Wagner's music.[13] One thing is plain: unlike Wagner, Hanslick found it possible to say some kind words about his enemy; like Wagner, Hanslick responded to a more than personal affront. He was, like Wagner, a representative figure, and he found it not merely insulting but ominous to witness the music of the future propagated so ruthlessly—with the manners of the future.

Nothing is easier than to detect the acid in Wagner's etching and to demonstrate its inaccuracies. In fact, a handful of scholars have tried to rescue Hanslick by separating him from Beckmesser.[14] But two obstacles have stood in the way of Hanslick's full rehabilitation: Wagner's caricature is cruel but it is funny, and it repossesses the general awareness with every performance of the *Meistersinger*. To cavil at this breathing statue to stupid self-importance must seem labored, humorless. As usual, the sober and complex truth limps helplessly behind the astute, simplistic libel—astute precisely because it is simplistic.

Moreover, Hanslick's defects, though far less crippling than Beckmesser's, are marked enough to invite a less than enthusiastic verdict on his critical performance. All pronouncements about a composer's work are bound to time and place; all are subject to shifts in educated taste. But even allowing for the inescapable changes produced by the passage of the years, it is evident from our twentieth-century perspective that Hanslick's capacity for

12. *Mein Leben*, III, 341–42.

13. *Aus meinem Leben*, II, 7–8. For a dignified defense against Wagnerian malice, see 227–34.

14. See especially Stewart Deas, *In Defence of Hanslick* (1940), essentially a pamphlet by a zealous advocate; Friedrich Blume's detailed encyclopedia article in *Musik in Geschichte und Gegenwart*, Vol. V (1956), cols. 1,482–93, an authoritative treatment, though somewhat marred by an unnecessary "defense" against the "charge" that Hanslick was of Jewish descent; and Werner Abegg, *Musikästhetik und Musikkritik bei Eduard Hanslick* (1974), which takes his ideas seriously. Henry Pleasants, ed., *Eduard Hanslick, Music Criticisms 1846–1899* (1950), makes a selection available in English.

musical appreciation was relatively constricted. The range of his enthusiasm was bounded on one side by Mozart and on the other by Brahms. Medieval and Renaissance music had little to say to him; even Bach seemed to him often dry, of greater historical than musical interest. Precisely because Hanslick was not merely opinionated but also witty—the apt German adjective, *geistreich*, was often applied to him—his sayings became notorious, and they have haunted his reputation ever since. It is hard to live down remarks like his casual comment that he would "rather see all of Heinrich Schütz go up in flames than the 'German Requiem.' "[15] Even Brahms's most uncritical admirers would nowadays find it embarrassing to accept so compromising a tribute as this. And, just as Hanslick proved deaf to many of the musical glories produced before the 1750s, he was deaf to many of the glories produced in his lifetime. He found Berlioz to be an "odd Romantic— *wunderlichen Romantiker*";[16] he denigrated Liszt as a charlatan, dismissed Bruckner as a madman, and warned against Wagner as a grave danger to music.[17]

Hanslick's detractors (except for the implacable Wagner and Bruckner) have felt compelled to admit that he prepared himself conscientiously for his reviewing assignments; he studied the scores of new symphonies and those of revived cantatas with equal diligence. He tried to understand what he could not love. But the point remains that he loved little, and that this is a serious handicap for a reviewer who attends concerts regularly, writes about them copiously and finds his word cited as authoritative. Even if one corrects for Wagner's malice, it seems plausible to

15. *Aus meinem Leben*, II, 304.
16. "Der Berlioz-Cultus," in Hanslick, *Musikalische Stationen* (1880), 190.
17. For Liszt, see individual reviews, especially in Hanslick, *Concerte, Componisten und Virtuosen der letzten fünfzehn Jahre, 1870–1885* (1886), 16–17, 39–47, 77–80, 133–34, and others, attractively supplemented by Hanslick's obituary article reprinted in Hanslick, *Musikalisches Skizzenbuch* (1896), 167–78; for Bruckner, see especially his review of the F-Minor Mass, in which he connects Bruckner's musical education with his incoherence, in Hanslick, *Fünf Jahre Musik* (1896), 279–83; and for Wagner, among many essays and reviews, especially those gathered under the rubrics "Richard Wagner," and "Nach Wagners Tod," collected in Hanslick, *Aus dem Opernleben der Gegenwart* (1889), 293–379.

hold that his Beckmesser remains in substance a telling, if heartless, depiction of a pedant in power.

Certainly Hanslick was a powerful man in his chosen sphere. Had he been merely ridiculous, Wagner would not have taken the trouble to ridicule him. Contemporary annals are filled with tributes, voluntary and involuntary, to his influence. In 1885, a Dr. Robert Hirschfeld, amateur of *a capella* choirs and of German Renaissance music, issued a pamphlet against *"the adroit moral pressure on the part of a critical authority."*[18] Critics like Hanslick, he wrote, in measured but resentful tones, could compel or prevent performances of music, and thus shape, or distort, the general taste. Hirschfeld found his readers: he brought out three editions of his pamphlet in the course of a single year. But patently his own courage frightened him: nothing bespeaks his anxiety more eloquently than his continued bows to Hanslick the professor (who, he wrote, is first-rate) in the midst of his attacks on Hanslick the critic (who is merely eighth-rate).[19]

Composers feared Hanslick quite as much as did the amateurs. In the very year, 1885, that Dr. Hirschfeld launched his little assault, Anton Bruckner told his friend and supporter Hermann Levi that it would be better to have his Seventh Symphony printed before it was performed in Vienna, lest "it be ruined by Hl Hanslick etc."[20] It is true that Bruckner was as timid as he was servile, but his pathetic appeal to Levi reflects a reality which Hanslick's friends cheerfully acknowledged: Hanslick the critic made a difference, often a decisive one, in the musical life of Vienna. And that difference, we can now see, was not always a beneficial one.

If, in the face of such reservations, I offer a plea for Beckmesser, I do so not to deny or to extenuate his flaws, but to place them in perspective. What I want to say is that Hanslick was engaged, and knew himself to be engaged, in a musical campaign in which the stakes were high. All his writings—his innumerable reviews and occasional essays, his informative history of musical

18. *Das kritische Verfahren Ed. Hanslick's* (1885), 19n.
19. *Das kritische Verfahren*, 10.
20. April 4, 1885. H.A., Staatsbibliothek Preussischer Kulturbesitz, Berlin. "Hl" is an abbreviation for the formula "Hochwohlgeboren."

life in Vienna and his charming autobiography—bear the mark of alert and unremitting partisanship. Hanslick was not a purely reactive writer; he early developed reasoned principles which he sometimes neglected and sometimes overstepped under the pressure of an immediate musical experience, but which generally guided his tastes through his long career. Yet these principles found their final definition in response to an adversary. In the 1850s, when Hanslick began to write serious music criticism and theory, Liszt, Wagner and their allies were moving to engross strategic posts in the musical world: they were beginning to edit respected periodicals, conduct famous orchestras, launch dependable followers. And in the ensuing decades, they took bastion after bastion. The Music of the Future became in Hanslick's lifetime very much the music of the present.

As politicians and strategists had known for centuries before George Bernard Shaw made his Devil say it: a good slogan is half the battle. Liszt and his disciples made an effective bid for the sympathetic attention of the public by parading their compositions as music that had broken with a dying tradition and was pregnant with new vitality. To be in the camp of Liszt and Wagner was to be original, to be youthful; to be opposed to the *Zukunftsmusiker* was to be uninventive and hidebound. To be sure, all parties in the combat claimed to respect the past, which is to say, Beethoven: just as Brahms was so much in awe of Beethoven's symphonic achievement that he hesitated for years before he dared to come before the public with a symphony of his own, so Wagner widely advertised his debt to Beethoven, and offered his willful interpretation of the Ninth Symphony as partial justification for his advocacy of the music-drama.[21] The *Zukunftsmusiker* saw themselves as Beethoven's rightful heirs, and their adversaries as mere epigones. While *they* were husbanding Beethoven's heritage with just the right mixture of piety and independence, Brahms and Hanslick were mechanically reproducing and thus effectively killing Beethoven's classicism. Hanslick could accept neither of these characterizations. He could not permit

21. See now Klaus Kropfinger, *Wagner und Beethoven: Untersuchungen zur Beethoven-Rezeption Richard Wagners* (1975). For Brahms and Beethoven, see above, 236.

the Wagnerites to monopolize the future by monopolizing the past.

3. A WORLD OF PURE BEAUTY

The document that most accurately reflects, and most conspicuously reveals, the pressure of partisan combat on Hanslick's musical theory is *Vom Musikalisch-Schönen*, a small treatise first published in 1854 and often reissued and revised; the last edition to appear in Hanslick's lifetime, in 1902, was the tenth. This is a rare tribute to a book, even a short and elegant one, on so recondite a subject as musical aesthetics; its sales are testimony not only to Hanslick's stylistic gifts, but also to the passionate, general interest in the questions to which *Vom Musikalisch-Schönen* addressed itself. The book is a treatise that its readers elevated—or debased—into a manifesto.

Hanslick was the first to recognize the political relevance of *Vom Musikalisch-Schönen:* in the Preface to the ninth edition he acknowledges the "rather sharp and rhapsodic manner" of his presentation, and expresses some regret that the issues of the day had pushed his theoretical principles into the background. In fact, these issues, which had dictated the original distribution of space, only grew more exigent as edition followed edition. His intention, Hanslick noted, had been to place his ideas about musical beauty into the center of his exposition; if "the polemical, negative element" had "gained the upper hand," the public, he hoped, would excuse this. "When I wrote this essay, the spokesmen of the Music of the Future had reached the height of their clamor," and men of his views felt compelled to respond. "When I brought out the second edition, Liszt had just added his program symphonies" to the general repertoire, compositions that "abdicate the independent significance of music" almost completely, and "make the listener swallow them only as a pill designed to promote ideas—*nur mehr als gedankentreibendes Mittel eingeben.* Since then we have had Richard Wagner's *Tristan, Nibelungenlied,* and his doctrine of the 'unending melody,'—

that is, formlessness raised to a principle, opium intoxication sung and fiddled, a cult, to which, as we know, a special temple has been opened at Bayreuth."[22]

The text of *Vom Musikalisch-Schönen* confirms the self-diagnosis of this late Preface. From the first edition onward, Hanslick reiterated his objections to what he took to be Wagner's central doctrine: the subordination of music to words.[23] And in later editions, he reiterated his "sharpest possible protest" against such productions as Liszt's symphonic poems.[24] It would be too simple, too personal, to say that Wagner obsessed Hanslick. On the one hand, the structure of Hanslick's argument was complete in 1854, when Wagner was a relatively unknown if promising composer of operas and a relatively uninfluential if provocative writer of manifestos. And on the other hand, Wagner came to obsess his age, not Hanslick alone: Hanslick once wrote a sarcastic little feuilleton from the resort of Karlsbad entitled, "What Do You Think of Wagner?" This, he noted, was the question that dominated the conversation of professional musicians and amateurs alike, disrupted formal dances and intimate suppers, threw christenings, funerals, even the peaceful shower after the steam bath into disarray. If the Holy Spirit were to descend in our time in the shape of a dove, and address the twelve apostles, he would ask them: "Gentlemen, what do you think of Wagner?"[25] What irritated Hanslick almost beyond the bounds of self-control was that Wagner was not merely so wrong, but that he seemed so important.

To be sure, political excitement, no matter how widespread, is no excuse for adopting indefensible theoretical positions or writing myopic reviews; it is precisely in the heat of combat that the rational judge should remain cool. But Hanslick's judgment was neither grossly nor permanently distorted by his detestation of

---

22. Eduard Hanslick, *Vom Musikalisch-Schönen: Ein Beitrag zur Revision der Aesthetik der Tonkunst* (1910), vi-vii. [henceforth *M-S*.]

23. *M-S*, 54–56. See the first edition of 1854, 31.

24. *M-S*, 73. This passage does not occur in the first edition. In the same paragraph, Hanslick pays tribute to Berlioz's "dazzling talent."

25. "'Was denken Sie von Wagner?'" (1889), in Hanslick, *Musikalisches und Litterarisches* (1889), 56–66.

Wagner, nor by memories of his unpleasant encounters with The Master. As I have said, he continued to write appreciative sentences about Wagner's compositions, especially the early ones, and at times publicly revised his first judgment in a favorable direction, even with the *Meistersinger*. Hanslick did not come to think about music as he did because he disliked Wagner. Rather, he came to dislike Wagner because he thought about music as he did. In fact, from the very outset, Hanslick presciently sought to disarm the charge of bias: "The musically beautiful, in the specific signification we have assigned to it, does not restrict itself to the 'classical.' Nor does it imply a preference for the 'classical' over the 'romantic.' It is valid for one school as much as for the other; it dominates Bach as much as Beethoven, Mozart as much as Schumann. Hence, our thesis contains not one hint of partisanship."[26] If it was inappropriate for Hanslick to have stigmatized Wagner's music as "formlessness," it is equally inappropriate for us to stigmatize Hanslick's aesthetics as "formalism." Hanslick was far from denying the place of invention or the power of the imagination; he did not denigrate feeling.[27] On the contrary, he criticized earlier systems of musical aesthetics, notably that of Hegel, for being too much oriented toward ideas and too little awake to "sensuousness—*Sinnlichkeit*."[28] He protested that his "passionate adversaries" had erroneously depicted him as launching a "polemic against everything that is called feeling"; it should have been obvious, he thought, that he was simply objecting to "the unjustified importation of feelings into science." His only real adversaries, to his mind, were "aesthetic enthusiasts who, claiming to enlighten the musician, merely interpret their sounding opium dreams."[29] As an experienced polemicist, he could hardly have expected his indignant disclaimers, justified though they were, to be taken at face value. Yet we are entitled, even obliged, to do so.

Hanslick's cardinal aesthetic principle is the autonomy of musi-

26. *M-S*, 80. This passage went through all the editions with only minute verbal changes.
27. See *M-S*, passim, especially 7 and 61.
28. *M-S*, 61–62.
29. *M-S*, iv–v.

cal beauty. The very title of his essay hints at this: just as it is an error to speak of "art" in the singular, since that does injustice to the variety of the arts, so one must not fail to differentiate the beauty of music from other types of beauty. To arouse feelings is not the aim of music. Nor are feelings its contents. The feelings of the composer at the moment of production, even when they are known, are irrelevant to the type of beauty he makes as he writes his notes. Music may awaken feelings, mainly through the associations that listeners bring to specific melodies or rhythms, to dances or marches; music can portray ideas and, by swelling or accelerating, represent certain emotional dynamics. Hanslick therefore argues, quite consistently, that one may legitimately assign to music descriptive epithets normally laden with emotional content—"charming, soft, fervent, energetic, delicate, fresh"[30]—as long as one employs these adjectives in their musical connotation alone. But when one insists, as most aestheticians have insisted, that music *expresses* feelings which the listener identifies and may come to share, one misinterprets activity for passivity, mistakes the importation of one's feelings into music for the reception of feelings *from* music. The listener to music and the insufficiently critical aesthetician (Hanslick might have said with Ruskin) commit the pathetic fallacy; they (he might have said with Freud) project their subjective states into the sounds they hear. The most expressive musical passages, Hanslick shrewdly observes, "are like silhouettes, which we normally recognize only after we have been told whom they represent."[31]

This is a sensible, even penetrating theory, designed to shift the weight of analysis from the producer and the consumer of music to the music itself.[32] It was only Hanslick's unhappy felicity that made him epitomize that theory with a memorable, but far too simple, sentence: "The contents of music are sounding moving forms—*Der Inhalt der Musik sind tönend bewegte Formen.*"[33]

30. *M-S*, 24.
31. *M-S*, 39.
32. See, on this point, Abegg, *Musikästhetik und Musikkritik*, Part II, "Allgemeine Probleme der Aesthetik und Kritik," 47–87 passim.
33. *M-S*, 59. In the first edition, this formula is more dogmatic: "*Sounding moving forms* are, solely and alone, the contents and matter of music" (32).

Hanslick had no intention of endowing musical beauty with the chilly perfection—frigid, asensual, obscenely chaste—of Canova's Venuses. Musical pleasure was, to him, very potent and very much a matter of feeling. But it was, he insisted, a feeling like no other: its vocabulary, its grammar, its means of expression and modes of communication were all its own. It was to underscore this point that Hanslick emphatically refused to resort to those analogies from architecture and mathematics that writers on music, in desperate search for telling description, like to employ. The beauty of music is not architectural or mathematical; it is musical.[34] The point of music, therefore, is to serve nothing and nobody, not even *Stimmung*—indeed, especially not *Stimmung*. One must listen to music, Hanslick wrote, austerely and nobly, "for its own sake."[35] Yet the force of this point, however cogently argued and circumstantially proved, was lost in Hanslick's formula that music is "sounding moving form," probably the phrase among his many good phrases that everyone remembered best. Once Hanslick had launched it, he had launched the myth of his formalism.

Hanslick recognized that his formula, even if correctly understood, did not exhaust what the theorist must say about musical beauty. The music itself, with its ascertainable properties, is central; but the total musical experience, which embraces composer, interpreter, and listener in a single, if complex, transaction, requires attention as well. Accordingly, Hanslick devoted a number of pages to the "subjective" side of music. Yet it was always to its objective side—to the structure that can be described, measured, analyzed—that Hanslick returned. "The layman and the man of feeling—*Gefühlsmensch*—like to ask if a piece is cheerful or sad; the musician, if it is good or bad."[36]

Welcome as the complexities are that Hanslick was prepared to introduce into his economical formulations, his combative aesthetics could not escape one potential embarrassment: vocal music. Hanslick did not scant music for the voice—how could he? He reviewed choral performances, lieder recitals, and operas as

34. M-S, 83–87.
35. M-S, 136.
36. Ibid.

extensively and sympathetically as symphonic or chamber music concerts. But the difficulty remains, and Hanslick did not resolve it with the discriminations he introduced for the purpose. Instrumental music alone, he argues, produces unalloyed musical beauty; it alone is the "pure, absolute art of sound—*reine, absolute Tonkunst.*"[37] He protests that this formulation implies no rank order: one may legitimately value vocal music as highly as, or more highly than, instrumental music. But music other than instrumental is an art that derives its total effect from non-musical means like poetry, visual devices, even the suspense of action; opera may be as exalted an art form as a string quartet, but it is another sort of art, calling for another sort of judgment.

Hanslick's solution is more verbal than substantive. It is true, by definition, that the art of pure sound is music without words and without visual action. But the meaning of vocal music, whether lied or opera, consists precisely in the union of sounds and words, not in their separation. On this union, and on the relation between its two elements, Hanslick has some persuasive things to say. His choice of Gluck's famous aria from *Orfeo*, "Che farò senza Euridice," is adroit: Orfeo's lament for his lost love moves along briskly and could as easily serve as a hymn of rejoicing. Its loveliness is independent of its message.[38] Hanslick's discussion of the worldly, erotic duets that Händel borrowed from himself for his sacred oratorio, *The Messiah*, is equally to the point.[39] And his cool comments on the extravagant uses to which Beethoven enthusiasts were putting the choral movement of the Ninth Symphony are worth reading today.[40] Few will dispute Hanslick's dictum, borrowed from Mozart, that in vocal compositions second-rate words will not spoil first-rate music, while second-rate music will spoil first-rate words. Yet few will find wholly satisfactory the rather offhand conclusion that Hanslick

37. *M-S*, 34. See on this issue, Abegg, *Musikästhetik und Musikkritik*, 120.
38. *M-S*, 37–39. But see the subtle objection of Joseph Kerman: "Hanslick's famous objection that the piece does not sound instantly gloomy misses the essential point: the aria is beyond grief, and represents a considered solution, a response to the catastrophe." (*Opera as Drama* [ed. 1959], 43.)
39. *M-S*, 41–42.
40. *M-S*, 90–92n.

draws from his observations: in opera, the union between music and poetry is a "morganatic marriage," with poetry in the role of the fortunate commoner.[41] The aesthetic experience of opera, which Hanslick sought to capture in many perceptive reviews, is too multifarious to be exhaustively described by such metaphors, charming though they may be.

Yet incoherence in theory should not obscure relevance to practice. Hanslick's quarrel with Wagner was symptomatic of a larger battle; his somewhat grudging theoretical treatment, as distinct from his candid enjoyment, of vocal music was part of an envenomed duel between the "purists" and the "tone-painters." His defense of "pure" music stood in irreconcilable opposition to Wagner's assertion that in "music-drama" the music is a means and the drama the end. With that assertion, Wagner meant to claim the glory of a historic achievement: he had restored the true relationship between word and sound—nothing less. He was, in one of those curious involutions and complications in which Modernism abounds, an innovator and a reactionary at the same time.[42] The grandiloquence of Wagner's claim, and its realization in Wagner's late compositions, were enough to make Hanslick wince and reach for his pen once more.

But Hanslick's opposition to Wagner does not make him into a "mere" conservative. What emerges from his engagement with Wagner is, once again, the problematic nature of polarities. The struggle between the two men is, I think, best read as a family quarrel within the Modernist camp. As I have insisted before, Modernists were no more united among one another than were their adversaries: in painting, Impressionists, neo-Impressionists, Post-Impressionists and, later, Expressionists, Cubists, Non-Objective painters battled one another only less ferociously than they did, united, the Salon. If German painting saw Secessions from the Academy, it saw Secessions from Secessions soon after that.

41. M-S, 57.
42. By calling Wagner a "reactionary," I am of course alluding to the appraisal by his admirer Hermann Levi. See above, 232. Nietzsche (whose view of music, by the way, has much in common with Hanslick's) described Wagner as *the modern artist par excellence,* the Cagliostro of Modernity." (*Der Fall Wagner, Werke,* 5 vols. (1972), III, 359.)

Much the same way, Hanslick's commitment to the idea of aesthetic autonomy was a distinctly Modernist idea, foreshadowing, though by no means directly influencing, Non-Objective painting, New Criticism and (though he would have been horrified) the twelve-tone system, and this idea was in conflict with the Modernist idea represented by Wagner: Art as Religion embodied in his Music of the Future. As long as Hanslick remains buried under Beckmesser, he becomes nothing more than an effigy among the waxworks of forgotten eminences. Even non-Wagnerians, to the degree that they subscribe to the theory of art-as-expression, must find Hanslick utterly dated. Yet once we rescue Hanslick from the caricature that Wagner so maliciously and effectively imposed on him, he emerges as a theorist who, however time-bound and polemical his language, has something to say to his posterity.[43]

To assign Hanslick this position, even within carefully defined limits, must seem more than paradoxical; it must seem perverse. I have already cautioned against enlarging the scope of "Modernism" to a point where the term embraces everything and thus defines nothing, or includes all those phenomena we choose to like. I have no intention of forgetting this injunction now. Certainly, the dual quality of Modernism in our age—the openness to all experience coupled with a rage for experiment—was alien to Hanslick. He would have wondered at the tendentious traditionalism of the modern sensibility; he would have been at a loss

---

43. In one rather wry way, one can define as Hanslick a "modern" through his presumed Jewishness, since to anti-Semites, Jews were the "moderns." As Hanslick noted in his autobiography, Wagner "accused" him of being Jewish, in the second edition of his *Judentum in der Musik* (1869), in which Wagner calls *Vom Musikalisch-Schönen* "a lampoon, written with extraordinary cleverness, in the interest of music-Jewry." Hanslick professes to be flattered at the chance of being burned at the same stake with Mendelssohn and Meyerbeer, but denies Wagner's charge by referring to his father's family as "arch-Catholic peasants." (*Aus meinem Leben*, II, 10.) He says nothing of his mother's family, and the notion that Hanslick was half-Jewish remains a staple. Thus William M. Johnston, *The Austrian Mind: An Intellectual and Social History 1848–1938* (1972), 132–33; and see above, note 14.) Whatever the truth, I am constrained to ask, as I did in some earlier essays, Does it matter? Did it stamp his work?

to account for the primitivism that punctuates the search for the modern self. To prefer (as Hanslick candidly confessed he did) Goethe to all of Sophocles and Racine, Mendelssohn to Palestrina, Schumann's and Brahms's quartets to Bach's concertos and sonatas,[44] meant that he was what the French Moderns approvingly called "de son temps." But while this placed him in the nineteenth century, it scarcely makes him a Modern for the twentieth. Even if one rejects the Wagnerites' insulting characterization of Hanslick as a timid reactionary, an epigone writing for epigones, one feels safe in calling him a traditionalist, essentially a defensive critic. And it is true that (in contrast to Lincoln Steffens describing the Soviet Union) Hanslick had seen the future, and it did not work. Reviewing Bruckner's Eighth Symphony in 1892, he ruefully noted that what he called his "dreamy, confused hangover style—*traumverwirrter Katzenjammerstil*" might well be the style of the future, "a future we do not envy on that account."[45] But we must respect Hanslick's appraisal of himself as a critic who could take pride in neither liking nor disliking the new because it was new any more than he liked or disliked the old because it was old. In the "Conversation on Music Criticism" with his friend Billroth, with which he concludes his autobiography, Hanslick looked back on nearly half a century of reviewing music and thought his "receptivity" in the 1890s as fresh as it had been in the 1840s. And he offered as proof of that receptivity contradictory accusations leveled against him: while some had charged him with being a camp follower of the successful, others had charged him with a one-sided preference for novelty. Whatever the others might say, Hanslick was cheerfully satisfied to call himself a Modern.

In this historic movement toward Modernism, thoughtful conservers like Hanslick had their part to play. By sorting out the independent, unique quality of the musically beautiful, he put a considerable measure of wit and learning at the disposal of those contemporary forces in the arts which assign a prominent place to the irrational, without permitting it the upper hand. Form—

44. See his list of preferences in *Aus meinem Leben*, II, 303–8.
45. Reprinted in *Fünf Jahre Musik*, 191.

this is the meaning of *Vom Musikalisch-Schönen* and the un-counted articles that accompany Hanslick's treatise like so many grace notes—form has pleasures and, indeed, profundities of its own. Hanslick's vision was limited, and his place in the history of our culture is likely to remain a modest one. But he deserves to be rescued from oblivion or opprobrium for his perceptiveness, his intelligence, his capacity to see the dangers of the unrestricted rule of the id. The army of modern culture cannot be staffed by generals alone.

INDEX

Ludwig, Emil, 120n
Ludwig II, 202, 219, 222, 225
Lukács, Georg, 120
Luther, Martin, 4, 143

Macaulay, Thomas, 144
Machine, Modernism and, 232
Magee, Bryan, 215
Magnus, Eduard, 102
Mallarmé, Stéphane, 22, 138
Manet, Edouard, 25, 107, 160, 254
Mann, Thomas, 49, 133, 157, 179;
  literature and, 24–25, 132, 138–
  39; quoted, 149
Marburg School, 118
Marc, Franz, 138, 141
Marr, Wilhelm, 15
Marsop, Paul, 247
Martini, Fritz, 143
Marx, Karl, 6, 21, 65, 133, 174,
  259
Marxists and Marxism, 97, 156;
  Simmel and, 124
Materialism, 10
Mayer, Gustav, 165
Mayer, Helene, 179
Meier-Græfe, Julius, 160
Mein Kampf (Hitler), 8
Meinecke, Friedrich, 3, 116n
Melbourne, Lord, 116
Mendelssohn, Felix, 103, 251, 276
Mendelssohn, Moses, 109, 173
Mensi-Klarbach, Alfred von, 214
Menzel, Adolf von, 167
Menzel, Hubert, 122n
Metaphors: archeological, in Freud,
  43–46, 53; of conflict, 258; of
  disease, 15
Metaphysics, 91
Meyer, Conrad Ferdinand, 49
Milch, General Erhard, 165
Miller, Jonathan, 34n
Milton, John, 144
Mobility, of Jews, 174
Modernism, 19, 100, 138, 254; af-
  firmation in, 25–28; Berlin and,

178; classical tradition and, 23;
  components of, 22, 24, 234–35,
  259–60, 275; Jews and, 21, 100–
  101, 104, 158–59; rationality in,
  70–71; thought structure in, 231–
  33
Modigliani, Amedeo, 104
Molière, 148
Moloch, Der (Wassermann), 150
Mommsen, Theodor, 4, 99, 121
Monet, Claude, 159, 253
Mosse, George, 13
Mosse, Werner E., 96n, 97n, 132n,
  142n, 156n
Mottl, Felix, 113n; quoted on Bay-
  reuth, 226
Mozart, Wolfgang Amadeus, 167,
  194, 236, 237, 246, 255, 265,
  270
Muehsam, Margaret T., 174n
Mühsam, Erich, 163
Munch, Edvard, 28, 100, 107, 138,
  159–60
Munich, culture in, 100, 107
Munich Opera Company, 222
Münzenberg, Willi, 179
Muschg, Walter, 50n; quoted, 144
Museum of Modern Art (New
  York), 104

Nacht des Dr. Herzfeld, Die
  (Hermann), 132
Nadel, Arno, 163
Nadler, Josef, 180
Nagel, Ernest, 79n
Names, changes in, 98n
Nature: civilization and, 229;
  theme of, in art, 108
Naumann, Emil, 246
Nazi regime: anti-Semitism in, 13;
  Berlin resistance to, 177; fore-
  shadowed in German past, 7–10;
  historians and, 3–7; Lessing and,
  198
Nelson, Benjamin, 40n
Neumann, Angelo, 226